Teaching Truth, Training Hearts

The Study of Catechisms in Baptist Life

Revised Edition

Teaching Truth, Training Hearts

The Study of Catechisms in Baptist Life

Revised Edition

By
Thomas J. Nettles
with
Steve Weaver

Founders Press

Cape Coral, Florida

Published by
Founders Press

P.O. Box 150931 • Cape Coral, FL 33915
Phone (239) 772-1400 • Fax: (239) 772-1140
Electronic Mail: founders@founders.org
Website: http://www.founders.org

Revised Edition ©2017 Founders Press
First Edition ©1998 Thomas J. Nettles

Printed in the United States of America

13 ISBN: 978-1-943539-03-1

Dedication

to the 1998 Edition

To Margaret,

without whose prayers and example
catechising would be like
clouds without water.

Contents

Preface

Tom Nettles

I confess that I love catechisms. I have enjoyed memorizing large portions of some of those in this volume. It is spiritually refreshing to meditate on the phrases of the responses and investigate the Scriptures used to develop those responses. That exercise has been as helpful in my personal theological education as any other single practice. I relished the time on Sunday afternoons and sometimes on week nights working with my children on ways to memorize the beautiful cadences of *The Baptist Catechism* after they had learned every response in the *Catechism for Girls and Boys*. They would come up with rhythms. I will never forget the swelling, booming response that always came after mastering the rhythm in "whereby we are renewed in the whole man after the image of God, and are enabled more and more to die unto sin and live unto righteousness," or acrostics (APJIP, "assurance..., peace..., joy..., increase..., and perseverance...."), and challenges to each other for methods of remembering. They were quicker and smarter than I and I probably relied on my position as the book-holding inquisitor sometimes to escape embarassment at the obvious reality that they knew the answer verbatim while I still struggled to get all the phrases.

Though it sometimes creates tedium, mostly what I remember about those sessions was the fun and the clear conviction that we were working together on something that was right, that honored God and his truth, and that held promise for the development of spiritual, intellectual, and emotional maturity. I pray that those truths will yet be effectual in them and that they will want to pass along the adventure in truth to their children. I thank them for the fun and for being my laboratory.

These catechisms could be used in five helpful ways. (1) I hope parents will be able to use it as part of a family worship time; (2) Church classes for both children and adults would find it helpful in guiding or supplementing a doctrine study; (3) Pastors could read through one and then another catechism regularly to discipline their exegesis and provide a guideline for achieving a balance in their teaching and preaching ministries; (4) Christian schools may find it beneficial as part of the doctrinal curriculum at several grade levels; (5) Seminary classes on denominational history and theology would be hard pressed to find a more succinct and clear witness to the doctrinal balance and persevering testimony of Baptists through the centuries.

Even though I have sought to describe several other catechisms in introductory material, I regret having to leave out their texts. It seemed practical to limit the selection to these with the intent that they provide a window to both historical information and practical usefulness. A special thanks to Steve Weaver for his contribution of the material on *An Orthodox Catechism* and Hercules Collins. *An Orthodox Catechism* is similar to *The Baptist Catechism*. It shows the solidarity with orthodox evangelicals in their desire to propagate the faith once delivered to the saints. *The Baptist Catechism* employs the *Westminster Shorter Catechism* and the *Orthodox Catechism* employs the *Heidelberg Catechism*. Teachers will find creative ways to mix and mingle responses and biblical proofs on common subjects from different catechisms to provide a fuller display of the doctrines involved.

I want to thank some conscientious and tenacious secretaries who have combined their efforts over the years to make this volume possible. Jackie Madon at Southwestern Baptist Theological Seminary, Camille Couch at Mid-America Baptist Theological Seminary, Matilda Hunsicker and Stacy Guzzardo (Moo) at Trinity Evangelical Divinity School all provided faithfulness and competence in critical steps along the way. Also I deeply appreciate Founders Press for a willingness to make this book and consequently these texts available.

Finally, because of the wonder, mystery, beauty and infinite grace to which the truths contained in this small volume bear witness, I say sincerely SOLI DEO GLORIA.

Steve Weaver

I would first like to express my appreciation to Tom Nettles for including me with him in the second edition of this important volume. I must confess that I share Tom's love for catechisms, largely due to his influence on my life. In fact, like for so many others, it was when I read the first edition of this volume that I became convinced of the importance of catechisms in Baptist life. Therefore, it is a distinct honor to have had the opportunity to pursue doctoral studies under the primary author of this volume and now to contribute in a small way to this second edition. My prayer is that this new edition will lead to the continued recovery of the use of catechisms in Baptist life today.

My contribution to this volume was to provide the text of and introductory essay for the *Orthodox Catechism*. First published in 1680, the *Orthodox Catechism* is a revision of the beloved *Heidelberg Catechism*, a Protestant catechism originally published in 1563. For over four-hundred and fifty years this catechism has provided comfort to God's people. What has been largely unknown, however, was the revision published by London Baptist pastor Hercules Collins in the latter half of the seventeenth century. It is hoped that the inclusion of the *Orthodox Catechism* in this volume will result in an increased knowledge and use among Baptists of this encouraging expression of Reformed piety.

In the *Orthodox Catechism*, the question numbers were not in the original. Those have been added for convenience of the reader. We have updated the language, punctuation, and spelling, but have kept the changes to a minimum. We have also corrected any scripture references that were believed to be typos in the original.

Special thanks to Richard Barcellos of Reformed Baptist Academic Press for permission to use the text of the catechism which was originally edited for publication in Hercules Collins, *An Orthodox Catechism*, ed. Michael A.G. Haykin and G. Stephen Weaver, Jr. (Palmdale, CA: Reformed Baptist Academic Press, 2014). Two significant additions to the catechism in this volume is the inclusion of the section on the laying on of hands and the appendix on hymn-singing, which were both omitted from the RBAP edition. A special word of appreciation is also due to Enrique Durán, Jr., who did the initial transcription of the catechism and assisted in proofreading the catechism.

Finally, I would like to thank Founders Press for their ongoing commitment to publish material that edifies the church, including the present volume. I am thankful for the vision of Executive Director Tom Ascol, for the work of Ken Puls in shepherding this work in its early stages, and for the important role of Jared Longshore in bringing this book finally to its completed form.

Introduction

An Encouragement to Use Catechims

Life at the beginning of the third millenium A. D. pulsates with witticisms, opinions, and even reasons that would assign a book on catechisms to the dust bin of antiquarian irrelevancies. In the same odd combination of agreement that saw pietists and rationalists gradually overthrow confessional Christianity in 17th-18th century Europe, some within historically evangelical denominations join with twentieth-century postmoderns to cast an eschewing eye on these quaint systematic arrangements of biblical doctrine. To be sure, they think they share a common antipathy from different perspectives; in reality, like pietism and rationalism, foundational commitments are frighteningly similar. Whereas rationalists, such as Descartes, made human consciousness in the form of pure rationalism the final criterion for truth, pietists made human consciousness in the form of religious experience the criterion of truth. The pietists accepted the Bible and enjoined its study; they believed in conversion and preached so as to engender it; they believed in right and wrong and sought holiness both in personal life and in social and cultural institutions. All of these practices are right and the churches would do well in every generation to emulate them. Nevertheless, in spite of these good things, their weariness of theological vigilance led to an eventual theological slumber. This slumber induced a nightmare of horrors. To this day, the evangelical church has not been able to exorcise these dream-wrought demons in order to live in the full glow of the light of Christ (Ephesians 5: 8–14).

Now in these last days of modernism, dubbed post-modernism in much contemporary literature, human consciousness still serves as the criterion of truth. A significant difference exists, however; the confidence that rationalism could unlock the secrets of the world and the meaning of life and present humanity with an exhaustive display of truth forever to un-

shackle the mind of man has evaporated. Rationalism has led to irrational-
ism; now, therefore, human consciousness in the form of individual desire
reigns supreme. Neither truth nor a uniform set of standards governs the
post-modern milieu. One life style, chosen in accordance with one's own
desires, is as good as another. "Do not absolutize" is the only rule.

Again, evangelicals somehow find this mentality useful in seeking to
do what evangelicals do. An appeal to the absoluteness of *Me* has an inordinate influence on worship, practice, and faith in evangelical churches
and organizations. The structure of buildings, the preaching of sermons,
the development of church programs, the formation of focus groups, the
provision of recreation, and even the engagement in missions tend to focus
on personal fulfillment, positive self-image, individual desires, and a non-
threatening atmosphere.

The powerful attraction, and even governing capacity, of these (non)
values, while showing up in such areas as the physical arrangement of the
building and the content of corporate worship, has its most devastating
effect on preaching and religious education. Both of these stewardships
of the "deposit of truth" are in severe distress. The post-modern ideology
has become an infatuation of the church. Its guardians have allowed, and
at times encouraged and even taught, a fondling and caressing of the *Me*
goddess to the dangerous point of spiritual adultery. Governing life and
church by Truth rather than personal opinion, personal pleasure, and personal experience may prove distasteful to many, but to those who have
tasted that the Lord is good, it will open a door to a banquet of spiritual
blessings and heavenly delights.

Baptists have shared in this dalliance with post-modernism and have
waded in both the religious and secular streams of it. To those, an approach
to religious commitment that includes teaching by catechism would seem
strange at best and even highly offensive for many. Others, however, maintain a continuity with pietism and still treasure the Baptist emphasis on
conversion and the principle of biblical authority so central in Baptist history. They would consider the words "Baptist catechism" as mutually exclusive. They may labor under the misconception that catechisms are used
in times and places where inadequate views of conversion predominate or
the fires of evangelism have long since turned to white ash. If the Bible
is preached, they continue, no catechism is necessary; catechisms tend to
produce mere intellectual assent where true heart religion is absent. For
good reasons, therefore, some harbor deep-seated suspicion of catechisms.

This concern reflects a healthy interest for the experiential side of true
Christianity. Of this number, some have come from main-line Protestantism or Roman Catholicism. In these contexts they learned a confession,
went to catechism class, and were confirmed and then later heard the gos-

pel and embraced Christ in saving faith. They have subsequently left their former denomination and have joined a more Bible-centered and conversion-centered congregation. In doing this, they have interpreted their experience with catechisms largely in negative terms. In reality, the impressions of those experiences probably served as preparation for understanding and receiving the gospel. Concern for conversion and fervor, therefore, should never diminish one's commitment to the individual truths of Christianity nor the necessity of teaching them in a full and coherent manner.

In fact, some who profess the Christian faith are so experience-oriented that their view of spirituality makes them antagonistic to precise doctrine. Any attempt to inculcate systematic arrangement of truth is considered either divisive or carnal. Such convictions may be held in all sincerity and may gain apparent support from selected facts, but the actual appropriateness of such fears cannot be sustained historically, biblically, or practically. It is the purpose of this book to remove those misconceptions and provide for Baptists of both the post-modern and pietist type a view of Christian instruction which can both inform the mind and arrest the heart.

History Commends the Usefulness of Catechisms

The early church was painfully familiar with the apostasy of professing Christians. Persecution and the continued power of heathen worship practices caused many to lapse and prompted the early church to develop methods of instructing apparent converts before baptism. The period of instruction and catechizing served two purposes: it allowed the candidate (catechumenate) to decide if he still wanted to submit to Christian baptism and gave the church opportunity to discern (as far as human observation can do this) the genuineness of his, or her, conversion. Then, after engaging in a period of fasting and prayer with the church, the candidates were baptized. This use of catechisms served as a safeguard for the purity of the church.

Men such as Tertullian and Augustine served as catechists within the church. Virtually all pastors (bishops) had large classes of catechumens. Some of the clearest and most vital statements of theological commitment come from the writings designed for *catechesis*. Julian the Apostate (ca. 360) so feared the effectiveness of this enterprise that he closed all Christian schools and places of public literature and forbade the instructing of youth.

With the union of church and state by the end of the fourth century and the gradual development of infant baptism, the nature of catechetical instruction changed. The procedure of pre-baptismal catechetical instruction shifted more and more to after-the-fact instruction in preparation for confirmation. In many places it vanished entirely. Mass christianization of barbarian tribes in the middle ages eventually gave new direction to the catechetical idea. Charlemagne insisted that each baptized person should know at least the Lord's Prayer and the Creed. This concern then extended to the children of such christianized tribes. Though minimal, instruction was necessary, and the guarantee for it came from godparents who themselves were required to know the Creed and the Lord's Prayer. As confirmation developed in significance, examination upon the basic points of Christian doctrine became a normal procedure. This kind of practice has led to the impression that catechisms substitute for conversion in some traditions.

The Golden Age of catechisms emerged in the Reformation. Both Luther and Calvin placed high priority on instruction by catechetical method and considered the success of the Reformation as virtually dependent on the faithfulness of Protestants to this process. In 1548, Calvin wrote Edward VI's protector Somerset concerning the means by which thorough reformation could be accomplished.

> In the first place, there ought to be an explicit summary of the doctrine which all ought to preach, which all prelates and curates swear to follow, and no one should be received to any ecclesiastical charge who does not promise to preserve such agreement. Next, that they have a common formula of instruction for little children and for ignorant persons, serving to make them familiar with sound doctrine, so that they may be able to discern the difference between it and the falsehood and corruptions which may be brought forward in opposition to it. Believe me, Monseigneur, the Church of God will never preserve itself without a Catechism, for it is like the seed to keep the good grain from dying out, and using it to multiply from age to age. And therefore, if you desire to build an edifice which shall be of long duration, and which shall not soon fall into decay, make provision for the children being instructed in a good Catechism, which may shew them briefly, and in language level to their tender age, wherein true Christianity consists. This catechism will serve two purposes, to wit, as an introduction to the whole people, so that every one may profit from what shall be preached, and also to enable them to discern when any presumptuous person puts forward strange doctrine. … thirdly, to take away all ground of pretence for bringing in any eccentricity or new-fangled doctrine on the part of those who only seek to indulge an idle fancy; as I have already said, the Catechism ought to serve as a check upon such people.[1]

[1] John Calvin, *Selected Works of John Calvin*, 7 vols., ed. Henry Beveridge and Jules Bonnet (Grand Rapids, MI: Baker Book House, 1983), 5:191.

The *Heidelberg Catechism* and the *Westminster Catechism* have had the most significant impact on Reformed Protestantism. The former, dating from 1562, begins with two questions which establish the format for the remainder of the document.

1:   **What is thy only comfort in life and in death?**

> That I, with body and soul, both in life and in death, am not my own, but belong to my faithful Saviour Jesus Christ, who with his precious blood has fully satisfied for all my sins, and redeemed me from all the power of the devil; and so preserves me that without the will of my Father in heaven not a hair can fall from my head; yea, that all things must work together for my salvation. Wherefore, by His Holy Spirit, he also assures me of eternal life, and makes me heartily willing and ready henceforth to live unto him.

2:   **How many things are necessary for thee to know, that thou in this comfort mayest live and die happy?**

> Three things: First, the greatness of my sin and misery. Second, how I am redeemed from all my sins and misery. Third, how I am to be thankful to God for such redemption.

The three parts of the catechism which follow are entitled "Of Man's Misery," "Of Man's Redemption," and "Of Thankfulness." Within these sections full question and answer expositions are given of the Fall, the Apostles' Creed, Baptism and the Lord's Supper, Perseverance, the Ten Commandments, and the Lord's Prayer.

Hercules Collins, a leading English Baptist of the seventeenth century and successor as pastor to John Spilsbury in the first Particular Baptist church, adopted the *Heidelberg Catechism* as the basis for his 1680 publication of *An Orthodox Catechism*. Collins felt that this virtual duplication of the *Heidelberg Catechism* should strengthen the usefulness of the work, "hoping an Athenian Spirit is in none of you, but do believe that an old Gospel (to you who have the sweetness of it) will be more acceptable than a new."[2]

---

[2] Hercules Collins, *An Orthodox Catechism: Being the Sum of Christian Religion, contained in the Law and Gospel. Published for Preventing the Canker and Poison of Heresy and Error* (London, 1680), "Preface" [unnumbered]. Collins also proposed the use of the Nicene Creed, the Athanasian Creed, and the Apostles Creed.

Part of his purpose was to demonstrate basic unity with the larger Protestant community. In the funeral oration for Collins, John Piggott, reminded the congregation that "his doctine … was agreeable to the sentiments of the reformed churches in all fundamental articles of faith."[3] Collins believed that the catechism was a "sound piece of divinity," and expressed his hope that readers would know, "I concenter with the most Orthodox Divines in the *Fundamental Principles and Articles of the Christian Faith*, and also have industriously expressed them in the same words." While he was a zealous Baptist working for the restoration of a pure church and a pure observance of the ordinances, he earnestly contended that "whatever is good in any, owned by any, whatever Error or Vice [in church constitution] it may be mixed withal, the Good must not be rejected for the Error or Vice sake, but owned, commended, and accepted."[4]

Although scores of catechisms were produced in English in the seventeenth century, the most influential catechisms were those that arose from the Westminster Assembly, the *Larger and Shorter Catechisms*. The *Shorter Catechism* especially influenced Baptist life, as it formed the basis for Keach's (or *The Baptist*) catechism and subsequently Spurgeon's catechism. In America, The Philadelphia Association catechism and the Charleston Association catechism were duplicates of Keach's catechism. Richard Furman, long time pastor of First Baptist Church, Charleston, SC, used it faithfully and effectively.

Several principles appeared to govern the theory of catechisms:

One, many catechists believed that catechisms of different levels should be produced. Luther had published two as did the Scottish divine Craig and the Puritan John Owen (*Two Short Catechisms*). Richard Baxter had three, suited for childhood, youth, and mature age. The Westminster Assembly's two catechisms are well known. Henry Jessey, another of the leading early Baptists, had three catechisms, all bound together. One of these, *A Catechism for Babes or Little Ones*, contained only four questions: What man was, is, may be, and must be. John A. Broadus includes sections of "advanced questions" at the end of each respective section in the body of his catechism. This graduated difficulty in catechism rests on the theory that the earlier the stamping on the mind, the more indelible the result.

Two, exact memory is generally considered important. The power of words to substantiate reality enforces the necessity of some precision at

---

[3] Joseph Ivimey, *A History of the English Baptists*, 4 vols. (London, 1811–1830), 2:435.

[4] Collins, "Preface" to *An Orthodox Catechism*.

this point. "I serve a precise God," said Richard Rogers. Luther instructed those teaching the *Small Catechism* "to avoid changes or variation in the text and wording." We should teach these things, he continued, "in such a way that we do not alter a single syllable or recite the catechism differently from year to year." Instruction to Dutch Reformed ministers insisted that the text of the five chapters should be memorized by students "fully and unadulterated, not substituting strange words which sometimes falsify the meaning and give the text an opposite meaning."

Three, heart knowledge, more than exact head knowledge, was the main purpose of catechetical instruction. Catechizing aims ultimately at the eyes of understanding—heart knowledge. Even in the Westminster Assembly some were concerned that "people will come to learn things by rote, and can answer it as a parrot but not understand the thing." The design of the catechism is, under God, to chase the darkness from a sinner's understanding, so that he may be enlightened in the knowledge of Christ and freely embrace him in forgiveness of sin. John Bunyan specifically wrote, *Instruction for the Ignorant* that God might bless it to the awakening of many sinners, and the salvation of their souls by faith in Jesus Christ. The major purpose of Henry Jessey's *Catechism for Babes* was to give instruction concerning how God could forgive those who "deserve death, and God's curse," and could still "be honoured in thus forgiving, naughty ones as we are."

Henry Fish, an American Baptist, wrote a catechism entitled *The Baptist Scriptural Catechism*, published in 1850 by Edward H. Fletcher. Fish, a great observer and promoter of revival and an advocate of pulpit eloquence, screwed in tightly the application of each section of his catechism by a poignant rhetorical question sealing discussion of each doctrine. For example, his section on faith closes, "Are *you* a believer, or does the wrath of God abide on you for unbelief?" His section on regeneration and the Holy Spirit asks, "Are *you* giving evidence of having been renewed by the Holy Spirit?" The discussion of election poses the question, "Judging by this standard [that is, repentance, faith and the maintenance of good works as evidences of election], have *you* any reason to hope you are an object of his electing love. If not, have you not reason for deep concern?" After a strong section of responses to the subject of the omnipotence and independence of God, Fish closes with the question, "Since you are wholly in the power of this Almighty being, have you reason to fear or rejoice judging from your present character and condition?"

A catechism written by John Sutcliffe pinpoints this same concern as the goal of catechetical instruction.

Q: To conclude: what do you learn from the catechism you have now
    been repeating?

A: I learn that the affairs of my soul are of the greatest importance, and
    ought to employ my chief concern.

That this has indeed been the result of catechetical instruction quite
often is a happy fact. Luther Rice, that great early promoter of missions in
America, said this in reflecting on his conversion.

> After finding myself thus happy in the Lord, I began to reflect in
> a day or two, whether touching this reconciliation with God, there was
> anything of Christ in it or not! It then opened very dearly and sweetly
> to my view that all this blessed effect and experience arose distinctly out
> of the efficiency of the statement made by Christ. That I was indebted
> wholly to him for it all, and indeed the whole of that luminous system
> of divinity drawn out in the *Westminster Catechism*, opened on my view
> with light, and beauty, and power. This I had been taught to repeat, when
> a child. I then felt and still feel glad that I had been so taught.[5]

A charming reminiscence of one of the children Furman catechized
gives a clear picture of the importance he attached to this process and these
doctrines. A 1926 edition of *In Royal Service* quotes the remembrance a
grandchild had of her grandmother's experience under Furman.

> We had no Sabbath school then, but we had the Baptist Catechism,
> with which we were as familiar as with the Lord's Prayer. At our quarterly
> seasons, we children of the congregation repeated the Baptist Catechism
> standing, in a circle round the font. We numbered from sixty to a hun-
> dred. The girls standing at the south of the pulpit, the boys meeting them
> in the center from the north, Dr. Furman would, in his majestic, winning
> manner, walk down the pulpit steps and with book in hand, commence
> asking questions, beginning with the little ones (very small indeed some
> were, but well taught and drilled at home). We had to memorize the
> whole book, for none knew which question would fall to them. I think
> I hear at this very moment the dear voice of our pastor saying, "A little
> louder, my child," and then the trembling, sweet voice would be raised
> a little too loud. It was a marvel to visitors on these occasions, the won-
> derful self-possession and accuracy manifested by the whole class. This
> practice was of incalculable benefit, for when it pleased God to change
> our hearts, and when offering ourselves to the church for membership,

---

[5] J. B. Taylor, *Memoir of Rev. Luther Rice* (Baltimore, MD: Armstrong and
Berry, 1840), 25, 26.

we knew what the church doctrines meant and were quite familiar with answering questions before the whole congregation, and did not quake when pastor or deacon or anyone else asked what we understood by Baptism, the Lord's Supper, Justification, Adoption, Sanctification. Oh, no; we had been well taught. … What a pity that such a course of instruction has been abandoned.

Four, cognitive understanding was necessary also. Couching profound truth of the Great "I Am" in language digestible and understandable for children takes great discipline and concentration. Henry Jessey recognized a deficiency at this point in some of the earlier catechisms for children in that some of the answers contained Latin and Greek phrases. Jessey "desired to see one so plain and easie in the expressions, as that the very Babes, that can speak but stammeringly, and are of very weak capacities, might understand what they say."[6]

John A. Broadus felt the same tension when writing his "Catechism of Bible Teaching," included in this volume. Reflecting on finishing Lesson 1 entitled "God," Broadus said, "It is, of course, an extremely difficult task to make questions and answers about the existence and attributes of the Divine Being, that shall be intelligible to children, adequate as the foundation for future thinking, and correct as far as they go." Those three guidelines should serve well to judge any catechism.

Baptist catechisms have existed virtually since the appearance of modern-day Baptists in the seventeenth century. Both Particular Baptists and General Baptists in England used catechisms to instruct children and adults. Typical of the Particular Baptist commitment to catechizing is an admonition that appears in the circular letter of 1777 from the Baptist ministers and messengers assembled at Oakham in Rutlandshire, England:

> Our confession of faith and our catechism for the instruction of our young people, are published to the world; and from these glorious principles we hope you will never depart … At present, blessed be God, we believe there is no apparent apostacy in our ministers and people from the glorious principles we profess; but, at the same time, we must in great plainness and faithfulness tell you, that catechizing of children is most sadly neglected, both in private families and in public congregations …
>
> Our honoured brethren, the ministers at Bristol, have lately encouraged the publication of two editions of our catechism, … and we do most earnestly intreat you to furnish yourselves with this excellent com-

---

[6] Henry Jessey, *A Catechisme for Babes or Little Ones* (London: Henry Hills, 1652), preface. This catechism was reprinted in the *Harvard Library Bulletin*, vol. 30, no. 1 (January 1982), 42–53.

pendium of true divinity, and that you would teach it diligently to your children in private, and desire your pastors to instruct them, at least for the summer season, in public.

Among the General Baptists, Thomas Grantham in the 17th and Dan Taylor in the 18th centuries saw the value of a catechetical approach to indoctrination. Grantham's *St. Paul's Catechism* (1687) inculcated Arminian theology and used the six principles of Hebrews 6 as its guide. It has an unusual format in that the son asks questions and the father answers them. Both the questions and answers are too long and unwieldy to be easily memorized.

Dan Taylor's catechism, *A Catechism of Instruction for Children and Youth,* went through eight editions by 1810. He made no bold attempt to inculcate the distinctive marks of Arminianism, but instead spent a great amount of space on the doctrine of sin, its heinousness, its debilitating effects, its consequences, and the resultant necessity of regeneration. In light of the Christological controversies among the General Baptists in which Taylor was a major player, the omission of a separate chapter on the person of Christ is an unusual fact.

In the early nineteenth century, Baptists in Virginia often considered the question as to how the religious education of children should be conducted. Both in the general meeting and in separate associations the answer was given, "By the use of catechisms."[7]

Semple described a debate in the Dover Association concerning the use of catechisms in which virtually every objection to their use was forwarded and answered. Catechisms were unnecessary since the Bible was sufficient and catechisms tended to lessen the dignity of the Bible in people's estimation. Catechisms, in addition, had been used to inculcate the most "corrupt and absurd sentiments."[8]

Semple summarized the reply of the advocates of the catechism:

that corrupt men could communicate corrupt sentiments through the most sacred channels; that the pulpit and the press, conversation, and even public prayer had been occasionally the vehicles of unsound doctrines; that it could be no indignity to the Scriptures to inculcate in the minds of children principles and duties completely sanctioned by the Scriptures; that such forms of instruction greatly assisted parents in

---

[7] Robert Baylor Semple, *History of the Rise and Progress of Baptists in Virginia* (Richmond, VI: Pitt & Dickinson, 1894), 117, 127.

[8] Ibid., 136.

the discharge of their duty, seeing there could be few parents capable of explaining the Bible suitably for the instruction of children; that the manners and morals of the children of Baptists lately grown up plainly evinced that religious education had been too much neglected.[9]

The Sunday School and Publication Board of the State Convention of North Carolina produced a catechism designed to teach specific knowledge of scriptural facts.[10] In 1864, the Baptist Banner Office in Augusta, Georgia, published *A Catechism for the Little Children* by *Uncle Dayton* (A. C. Dayton) again focusing chiefly on scriptural knowledge.

At least two catechisms were produced by American Baptists in 1866. One, published by the American Baptist Publication Society, came from a contest held by the society. A committee edited the winning contribution and issued "The Prize Catechism" as *The Baptist Catechism*. It follows the order, and sometimes the wording of Keach's catechism. Its theology is a clear, forceful, and evangelistic Calvinism. The following exchanges illustrate the clarity and openness with which the doctrines of grace were embraced.

30. **If men were left to themselves, would any embrace the offer of salvation?**

    Men are so sinful, that not one would embrace the offer of salvation, but for the gracious working of the Holy Spirit.

32. **What is regeneration?**

    Regeneration is a work of the Holy Spirit, by which the heart is renewed so that it turns from the love of sin to the love of holiness, and from enmity and disobedience to the love and service of God.

33. **Will any who are truly regenerated be lost?**

    None who are truly regenerated will be lost, for they are kept by the power of God, through faith, unto salvation.

[9] Ibid.

[10] The copy owned by the author is photocopied from microfilm in the library of Southwestern Baptist Theological Seminary. Inadvertently, pages 2, 3 were omitted in the copying. These pages probably contain the date of publication. I would guess that the publication is in the early 1860's.

38. **Do all men receive these benefits of the atonement?**

All men do not receive these benefits of the atonement, but those only who have been elected in Christ Jesus.

39. **What is election:**

Election is the purpose of God, by which those who are saved were before the foundation of the world, chosen to be conformed to the image of his Son, to whom they were given as his people.

The second catechism by American Baptists in 1866, written by W. W. Everts, was entitled *Compend of Christian Doctrines Held by Baptists*. Originally published in Chicago by Church & Goodman publishers, it was reissued in 1887 by the American Baptist Publication Society in the *Baptist Layman's Book*. This later edition employed the *New Hampshire Confession of Faith* as the ordering principle and shares the same clear Calvinism as before. In fact, in the 1887 edition, Everts indicates no embarrassment about the term "Calvinist" in his answer to a question on perseverance: "The chief assailants of the doctrine admit that there is a stage of experience from which none can fall. Calvinists made that experience coincide with the new birth." This catechism contains an exposition of the Beatitudes. For example, in answer to how the blessing of comfort is bestowed on those that mourn, Everts writes, "By alleviating, terminating and sanctifying sorrow, and crowning it with heavenly hope."

Southern Baptists developed catechisms as valuable tools for the religious education and evangelization of slaves. In 1848, Robert Ryland published *A Scripture Catechism for the Instruction of Children and Servants* and, in 1857, E. T. Winkler published *Notes and Questions for the Oral Instruction of Colored People*. Each of these catechisms contains fifty-two lessons, one for each Lord's Day of the year. Ryland's catechism is described more fully later in this volume. Examples from Winkler's *Notes and Questions* are included.

In 1863, when the Sunday School Board of the Southern Baptist Convention was founded, one of its first publications was *A Catechism of Bible Doctrine*, by J. P. Boyce. Within a four-month period in 1864, ten thousand of these were printed and distributed. In 1879, Southern Baptists requested J. L. Dagg to write "a catechism … containing the substance of the Christian religion, for the instruction of children and servants." Evidently this catechism was never completed. When the Southern Baptist Convention was considering the reestablishment of the Sunday School Board in 1891, the first new project it proposed was the publication of a catechism by John A. Broadus. This was printed and used widely and advantageously.

Today's Baptist community would benefit from a resuscitation of the advice given in Cathcart's *The Baptist Encyclopedia* which encourages "parents to employ the Catechism in their own homes" because "this neglected custom of the past should be revived in every Baptist family in the world."

Summary and Conclusion

Catechisms have served in several capacities historically. During the early centuries of Christian history they were used for prebaptismal instruction. Later, after infant baptism began to become prominent, they were used to educate the masses baptized in infancy. Charlemagne in particular arranged that catechetical instruction should be given in his era of embarrassing ignorance.

During the Reformation, catechisms met several important and pressing needs. As a type of personalized confession, they helped establish clearly the distinguishing doctrines considered paramount by the reformers. Also, their polemical power assisted in the task of bringing a corrective cordial to the deceptive spiritual sickness propagated by Roman Catholicism. Additionally, they were effective in teaching biblical truth as an ongoing enterprise in cities and countries that adopted the Reformation. Puritans and their heirs utilized catechisms as an evangelistic tool. Baptists, including Southern Baptists, produced scores of catechisms for use in this variety of ways.

We see, then, that like all good ideas, catechisms are subject to abuse, and their evil lives after them. We should not, however, let the good be interred with their bones, but resurrect it as an effective instrument for a new day of Reformation.

The Bible Encourages The Use of Catechisms

Precedence of history alone, however, does not provide sufficient justification for the use of a method in teaching Christian truth. For those committed to the regulative principle of Scripture, biblical warrant, either directly commanded or legitimately inferred from a robust grasp of revealed rationale, cannot be sidestepped. It is necessary to establish, therefore, that in addition to these lessons of history, Scripture itself encourages the use of catechisms. The means by which God brings about justification and subsequent transformation embody the biblical message in a way remarkably consistent with the purpose, content, and arrangement of catechisms in the reformation tradition. The divine out-breathings which produced Scripture create both an assumption and a purpose which are consistent with this approach to instruction. The assumption is the authority, sufficiency, and consistency of Scripture; the purpose is preparation of the mind and conscience for the Spirit's work of regeneration and the increase of spiritual maturity in the children of God.

Examples or models of instruction used by the first-century church abound in Scripture, both in method and content. These make it clear that the use of summaries, readily digestible portions of revelatory truth, make for effective instruction in the church. In addition, implicit admonitions for this form of education are scattered throughout the pages of the Bible and mixed with the models mentioned above.

The catechetical approach should not be used to serve any fascination with systems and abstractions or to puff one's self up with speculative knowledge instead of increased love for God (1 Corinthians 8:1). Instead, it is one way that Christians may enhance their ability to use Scripture in accordance with its purpose. Instruction with this kind of precision constitutes an obedient response to the Bible itself and fulfils biblical principles undergirding the process of disciple-making.

Fulfilment of Scripture's Purpose

Preaching, teaching, and meditation (all biblical means of spiritual growth) require slightly different emphases in the use of Scripture and accomplish slightly different tasks in conforming us to Christ. Preaching comes in the form of a proclamation, challenging and correcting our thoughts and actions, teaching us of the grace of God in the gospel, and calling us to deeper repentance and obedience. Teaching, no more content-oriented nor less confrontive than preaching, employs a format less monologic and more oriented toward questioning and discussion. Meditation involves extended personal appraisal of one's own thoughts and actions in comparison to the beauty and holy character of God as revealed in Scripture and impressed on the heart by the Holy Spirit.

In each of these, not only does the person who is well-catechised have a distinct advantage, the use of a catechetical approach is a basic element of the procedure itself. Those who have good scripture knowledge gain more from good preaching. If, in addition, they have been trained to see the coherent structure of biblical truth and can define its leading principles, their knowledge of Scripture is more precise and thorough. The consequent benefit from preaching increases. More will be said about this in the discussion of practical advantages.

A well-catechised hearer doesn't view the words and ideas of the preacher as isolated fragments of truth; he understands them as constituent elements of the "one faith" which must govern our efforts to achieve "unity in the faith." Matthew Henry, a seventeenth-century Puritan biblical scholar and pastor, states, "Catechizing does to the preaching of the word the same good office that John the Baptist did to our Saviour; it prepares the way, and makes its paths straight, and yet like him does but say the same things."

This relationship between preparatory instruction and purity of worship was woven into the very fabric of the history of Israel. The people were commanded to instruct their children in the ways of God. When an Israelite child asked his father, "What mean the testimonies, and the statutes, and the judgments, which the Lord our God hath commanded you?" the parent was to answer with a summary of the mighty works of God for the redemption of the people (Deuteronomy 6:20–25). These acts of God might be more fully expounded in other contexts, but the summary served as a basis of all conduct and worship.

One could conclude that the entire history of Israel was catechetical preparation for Peter's sermon at Pentecost. Of course, it was much more than that. Peter explained what the people observed with the words, "This is what was spoken by the prophet" (Acts 2:16) and the explanation was sufficient. His appeal to the attestation of Jesus' ministry by miracles, wonders, and signs (Acts 2:22) was consistent with their understanding of God's activity in pivotal redemptive eras of their history (Moses and Elijah). His recitation of the Messianic prophecies through David made immediate appeal to the orientation of his audience. Also, his references to the pouring out of the Spirit did not refer simply to Jesus' promises during his earthly ministry about the coming of the comforter. This would have meant little to Peter's audience. More likely he referred to the coming of the Spirit as the sign of ultimate redemption and the new covenant (Ezekiel 11:19; 18:31; 36:27; 39:29; Jeremiah 31:31–34). Peter's announcement of Jesus as both "Lord" and "Christ" met with immediate understanding and conviction. Both words were filled with meaning for the hearers and the string of evidence he presented pointed to the conclusion they drew.

I am not contending that a strong background of knowledge when combined with a compelling argument always makes a convert. No conviction or conversion will come without the effectual working of the Spirit of God (Ephesians 1:19; Colossians 2:11, 12). A connection, however, between prior knowledge and proclamation is a part of God's ordained means of salvation.

The same is seen in Paul's sermon at Athens. He appealed to what he knew they had discerned from general revelation and had put within their system of worship (Acts 17:22–29). In a sense, nature and conscience had catechised them. Many misunderstandings and erroneous applications, however, dominated the Athenians religious scheme as they tortured the message of creation and conscience into superstitious paganism. In addition to some elemental truths to which Paul could refer, he had the more monumental task of deconstruction in his preaching to these proud pagans, as he confronted their woefully diminutive theology and moral ignorance. The unregenerate condition is deadly whether one is in pagan ignorance or lives in a flourishing Christian context. Given this element of equality, the one who is well-catechised has his natural capacity more greatly enlarged to comprehend the preaching of the Christian gospel.

Also, more quickly than those not so trained, those catechised become capable of preaching and teaching. The appeal of preaching lies in proclaiming the new (whether it be insight into content or application) based on known truth. Jesus said, "Every scribe who has become a disciple of the kingdom of heaven is like a head of a household, who brings forth out of his treasure things new and old" (Matthew 13:52). The scribes were the most thoroughly educated people of Israel during the time of our Lord. They were professional students of the law and gathered around themselves pupils to whom they taught the law and the oral tradition which accompanied it, much of which they themselves produced. They taught their students to pass on this content without alteration. Jesus indicates that the person with scribal training, when converted and freed of the idol of human tradition, is capable of teaching others the truths of the kingdom of God. He can understand and communicate how Christian revelation relates to the new challenges the world constantly presents. He gives insight into how one can make fresh applications of the unchangeable truths of divine revelation.

The Apostle Paul prototypically exemplifies one whose zeal for knowledge prior to conversion affected proportionately his impact as an evangelist and teacher of the church. Prior to his experience of transforming grace, Paul "advanced in Judaism beyond many of [his] contemporaries" (Galatians 1:14). He was zealous for the ancestral traditions, that is, in his knowledge of the Law [Scripture] and his commitment to its centrality for the healthy state of God's people, he was a Pharisee (Galatians 1:14; Philippians 3:5). This knowledge created a zeal hostile to the church. When, however, God revealed His Son in Paul, his capacity for the reception of the new revelations connected with Christ's fulfilment of the Old Covenant was immense. Though he was set aside to "go to the Gentiles," (Galatians 2:9), he often reasoned from the Scriptures in the synagogues seeking to convnce the Jews that Jesus was the Christ. His defense of justification by faith alone by grace alone through Christ alone was done on the basis of careful exposition of the Old Testament. His commitment to Scripture as that which is able to make one wise to salvation and thoroughly furnish the Christian with all that he needs for spiritual maturity was only intensified by the gracious opening of his eyes to see the glory of God in the face of Jesus Christ. Apart from Christ himself as the incarnation of the "scribe" who takes out of the law things new and old, Paul fits the pattern most neatly. His thorough catechising in Scripture and theological literature prepared him for his trying and arduous work as an apostle.

Apollos, before he met Aquila and Priscilla, was literally "catechized" in the way of the Lord and was teaching with accuracy the things concerning Jesus (Acts 18:25). Upon receiving more accurate instruction concerning some details he continued his teaching being of great help to believers and an irrefutable apologist for the faith in public debate with the Jews (Acts 18:27, 28). It was no small contribution to his eventual effectiveness that he was so thoroughly "catechized."

Admonitions and Examples

The biblical evidence for the value of catechisms is not derived solely from inference. The specific admonitions of Scripture support the use of this method. "Teach them diligently to thy children" and "talk of them when thou sittest in thine house, and when thou walkest by the way, and when thou liest down, and when thou risest up" were the instructions accompanying the second giving of the commandments (Deuteronomy 6). This sort of instruction included memorization of fundamental precepts. The Psalmist assumes the existence of this knowledge in his numerous exhortations to meditate in the law of the Lord. No meditation can occur where no content is present; and the more accurate and precise the content, the more edifying and uplifting the meditation.

David says, "The unfolding of thy words gives light" (Psalm 119:130 NASB). The word for "unfolding" may mean "entrance" or "opening." Its root often is used metaphorically for "understanding" or, in a phrase, "grasping the true meaning." The illumination of the Holy Spirit alone accomplishes this, particularly as it relates to one's transformation by the renewing of the mind (Romans 12:2). From a human standpoint, however, the purpose of a catechism is to present true contextual understanding of the biblical revelation. It can give significant and enlightening help in the Christian privilege of meditation on the truths of divine revelation, a practice which gives understanding to the simple.

Much of the educational task of the church today is parallel with that of the Levites in Nehemiah's day. When the Israelites were at the threshold of recovering their significance as the people of God, central to this reorientation was the learning of the word of God. Ezra led the scribes and the Levites in intensive sessions with the people (Ezra 8:1–8). Scripture says, "They read in the book of the law of God distinctly, and gave the sense, and caused them to understand the reading."

Scripture itself gives clear warrant to the use of external aids in order to enhance and accelerate biblical understanding. The Levites "gave the sense." Preeminently, the preacher serves in that capacity; but providing the same kind of touchstone given by the "rule of faith" in the early Christian centuries, a catechism helps perform the same function. When it has a comprehensive scriptural orientation and is organized logically, a catechism can enhance understanding and give immense help in grasping the sense of Scripture.

Summaries of faith, either in confessional or catechetical form, appear in the New Testament. These are used in situations where strong clear reminders of the distinctiveness of the Christian faith are needed. They serve to exhort, encourage, warn and edify. Bits and pieces of confessions, or perhaps catechetical responses, are very likely present in such passages as Ephesians 4:4–6; 1 Timothy 1:15–17; 3:12–16; 6:12-16; 2 Timothy 1:8–10; 2:11–13; and Titus 2:11–14.

The faith Paul mentions in Ephesians 4:5, 13 ("one faith … unity of the faith") could be the experience of grace of faith. Another, and more likely, possibility is that it denotes an objective faith, that is a body of teaching. The context seems to favor that understanding. Paul emphasizes the gift of pastor-teacher in verse 11 and, in verse 13, has in mind a doctrinal core around which believers should be united. This is contrasted to the instability of the doctrine characteristic of deceitful teachers (v. 14). At any rate, the words in verses 5 and 6 have an easily memorable form which expressed a foundational and minimal confessional standard for some first-century Christian churches. This simple but clear and exclusive confession could serve as an effective shield of faith against many fiery first-century darts of false teaching.

The phrase "a faithful saying" (literally "Faithful the word"), in 1 Timothy 1:15 and 3:1 and 4:9, introduces a confessional, or perhaps catechetical formula. The sentences which follow could possibly stand alone as pithy and pregnant epigrams, "one-liner" confessions such as "Christ Jesus came into the world to save sinners." More likely they are part of larger statements as in 1 Timothy 3:16. That particular confession called by Paul "The Mystery of Godliness" begins with a phrase which contains an adverbial form of the word "confess" and literally translates "confessedly great." Idiomatically it means "undeniably." That which is "confessed" with such certainty is a six-article Christological confession.

Apparently, Paul considered this confession a helpful safeguard against the encroachment of heresy, for immediately in 1 Timothy 4:6, Paul warns Timothy about the errors of ascetic dualism. That heresy by implication denies the goodness of creation as well as the reality of the incarnation, death, resurrection, and bodily ascension of Christ into heaven. Paul points to the "words of faith" and the inherently good, noble, and praiseworthy doctrine he has been following. He uses the same word to describe the "teaching" (v. 6) as he does to describe the inherent goodness of the creation (v. 4).

The phrase "words of faith" in verse 6 has a strong verbal relationship to the "faithful sayings" in 1 Timothy 1:15, 3:1, 4:9, and 2 Timothy 2:11. The first uses the noun form of "faith" and the second uses the adjective form. Conceptually, Paul is making the same affirmation. A "faithful saying" incorporates words which summarize certain truths of the faith; thus, "words of faith" becomes "faithful words," or "faithful sayings." These are in turn identified with "the sound doctrine" (NASB) Timothy has been following.

Paul is reminding Timothy that spiritual and doctrinal nourishment he received in his early instruction is a strong, and even essential, foundation for an effective ministry with the people of God. Verse 9 then repeats the formula "It is a faithful saying and worthy of full acceptance" that exercising oneself to godliness (v. 7), striving and laboring for life now and to come (vv. 8, 10) are all part of putting one's hope in the living God "who is the saviour of all men, especially those who believe."

These faithful sayings consisted of the teachings of the apostles and New Testament prophets (the foundational gifts to the church). In addition, they served as the Christ-centered guide to the interpretation of the Old Testament Scriptures and as paths to life in the presence of the Living God.

In 2 Timothy 1:8, Paul encourages Timothy not to be ashamed of the "testimony of our Lord." The word "testimony" which serves to translate two Greek words contains a rich fabric of meaning. Among the several things that both unite are the following: an event, word, or thing that serves as proof or evidence (John 8:17); a personal conviction about the truth which can not be compromised no matter what the consequences (2 Corinthians 1:12); the spoken message about Christ's person and work (1 Corinthians 1:16); and, in *The Martyrdom of Polycarp*, it refers specifically to the martyr's death. In 1 Timothy 2:6 the word "testimony" is used as an appositive to "ransom." The death of Christ was thus Christ's personal witness to and irrefutable evidence of the truth that there is one God and that reconciliation is possible only through a mediator who provides an effectual ransom (*antilutron*). The death of Christ speaks volumes, infinite volumes, about the unique efficacy of the gospel; it is the testimony in God's ordained time. And to that specific testimony that Christ made in his death Paul was appointed a preacher, and apostle, and a teacher. When he speaks of the "testimony of our Lord," therefore, in 2 Timothy 1:8 he has in mind that historical witness of Christ in his passion which is communicated to all generations in the words called the Gospel ("be a fellow-sufferer in the gospel).

John's Angel in Revelation 19:10 speaks of those messengers who "hold the testimony of Jesus." Indeed, the angel continues, the "testimony of Jesus is the Spirit of prophecy." Isaiah, when hounded by the false religionists of his day to consult mediums, replied, "To the law and to the testimony! If they do not speak according to this word, it is because they have no dawn" (Isaiah 8:20 NASB).

The testimony of our Lord, or the testimony of Jesus, is the fulfilment of all the prophets. This testimony (*marturion*) is given a form so that witnesses (*martus*) may testify (*martureo*) verbally. An elevated prose portion of that testimony is presented in the words of 2 Timothy 1:9–10:

> Who has saved us and called us with a holy calling
>   not according to our works
>   but according to his purpose and grace
>   which was given us in Christ Jesus before the world began
> But has now been manifest by the appearing
>   of our Saviour Christ Jesus
>   who destroyed death on the one hand, and,
>   on the other, brought life and immortality to light through the gospel.

Timothy also is admonished to "guard the deposit" and follow the pattern or standard of "sound words" given him. This deposit and these sound words he was to entrust to faithful men who would be able to teach others. Paul had already warned against those who lived in a moral squalor opposed to the "sound teaching which is according to the glorious gospel of the blessed God" (1:10). In 1 Timothy 6:3, Paul warns Timothy against those who want to teach other things and will not receive "sound words," that is, those about our Lord Jesus Christ. Nor will they receive "the teaching" that is according to godliness. Instead, they are men who understand nothing and, among other things, are deprived of the truth. He gives similar instruction to Titus that he would select overseers who hold firmly to the sure word which is in accord with "the teaching." This is so they may exhort others in "the teaching, the sound teaching" and may reprove those who oppose them.

Second Timothy 3:14, 15 pictures Timothy as having learned from his grandmother, mother, and Paul sets of truths stated not exactly in Scripture language but foundationed upon Scripture truth. In conformity with this same idea the writer of Hebrews speaks of the need of some to be instructed in the "elementary principles of the Oracles of God" (Hebrews 5:12).

Paul's emphasis on "the teaching," the "deposit," the "sound teaching," the "sound words," and his instruction that it serve as a corrective guideline to false teachings, false teachers, and non-essential subtleties creates a form with clearly recognizable features. The Puritans Thomas Watson and Matthew Henry are convinced that the "form, pattern, standard of sound words" is a type of catechism: "the first principles of the oracles of God."

The apostles and other teachers in the New Testament worked with several clear, concise, verbally friendly confessional and catechetical devices to establish a foundation for the entire teaching ministry. The practice of learning by exact verbal patterns was well-established, by divine mandate, in Jewish culture. A continuance of that would not only be natural but an expected response to the divine disclosure of the words of the gospel. Nothing should hinder the conclusion that memorization of the deposit of truth is biblical. The catechism appears to meet this need most acceptably.[11]

Sola Scriptura

Some object to catechisms because they fear a tendency to replace Scripture. If viewed in terms of the medieval practice, such a fear might have legitimacy. In addition the period of Lutheran Orthodoxy produced an implicit creedalism that was opposed by the founder of the pietist movement. While Pietism developed its own set of problems, its renewed emphasis on Bible study was a needed practical application of the protestant emphasis on *sola scriptura*. The most consistent practice in protestantism, however, gives positive relief to this important concern. Spurgeon noted the tendency of this fear and addressed it forcefully:

> If there were any fear that Scripture would be displaced by handbooks of theology, we should be the first to denounce them; but there is not the shadow of a reason for such a dream, since the most Bible-reading of all nations is that in which the Assembly's Catechism is learned by almost every mother's son.[12]

---

[11] Birger Gerhardsson, *Memory and Manuscript: Oral Tradition and Written Transmission in Rabbinic Judaism and Early Christianity*.

[12] Cathcart, *The Baptist Encyclopedia*, s.v. Creeds, advantageous.

Matthew Henry, in his "Sermon Concerning the Catechizing of Youth," expressed, over a century earlier than Spurgeon, the same confidence:

> Bear us witness, we set up no other rule and practice, no other oracle, no other touchstone or test of orthodoxy, but the Holy Scriptures of the Old and New Testament: these are the only fountains whence we fetch our knowledge; … and far be it from us that we should set up any form of words in competition with it, much less in contradiction to it; or admit any rival with it in the conduct and guardianship of our souls, as some do the traditions of the church, and others I know not what light within. Every other help we have for our souls we make use of as *regula regulata* — "a rule controlled"; in subordination and subserviency to the Scripture; and among the rest our catechisms and confessions of faith.[13]

Allow a contemporary to testify to the eminently safe and edifying character of a scriptural catechism. In his introduction to his own revised version of Keach's catechism, Paul King Jewett anticipates this objection with a strong answer:

> It would be anomalous indeed to say that in teaching that the Scripture is the only rule of faith and practice, the catechism is setting itself in the place of Scripture. All that the authors of our catechism have sought to do is to state in a plain, orderly and concise manner what the Scripture teaches. And do we any less in the sermon, which is the very central act of evangelical worship? What is a sermon, or at least what ought it to be, but a clear and forceful statement in the preacher's own words of what the Scripture means? And if this may be done in a sermon, why may it not be done in a catechism?[14]

Catechizing is Practical

The practicality of such an exercise can be demonstrated at several points. First, catechizing forces one to redeem the time. There are many good and helpful ways for parents and children to spend time together. Many parents struggle, however, with finding a means of creating spiritual and biblical discussions with their children. The discipline of catechising draws parent and child, student and teacher, together in the most helpful and edifying of all activities—the submission of heart and mind to the

---

[13] *The Complete Works of Matthew Henry*, 2 vols. (Grand Rapids, MI: Baker Book House, 1979), 2:159, 160.

[14] Paul King Jewett, *The Baptist Catechism: Commonly called Keach's Catechism* (Grand Rapids: Baker Book House, 1952), vii, viii.

teachings of the Bible. Other activities may draw the parties together, but time could not be so well spent in any other endeavor. As Matthew Henry affirms, "Your being catechized obliges you to spend at least some part of your time well, and so as you may afterwards reflect upon it with comfort and satisfaction above many other, perhaps above any other, of your precious moments."

Second, catechizing gives the building blocks from which all Scripture can be comprehended. I considered this idea briefly when considering how a catechism is in conformity with the purpose of Scripture. One of the church's most influential and, from a teaching standpoint, successful theologians, John Calvin, saw the truth of this principle and employed it brilliantly. He wrote a catechism to be used in all the homes in Geneva and explains his commitment to this idea in the preface to his 1545 French edition of the *Institutes of the Christian Religion*. He spoke of the benefits to the church of having in writing a treatment "in succession of the principal matters" which comprise Christian truth. He who takes advantage of this benefit will "be prepared to make more progress in the school of God in one day than any other person in three months" since he knows "to what he should refer each sentence and has a rule by which to test whatever is presented to him."

Marion Snapper calls this the Lodestar hypothesis. In the absence of sophisticated electronic equipment, a maritime navigator must focus on several brilliant and pivotal stars out of the vast and dazzling array of heavenly splendours. The catechism provides these guiding lights. An artist begins learning his gift by observing the forms of circles, triangles, ellipses, squares, and adds understanding of shading, symmetry, and depth. He then combines these into beautiful creations by the skilful addition of detail. A theologian begins with the first basic principles of faith, which, if learned well provide the immovable stones which support massive and comprehensive treatments of all the revealed counsels of God.

The first level of scholastic education, the trivium, involved the study of three disciplines: grammar, logic, and rhetoric. Grammar supplied the basic laws of language—vocabulary, precise diction, declensions, conjugations, and syntax. Logic involved the arrangement of these well constructed sentences composed of clearly defined terms into arguments which were free of fallacies in reason. Rhetoric consisted of the art of presenting this well reasoned position in an attractive compelling style. The "grammar" of Christian witness and world-view is Scripture memory and catechism. The "logic" is more catechism and systematic theology. The "rhetoric" is preaching (Acts 18:5), persuasion (Acts 18:4), public debate (Acts 18:28), purposive extended argumentation (Acts 19:8), tactical apologetics, and world-view confrontation (Acts 17:22, 23). Paul had so mastered the fundamental points, the "grammar," that he could use them in a dazzling variety of complex situations. One could add to this category all aspects of the apostolic letters of the New Testament such as practical instruction, ethical admonition, and theological application. The catechism, however, helps provide the "grammar" for all of this development.

Though a catechism cannot contain all the beauty of the Scriptures, it may contain "the essentials of religion, the foundations and main pillars" upon which the rest stands. Matthew Henry compares a catechism to a "map of the land of promise, by the help of which we may travel it over with our eye in a little time." A catechism can no more replace the Bible than a map can replace travel. Though a map does not render the smell of flowers, the heat of the sun, the refreshment of a breeze, or the height of a mountain, the serious traveler would never want to be without one. Travelling from Cuckfield to Canterbury or from Gary, Indiana, to Soddy Daisy, Tennessee, a trip can turn into quite a disaster without a good map for guidance. The terrain is not altered to fit the map; rather, the map is carefully designed to show what the terrain is like. Nor does one sit at home admiring the wonderful map, thinking that he has seen the world because he has studied the map. No, the map aids in travel and gives a person courage to try it. The map gives an overall view of the journey, and, conversely, the journey even helps the traveler better understand the map. Even so is a catechism to Scripture.

Third, a catechized congregation makes better sermons and better preachers. Thomas Watson says, "To preach and not to catechise is to build without foundation." The writer of Hebrews felt that the inadequate theological foundation of his readers restricted his scope in instructing them further. They desperately needed a more mature grasp of elementary theological principles (Hebrews 5:11–14). What might the writer have told us about the priesthood of Christ had his addressees been mature doctrinally and well catechized? Even so, if a significant portion of one's regular congregation sees clearly the lodestars of the Faith, more detailed textual exposition becomes possible, if not necessary. Thus, the people are in a position to feed on the sincere milk of the word and the pastoral dimension of feeding the flock of God takes on new and highly challenging dimensions.

Two dangers lurk surreptitiously within this strength and must be avoided. An elevated quality of understanding in a portion of the congregation must not force one into a weekly display of esoteric interests. While every message must have something to stretch and challenge the mature, it must also speak plainly to the children and the uncatechized. Two, one must avoid the spirit of novelty. A strong foundation must not be interpreted to grant one licence to produce cute little doctrinal embellishments of one's own whims derived from hermeneutical oddities and hidden meanings. Such enterprises, in reality, produce only disproportionate, grotesque monstrosities composed of wood, hay, and stubble to be consumed, for they have no coherence or harmony with the foundation, which is Christ. In fact the tendency of the preacher involved in catechetical training with his congregation would be to emphasize the great central truths of the gospel: sin, the cross, atonement, regeneration, repentance unto life, saving faith, justification, the person and work of Christ, the convenantal working of the Triune God in the salvation of sinners.

The fourth practical use of a catechism is its witness to our belief that Scripture is consistent, clear, and can be taught systematically. Popular skepticism towards the possibility of revealed truth produces raised eyebrows and dropped jaws at the mention of "systematic" theology or catechisms of Bible doctrine. Such materials presuppose that the Bible's teachings on any number of subjects can be arranged in such a manner as to present a consistent, non-contradictory picture of that subject. Catechisms may present real problems to those who feel uncomfortable affirming full biblical truthfulness and consistency; but, for those who accept that position as necessary for the Christian faith, catechisms should be not only welcomed but aggressively sought.

Fifth, arising from the Christian's commitment to truthfulness, which includes coherence and non-contradiction, the catechism aids in producing minds which are congenial to logic and analysis. A well-constructed catechism weaves itself into a tapestry of truth. All parts depend upon and are informed by all others. The learner does not see items of information as meaningless and disconnected from reality as a whole. Instead, without eliminating the sense of mystery and intruding on things hidden from our view by God himself, a confidence in the coherence of truth is paramount. Everything begins with God as creator, subsists and maintains its being through divine providence, and ultimately is consumed in the divine purpose to God's glory.

Not only is the created order meaningful, but history is meaningful, and the words used to describe creation and history are meaningful. The God who *spoke* the world into existence and maintains it by the *word* of His power, has by those acts vested in written language the possibility, in fact the necessity, of accurate communication. Observe the logical procession and analytical integrity of the following series of exchanges:

Q. **Into what estate did the fall bring mankind?**

A. The fall brought mankind into an estate of sin and misery (Rom. v. 1,2).

Q. Wherein consists the sinfulness of that estate whereinto man fell?

A. The sinfulness of that estate whereinto man fell, consists in the guilt of Adam's first sin, the want of original righteousness, and the corruption of his whole nature, which is commonly called original sin; together with all actual transgressions which proceed from it (Rom. v.12, to the end; Eph. ii. 1, 2, 3; James i. 14,15; Matt. xv. 19).

Q. Wherein consists the misery of that estate whereunto man fell?

A. All mankind by this fall lost communion with God, are under his wrath and curse and so made liable to all miseries in this life, to death itself, and to the pains of hell forever.

Q. Did God leave all mankind to perish in the estate of sin and misery?

A. God having out of his mere good pleasure, from all eternity, elected some to everlasting life (Eph. i. 4,5), did enter into a covenant of grace, to deliver them out of the estate of sin and misery, and to bring them into an estate of salvation by a Redeemer (Rom. iii. 20–22; Gal. iii. 21, 22).

The fall leads to an estate of Sin and Misery. The two estates are defined and their several parts delineated, and deliverance from sin and misery is introduced. This, of course, leads to a section describing the person and work of the Redeemer. These responses are from *The Baptist Catechism* used by London Particular Baptists, the Philadelphia Association and the Charleston Association. It is based on the *Westminster Shorter Catechism*, a cut above most other catechisms, but the advantage under discussion still stands for any well-organized catechism.

Sixth, godly catechizing bolsters the faith of those in conflict with the world, the flesh, and the devil. In 1630, Hugh Peters encouraged parents to catechize their children by reminding them, "If ever your poore Infants bee driven to wildernesses, to hollow caves, to Fagot and Fire, or to sorrowes of any kinde, they will thank God and you, they were well catechized." Marion Snapper characterizes this as the "Prison Camp hypothesis." His judgment is that this is about as realistic as "arguing for obesity in anticipation of landing in a Vietnamese prison camp; it is simply too far removed from the realities of life."

Though "wildernesses, … Fagot and Fire" may not be a present threat, persecution and opposition of a different sort are just as real and perhaps more subtly destructive. Biblical views of both God and man undergo incessant bombardment in the educational structure of modern society. And now that modernity has been stretched into post-modernity, toleration of all viewpoints has theoretically increased, but confidence in the existence of real truths has correspondingly diminished. In reality, everything is tolerated but Christian certainty.

What Christian young person hasn't found herself in the wilderness of a university classroom, or high school class room for that matter, wishing she knew concretely the argument for a belief that her parents and pastor hold dearly. And how many who have only vague impressions of doctrine but no lively and coherent apprehension of them find themselves overwhelmed by the apparent massive scholarship and acute philosophical insights of an unbelieving teacher?

Such an experience tends to isolate "religious" ideas to a corner of knowledge merely mystical and devotional, tangent to reality only at the point of personal value judgments but not considered worthy of the status of absolutes in any sense. Christianity becomes only a matter of private opinion, but certainly not a case to be argued. Catechizing from an early age sensitizes and conditions the person to consider God and his attributes as an essential part of knowledge, indeed foundational for all true learning. In addition, one learns to evaluate man properly both as to his dignity from creation and his intellectual/moral capabilities as modified by the fall.

Seventh, catechisms provide the theological foundation to bring reformation, prepare for revival, and avoid fanatical enthusiasm. Reformation is the recovery and propagation of central gospel truth and the ordering of the church—worship, ordinances, officers, and preaching—in its light. Revival is the recovery of love for God and man and results in the establishing of priorities in life on the basis of that love. Enthusiasm, the teaching that special leading and the revelation of truth are given privately to individuals, has been the source of divisive and dangerous error. Catechizing provides a doctrinal and biblical foundation which disarms and disciplines the tendency toward privatization of religious truth.

J. B. Gambrell, the great Baptist commoner, advocated the teaching of strong doctrine to maintain Baptist distinctives. When he was editor of *The Baptist Standard*, he challenged the readers to consider the benefits of a creed for vital Christian witness. A digest of his arguments applies just as forcefully to the use of catechisms.

> In this discussion a good start is to say that no one can be a Christian without a creed. ... In Christianity the holy Scriptures are the measure and criterion of creeds. To say it is right to believe a doctrine, but wrong to write what you believe, is not even respectable baby talk. ... In times of looseness, vague expression, cunning craftiness in dealing with religious things a creedal statement, drawn on scriptural lines, perspicuous and forceful, has cleared the thinking of the people, separated between truth

and all the outlying terriory of error like a staked and ridered fence. ...
A creedal statement is a challenge to seekers for truth to see whether
the things stated are so, taking each separate statement and comparing
it with the Scriptures. It gives definiteness to inquiry and greatly helps
in the study of the Bible by drawing attention to one great cardinal doctrine at a time. ... A worthy creedal statement has a fine unifying effect.
It clarifies the minds of many who are right in their trend and feeling,
but have not condensed their feeling and thoughts into words. ... A clear
statement of any case will unify those whose minds are impregnated with
the truth, but in whose minds the truth has not crystallized into form. ...
A worthy creedal statement is helpful in dissipating misunderstandings.
Only the devious, the sophist, the deceitful workers, the man with unworthy purposes opposes clear statement in dealing with religious matters. ... The cry against creeds is lacking in sound judgment. It comes
mostly from those who wish to evaporate religious thought into theological mist that it may be crystallized into other forms. ... The practical
value of clear, creedal statements in propagating the truth is and always
has been immense. ... It is almost impossible to say too much for clear,
crystallized creedal statements in which little words are used edgewise to
carve the outlines of truth deep in the minds of men.[15]

If so much can be said for writing a creed, how much more helpful is
memorizing a catechism built on the creed.

[15] J. B. Gambrell, *The Baptist Standard*, vol 26, no. 4, January 22, 1914.

1

An Orthodox Catechism

An Introduction

In the year 1680, a thirty-four year old Baptist pastor in London by the name of Hercules Collins published a revised edition of the *Heidelberg Catechism* which he titled, *An Orthodox Catechism*.[1] As the title suggests, Collins was interested in asserting the orthodoxy of Baptists in a day in which their credentials as such were being seriously questioned. This catechism is also thoroughly Protestant. In this introduction to the catechism, the similarities between the *Heidelberg* and *Orthodox* catechisms will be explored, as well as the changes and additions which Hercules Col-

---

[1] Hercules Collins, *An Orthodox Catechism: Being the Sum of Christian Religion, Contained in the Law and the Gospel. Published for preventing the Canker and Poison of Heresy and Error* (London, 1680). For the purpose of comparing the *Heidelberg* and *Orthodox* catechisms, I will reference James M. Renihan, ed., *True Confessions: Baptist Documents in the Reformed Family* (Palmdale, CA: Reformed Baptist Academic Press, 2004) which places edited versions of *An Orthodox Catechism* and the *Heidelberg Catechism* side by side to highlight the similarities, changes, and additions. For accuracy I have compared Renihan's edition with the original printing of *An Orthodox Catechism* listed above and the *Heidelberg Catechism* as contained in Zacharias Ursinus, *The Summe of Christian Religion* (London: James Young, 1645). This edition, according to James Renihan "is obviously the edition used by Collins." Renihan, *True Confessions*, 236. For a more accessible edition of the *Heidelberg Catechism*, see *The Heidelberg Catechism: A New Translation for the 21st Century*, trans. Lee C. Barrett, III (Cleveland, OH: The Pilgrim Press, 2007).

[2] Portions of this introduction appeared in Michael A.G. Haykin and Steve Weaver, "To 'concenter with the most orthodox divines': Hercules Collins and his An Orthodox Catechism—a slice of the reception history of the Heidelberg

lins elected to make in this historic Protestant document.[2] The purpose of this analysis will be to demonstrate that where Collins deviates from the *Heidelberg Catechism*, he does so based upon the Reformation's own regulative principle of worship. Thus, the *Orthodox Catechism* is even more "Protestant" than the *Heidelberg Catechism*.

The Place of the *Heidelberg Catechism* in Reformed Protestantism

The *Heidelberg Catechism* is a classic exposition of the Reformed Protestant faith. It has been described as "a defining confessional document of Reformed Protestantism" and as "a document that has proven itself to be an enduring and inspiring monument to the Reformed faith."[3] On the tercentenary of the Heidelberg Catechism's original publication, in a new edition of the catechism published by the German Reformed Church in America, it was asserted that: "Nowhere else have we the proper genius and life of the Reformed Church, as it stood in the latter half of the sixteenth century, exhibited and portrayed in the same happily comprehensive form."[4] Philip Schaff adds that the catechism "is an acknowledged masterpiece, with few to equal and none to surpass it" and that it "is the most catholic and popular of all the Reformed symbols."[5] Clearly the *Heidelberg Catechism* is a key representative of the Protestant Reformed tradition. Considering the prominence of the *Heidelberg Catechism* in Reformed Protestantism makes it all the more interesting that this catechism was chosen by a seventeenth-century Baptist pastor in London named Hercules Collins as a basis for his *An Orthodox Catechism*.

Historical Setting for the *Heidelberg Catechism*

In the year 1562, Frederick III, elector of the principality of Palatinate in the Holy Roman Empire, issued an order calling for the preparation of

Catechism," in *Power of Faith: 450 Years of the Heidelberg Catechism*, ed. Karla Apperloo-Boersma and Herman J. Selderhuis (Göttingen, Germany: Vandenhoeck & Ruprecht, 2013), 71–81.

[3] Charles D. Gunnoe, Jr., "The Reformation of the Palatinate and the Origins of the Heidelberg Catechism," in *An Introduction to the Heidelberg Catechism: Sources, History, and Theology*, ed. Lyle D. Bierma (Grand Rapids, MI: Baker Academic, 2005), 15.

[4] *The Heidelberg Catechism, in German, Latin and English: With An Historical Introduction. Prepared and Published by the Direction of the German Reformed Church in the United States.* Tercentenary Edition (New York, NY: Charles Scribner, 1863), 11.

[5] Philip Schaff, *The Creeds of Christendom: With a History and Critical Notes*, Vol. I (Grand Rapids, MI: Baker Book House, 2007), 1:540.

a new catechism.[6] This event would be looked back upon as "a major step in the transformation of the Palatinate into a Melanchthonian-Reformed territory."[7] Although traditionally Zacharias Ursinus and Caspar Olevianus have been credited with the co-authorship of this document, the most recent scholarship argues that the production of the catechism was the result of the efforts of a larger group of scholars that had been assembled by Elector Frederic III. Among these scholars was Caspar Olevianus, but his role was not as prominent as was once thought. Zacharias Ursinus, however, is acknowledged by scholarly consensus as being "responsible for crafting the final text of the HC."[8] Ursinus' role is significant in that he had spent time studying at two great centers of the Reformation: in Wittenberg under Philip Melanchthon and in Zurich under Peter Martyr Vermigli.[9] Ursinus had also visited Geneva where he met the French Reformer John Calvin, and received a set of his works as a personal gift.[10] Thus, Ursinus had connections to all three strands of the Magisterial Reformation. Ursinus' role in the final product of the document helps to explain why the *Heidelberg Catechism* would become a statement of such "remarkable consensus" between "the followers of Zwingli and Bullinger, Calvin, and Melanchthon."[11] In January of 1563, the catechism was adopted at a synod convened in Heidelberg.[12] This catechism has gone through numerous editions and translations. As Philip Schaff has noted: "It has the pentecostal gift of tongues in a rare degree. It is stated that, next to the Bible, the 'Imitation of Christ,' by Thomas à Kempis, and Bunyan's 'Pilgrim's Progress,' no book has been more frequently translated, more widely circulated and used."[13]

The Rise of the Particular Baptists

Approximately seventy-five years after the publication of the first edition of the *Heidelberg Catechism*, there arose a group in London who had

[6] Lyle D. Bierma, "The Purpose and Authorship of the Heidelberg Catechism," in *An Introduction to the Heidelberg Catechism: Sources, History, and Theology*, ed. Lyle D. Bierma. (Grand Rapids, MI: Baker Academic, 2005), 49.

[7] Ibid.

[8] Ibid., 71.

[9] Ibid., 68–70.

[10] Ibid., 68.

[11] Lyle D. Bierma, "The Sources and Theological Orientation of the Heidelberg Catechism," in *An Introduction to the Heidelberg Catechism: Sources, History, and Theology*, ed. Lyle D. Bierma (Grand Rapids, MI: Baker Academic, 2005), 81.

[12] Bard Thompson, "Historical Background of the Catechism" in *Essays on the Heidelberg Catechism* (Philadelphia, PA: United Church Press, 1963), 26.

[13] Schaff, *The Creeds of Christendom*, 1:536.

become convinced that the New Testament teaches the baptism of believers by immersion. This group had left the Separatist congregation pastored by John Lathrop in 1633 to form their own Independent congregation after having become convinced that the New Testament taught the baptism of believers, although they remained unconvinced of the importance of the mode.[14] By 1638, John Spilsbury[15] had become the pastor of this congregation which met on Old Gravel Lane in Wapping[16] and by 1641 the congregation had become committed to the position that the baptism of believers by the mode of immersion was the only valid New Testament baptism.[17] This congregation would become the first Particular Baptist church, and until only recently it remained in existence as the oldest Baptist church in London. Each of the first three pastors would write treatises on the subject of believers' baptism.[18]

The third pastor of the Wapping congregation was Hercules Collins[19] (1646/7–1702). Collins served as the pastor of this congregation from 1677 until his death in 1702. Collins followed John Spilsbury and John Norcott[20] as pastor of this historic congregation. For the first half of

[14] James Edward McGoldrick, *Baptist Successionism: A Crucial Question in Baptist History* (Lanham, MD: Scarecrow Press, 2000), 130.

[15] For biographical information on Spilsbury, see James M. Renihan, "John Spilsbury (1593–c.1662/1668)," in Michael A. G. Haykin, ed., *The British Particular Baptists 1638–1910* (Springfield, MO: Particular Baptist Press, 1998), 1:21–37.

[16] For the history of the church, see Ernest F. Kevan, *London's Oldest Baptist Church: Wapping 1633–Walthamstow 1933* (London: Kingsgate Press, 1933).

[17] McGoldrick, *Baptist Successionism*, 131–132.

[18] John Spilsbury, *A Treatise Concerning the Lawful Subject of Baptism (London, 1643); John Norcott, Baptism Discovered Plainly & Faithfully, According to the Word of God* (1672); and, *Hercules Collins, Believers-Baptism from Heaven, and of Divine Institution. Infants-Baptism from Earth, and Human Invention* (London, 1691).

[19] For details on the life of Hercules Collins see G. Steve Weaver, Jr., Orthodox, Puritan, Baptist: Hercules Collins (1647–1702) and Particular Baptist Identity in Early Modern England (Göttingen: Vandenhoeck & Ruprecht, 2015). See also Michael A.G. Haykin, "The Piety of Hercules Collins (1646/7–1702)," in *Devoted to the Service of the Temple: Piety, Persecution, and Ministry in the Writings of Hercules Collins*, ed. Michael A.G. Haykin and Steve Weaver (Grand Rapids, MI: Reformation Heritage Books, 2007), 1–30.

[20] For details about John Norcott, see Joseph Ivimey, *A History of the English Baptists* (London: B. J. Holdsworth,1823), 3:295–301; Kevan, *London's Oldest Baptist Church*, 62–64; Geoffrey F. Nuttall, "Another Baptist Ejection (1662): The Case of John Norcott," in *Pilgrim Pathways: Essays in Baptist History in Honour of B.R. White*, ed. William H. Brackney and Paul S. Fiddes with John H. Y. Briggs (Macon, GA: Mercer University Press, 1999), 185–188.

Collins ministry (until the Act of Toleration in 1689) the congregation had to meet in secret for fear of persecution. Collins was imprisoned for his nonconformity in 1684. While in the infamous Newgate Prison, Collins penned two of the most devotional of his twelve writings.[21] However, it is his first work, *An Orthodox Catechism*, which is the subject of our inquiry in this chapter. Given the persecution that the Baptists faced in the late seventeenth century, it should come as no surprise that Collins chose the *Heidelberg Catechism* for the basis of his catechism since it was, as Mark Noll has stated,

> … a superb statement of faith for a persecuted people. Its stress, from the very first question, on God's desire to comfort his own, as well as its emphasis on the transcendent goodness of God's providence, brought reassurance to those who felt that they had been abandoned by all earthly powers.[22]

The significance of Hercules Collins among the Particular Baptists of the late seventeenth century can be seen in at least three areas. First, he was a relatively prolific author among the Particular Baptists of the period,[23] publishing at least twelve distinct works between the years 1680 and 1702. Second, Collins was among the original signatories of the *Second London Confession of Faith* (1689). Third, Collins' name was affixed to the recommendatory epistle of *The Gospel Minister's Maintenance Vindicated* along with ten other prominent London Baptist pastors, including such luminaries as Benjamin Keach, Hanserd Knollys and William Kiffin.[24] Combined these facts demonstrate, not only that Collins was an important figure in late seventeenth-century Baptist life, but that he can also serve as a faithful representative of the broader Baptist community of which he was a part.

---

[21] *A Voice from the Prison. Or, Meditations on Revelations III.XI. Tending To the Establishment of God's Little Flock, In an Hour of Temptation* (London, 1684) and *Counsel for the Living, Occasioned from the Dead: Or, A Discourse on Job III.17,18. Arising from the Deaths of Mr. Fran. Bampfield and Mr. Zach. Ralphson* (London, 1684). A complete list of Collins works can be found in Haykin and Weaver, *Devoted to the Service of the Temple*, 135–137.

[22] Mark A. Noll, *Confessions and Catechisms of the Reformation* (Vancouver, BC: Regent College Publishing, 2004), 135.

[23] The only author during this period which could rival his production being his friend Benjamin Keach (1640–1704), pastor of the Horsley-Down congregation. For more on Keach, see Austin Walker, *The Excellent Benjamin Keach* (Dundas, ON: Joshua Press, 2004).

[24] Benjamin Keach, *The Gospel Minister's Maintenance Vindicated* (London, 1689).

Purposes of An Orthodox Catechism

Hercules Collins seems to have had at least three purposes in publishing his *Orthodox Catechism*. The catechism functions as a tool for pastoral instruction, as a polemic against false teaching, and as a plea for doctrinal unity. Having become the pastor of the Wapping congregation only four years earlier, Collins clearly modifies the *Heidelberg Catechism* for use as a tool in fulfilling his pastoral duties. A comparison of the two documents side by side reveal a number of relatively minor edits, many of which are best explained as Collins' attempts to make the catechism more accessible to his local congregation. One example of this type of editing is found in Collins' rearrangement of the section dealing with the Ten Commandments. Whereas the *Heidelberg Catechism* lists the Ten Commandments all together then later explains them individually, Collins rearranges this section to allow for each commandment to be listed separately along with its explanation and application. This rearrangement has an obvious pedagogical benefit for the *Orthodox Catechism*. Elsewhere, Collins more explicitly states his concern for the local congregation to which he ministered in the following benediction which concluded his Preface to the catechism:

> And for those whom the Lord hath committed to my Charge, that the Eternal God may be your Refuge, and underneath you everlasting Arms; that Grace may be opened to your Hearts, and your hearts to Grace; that the blessing of the God of Abraham, Isaac and Jacob may be upon you, and the eternal Spirit may be with you, shall be the Prayer of your unworthy Brother, but more unworthy Pastor,
> H. C.

A second use of *An Orthodox Catechism* is clearly stated by Collins on the title page: "Published For Preventing the Canker and Poison of Heresy and Error." This polemic function of the catechism was necessary, because in the mid-seventeenth century the writings of a man associated with the Particular Baptists named Thomas Collier,[25] had brought the

---

[25] Thomas Collier was a significant Particular Baptist leader in England during the mid-seventeenth century. A native of Somerset, he was a key leader in the Western Association's adoption of the *Somerset Confession* in 1656. His career is riddled with doctrinal instability, with some writings which are orthodox, while others were filled with heresy. For more information on the life and writings of Thomas Collier, see Richard D. Land, "Doctrinal Controversies of English Particular Baptists (1644–1691) as Illustrated by the Career and Writings of Thomas Collier" (PhD diss., Oxford University, 1979).

Baptists into disrepute. In 1648, Collier had denied the historic orthodox understanding of the Trinity. Collier wrote that God:

> … is not, first, as some imagine, *Three Persons yet one God*, or three sub-sistings, distinguished though not divided; Its altogether impossible to distinguish God in this manner, and not divide him; thus to distinguish is to divide; for three persons are three not only distinguished, but divided: Some say there is, *God the Father, God the Son, and God the Holy Ghost, yet not three, but one God*; Let any one judge if here be not three Gods, if three then not one;[26]

Thomas Hall's subsequent labeling of Collier as an "Arian, Armin-ian, Socinian, Samosatenian, Antinomian, Anabaptist, Familist, Dona-tist, Separatist, Anti-Scripturist, &c. An Open enemy to God, to Christ, to the Holy Ghost, to Scripture, Law, Gospel, Church, Commonwealth, Magistracy, Ministry, Army, &c."[27] was no doubt applied to other Baptists without distinction. Collins was clearly concerned with defending Baptists against charges of heresy while at the same time providing an instrument of instruction in order to prevent the spread of more false teaching among their number.

A final reason that Collins published *An Orthodox Catechism* was to identify himself and his fellow Particular Baptists with the orthodoxy of the Protestant divines of Europe. As Collins noted in his preface, "I con-center with the most orthodox divines in the fundamental principles and articles of the Christian Faith."[28] This catechism served as an attempt to express the agreement of the Baptists with other bodies of Reformed be-lievers on the most essential matters of Christianity. To that end, Collins writes:

> Now albeit there are some differences between many godly divines and us in church constitution, yet inasmuch as those things are not the es-sence of Christianity, but that we do agree in the fundamental doctrine thereof, there is sufficient ground to lay aside all bitterness and prejudice, and labor to maintain a spirit of love each to other, knowing we shall never see all alike here. [29]

---

[26] Thomas Collier, *A General Epistle, To The Universal Church of the First Born: Whose Names are written in Heaven* (London, Giles Calvert, 1648).

[27] Thomas Hall, *The Collier in his Colours: or, The Picture of a Collier* (London: n.p., 1652). This work is actually included (with a separate title page) in Hall's *The Font Guarded With XX Arguments* (London: 1652).

[28] Collins, *An Orthodox Catechism*, Preface.

[29] Ibid.

Both the choice of the *Heidelberg Catechism* as the basis for his catechism and the use of the word "orthodox" in the title of his catechism highlight Collins' interest in identifying himself with historic Protestant orthodoxy. As James Renihan writes of Collins' choice of a title: "While it obviously refers to the true character of the doctrines it promotes, it also identifies the source of those doctrines, the so-called Protestant Orthodox divines of Europe. Collins was making an emphatic statement: just as they are Orthodox, so also are we."[30]

Similarities between the *Heidelberg* and the *Orthodox* Catechisms

When comparing the *Orthodox* and *Heidelberg* catechisms it is striking to note how very similar they are. Out of 129 questions in the *Heidelberg Catechism* (the *Orthodox Catechism* is not numbered), there are only eleven substantial changes: ten questions added and one omitted. Collins follows the *Heidelberg Catechism* in beginning with the question which Philip Schaff called "the whole gospel in a nutshell."[31]

Q.   **What is thy only comfort in life and death?**

A.   That both in soul and body whether I live or die, I am not mine own, but belong wholly unto my faithful Lord and Savior Jesus Christ: who by his most precious blood, fully satisfying for all my sins, hath delivered me from all the power of the devil, and so preserveth me, that without the will of my heavenly Father, not so much as an hair may fall from my head; yea all things must serve for my safety: Wherefore by his Spirit also he assureth me of everlasting life, and maketh me ready and prepared, that henceforth I may live to him.[32]

The basic structure of the catechism follows the pattern of the *Heidelberg Catechism* which is outlined in the second question:

Q.   **How many things are necessary for thee to know, that thou enjoying this comfort mayest live and die happily?**

A.   Three. The first, what is the greatness of my sin and misery. The second, how I am delivered from all sin and misery. The third, what thanks I owe unto God for this delivery.[33]

---

[30] Renihan, *True Confessions*, 235.
[31] Schaff, *Creeds of Christendom*, 1:541.
[32] Collins, *An Orthodox Catechism*, 1.
[33] Ibid., 2.

The rest of the catechism from the third question to the end follows the basic outline seen in this question of 1. Of Man's Misery; 2. Of Man's Redemption; and, 3. Of Thankfulness.[34] All the topics contained in the *Heidelberg Catechism* are also covered in *An Orthodox Catechism*.[35] The rest of this introduction will be devoted to three topics which are retained in *An Orthodox Catechism*. These are the Apostles Creed, Sacraments, and the Lord's Supper.

Apostles' Creed

Both the *Heidelberg Catechism* and its Baptist counterpart are concerned with historic catholic teaching. The Apostles' Creed is stated by Philip Schaff to be "an admirable popular summary of the apostolic teaching, and in full harmony with the spirit and even the letter of the New Testament."[36] The Apostles' Creed provides the Trinitarian structure of the second section of the catechism which highlights man's redemption. The rest of this section continues in outline form as indicated in the response to the question: "Into how many parts is this Creed divided?" The answer, "Into three: the first of the eternal Father, and our creation: the second, of the Son and our redemption: the third, of the Holy Ghost, and our sanctification."[37] In clear contrast to the heterodoxy expressed by Thomas Collier in regard to the doctrine of the Trinity, the *Orthodox Catechism* asserts the biblical doctrine in these words:

Q. **Seeing there is but one only substance of God, why namest thou those three, the Father, the Son, and the Holy Ghost?**

A. Because God hath so manifested himself in His Word, that these three distinct persons are that one true everlasting God.[38]

Although following the *Heidelberg Catechism* fully in its exposition of the Apostles' Creed, Collins does see fit to make a couple of important distinctions. In the margin alongside the text of the Apostles' Creed, Collins provides the following caveats. On the phrase "He descended into Hell," Collin adds: "Not that he, (to wit, Christ) went into the place of the

---

[34] These headings are given by Zacharias Ursinus in his *The Summe of Christian Religion*. They are not present in *An Orthodox Catechism*, but the structure is inherent to the questions whose order Collins follows without exception.

[35] Although the section on baptism is dramatically altered, the topic is still covered. There are also questions added to certain topics by Collins.

[36] Schaff, *Creeds of Christendom*, 1:14.

[37] Collins, *An Orthodox Catechism*, 9.

[38] Ibid.

damned, but that he went absolutely into the state of the dead. See Dr. Usher of Christ, in his body of divinity, pag. 174. and Mr. Perkins on the Creed."[39] Similarly, on the phrase "I believe in … the holy catholic church," Collins adds: "Not that we are to believe in, but that there is a catholic church, and by catholic, we mean no more than the universal church, which is a company chosen out of whole mankind unto everlasting life, by the Word and Spirit of God."[40] But even with these caveats, Collins is not deviating from the common Protestant understanding of the Creed.[41] He is merely providing explanatory glosses for those who might be newly exposed to this language through his catechism.

Sacraments

Whereas the *Second London Confession of Faith* (1677, 1689)[42] changes the term "sacrament" in the *Westminster Confession of Faith* (1646) to "ordinance" no such alteration is present in the *Orthodox Catechism*. As will be clear later in the discussion of Collins alteration of the *Heidelberg Catechism's* treatment of baptism, Collins was at the very least aware, if not involved in the original composition of the *Second London Confession of Faith*. But his choice to retain this language indicates a lack of unanimity on the subject among the Particular Baptists.[43] Although Hercules Collins was

[39] Ibid., 8. In this note, Collins refers to Bishop James Ussher's *A Body of Divinity: Being the Sum and Substance of the Christian Religion* (Birmingham, AL: Solid Ground Christian Books, 2007) and the Puritan William Perkins' *An Exposition of the Symbole or Creed of the Apostles* (Cambridge: John Legatt, 1595).

[40] Collins, *An Orthodox Creed*, 8.

[41] This can be seen in the works by Ussher and Perkins referenced by above.

[42] This popular Confession of Faith was first published in 1677, but was officially adopted by the London General Assembly when they met in 1689. It was subsequently published with a list of signatories. Hercules Collins (along with men like Hanserd Knollys, William Kiffin, and Benjamin Keach) was one of the original signers of this historic document. This confession may be accessed in William L. Lumpkin, *Baptist Confessions of Faith* (Valley Forge, PA: Judson Press, 1969), 235–295.

[43] In fact, Stanley K. Fowler argues in his *More Than A Symbol: The British Baptist Recovery of Baptismal Sacramentalism* (London: Paternoster Press, 2002) that the changing of the terminology from "sacrament" to "ordinance" in the *Second London Confession* does not mean that Baptists had embraced a non-sacramental view of baptism. Among the reasons that he cites for this conclusion are: "the terms 'sacrament' and 'ordinance' were often used synonymously by Baptists of that era, including signatories of this confession" and "Chapter XXX of the *Second London Confession* interpreted the Lord's Supper in the Westminster tradition along the lines of a 'spiritual presence' of Christ which is mediated through the Supper, i.e., the Calvinistic as opposed to the Zwinglian view." Ibid., 17.

not hesitant to alter this catechism where he believed it to be warranted by Scripture, he obviously had no problem using the word "sacrament" and retaining the definition used in the *Heidelberg,* language which can be traced back to men such as John Calvin, Heinrich Bullinger, and Philip Melanchthon.[44] For example, in stating the source from which the faith that alone makes us "partakers of Christ and his benefits," both catechisms state: "From the Holy Ghost, who kindleth it in our hearts by the preaching of the Gospel, and confirmeth it by the use of the Sacraments."[45] The sacraments, which are limited to baptism and the Lord's Supper, are then defined as the "sacred signs, and seals, set before our eyes, and ordained of God for this cause, that he may declare and seal by them the promise of his Gospel unto us."[46] Thus, the sacraments function to assure us "that the salvation of all of us standeth in the only sacrifice of Christ, offered for us on the Cross."[47]

Lord's Supper

Some modern-day Baptist theologians might be surprised to learn that there is virtually no change between a sixteenth-century Reformed document and a seventeenth-century Baptist document on the issue of the Lord's Supper,[48] but that is exactly what one finds when the sections in the *Heidelberg* and *Orthodox* catechisms are examined side by side. For example, the catechisms state that when a believer partakes of the Lord's Supper he may say, "my soul is no less assuredly fed to everlasting life with his body, which was crucified for me, and his blood, which was shed for

[44] Previously scholars have sought to determine whether the *Heidelberg Catechism* was Zwinglian, Melanchthonian, or Calvinistic in its description of the Sacraments, Lyle D. Bierma has argued persuasively in his monograph *The Doctrine of the Sacraments in the Heidelberg Catechism.* Studies in Reformed Theology and History 4 (Princeton Theological Seminary, 1999) that the language of the *Heidelberg Catechism* on the sacraments is intentionally vague on matters on which the major leaders of the Reformation would disagree. This language was specifically chosen to accommodate all the viewpoints of the Reformation (with the exception of the pre-Melanchthonian unmodified Lutheran view). For the purpose of this chapter's argument, it is sufficient to note that the language on the sacraments is grounded in a Reformation understanding, albeit a consensus statement.

[45] Collins, *An Orthodox Catechism,* 25.

[46] Ibid.

[47] Ibid., 26.

[48] The only real change of note is the change of the title of the section from "Of the Holy Supper of Our Lord Jesus Christ" in the *Heidelberg* to "Of the Lord's Supper." This change was probably made because the former smacked of the High Anglicanism of the late seventeenth century.

me; than I receive and taste by the mouth of my body the bread and wine, the signs of the body and blood of our Lord, received at the hand of the minister."[49] Further, the one who partakes of the body of Christ at the Lord's Table can be said to be made "more and more to be united to his sacred body, that though he be in heaven, and we on earth, yet neverthe-less are we flesh of his flesh, and bone of his bones: and as all the members of the body are by one soul" through the work of "the Holy Ghost, who dwelleth both in Christ and us."[50] Likewise, Collins affirms that in the Lord's Supper, which he calls a "visible sign and pledge," God assures us that we are "partakers of his body and blood, through the working of the Holy Ghost."[51] According to Michael Haykin, this statement means that: "From Collins' perspective, although Christ's body is in heaven, we can have communion with the risen Christ in the Supper through the Spirit."[52] By retaining this language, Collins is assenting to the spiritual presence view of the Lord's Supper originally articulated by John Calvin.[53]

Changes to the *Heidelberg Catechism* in the *Orthodox Catechism*

The most noticeable change made by Hercules Collins in the *Orthodox Catechism* is the change of the section dealing with baptism. Collins' desire to promote unity between Baptists and other Protestant groups did not cause him to compromise this Baptist distinctive. In fact, in his preface which calls for unity on the "essence of Christianity," Collins stated that he only differed with the "orthodox divines" in "some things about Church-constitution, wherein I have taken a little pains to show you the true form of God's house."[54] The first hint within the catechism that Collins will make a significant change on the subject of baptism is found when he inserts the phrase "figured out in holy Baptism"[55] into the answer to ques-tion 43 of the *Heidelberg Catechism*. This question describes the believer's sharing with Christ in His crucifixion, death, and burial. Collins insertion of the above phrase demonstrates the importance of the symbol's corre-spondence to the thing signified for Baptists.

[49] Collins, *An Orthodox Catechism*, 39.

[50] Ibid.

[51] Ibid., 42.

[52] Michael A.G. Haykin, "'His soul-refreshing presence': The Lord's Supper in Calvinistic Baptist Thought and Experience in the 'Long" Eighteenth Cen-tury," in *Baptist Sacramentalism*, ed. Anthony R. Cross and Philip E. Thompson. Studies in Baptist History and Thought 5 (London: Paternoster Press, 2003), 181.

[53] See John Calvin, *Institutes of the Christian Religion*, Book IV, Chapter VII.

[54] Collins, *An Orthodox Catechism*, Preface.

[55] Ibid., 16.

Though the questions describing the meaning of baptism remain unchanged in the *Orthodox Catechism*, Collins has added a complete section on the mode of baptism. This illustrates that the Baptists' quarrel with the Reformed bodies was not over their understanding of the meaning of baptism (at least as applied to adults). Their disagreement was over the mode of baptism and the identity of the proper recipients. In answer to the question "What is Baptism?" (which is conspicuous by its absence in the *Heidelberg Catechism*), Collins reproduces the description of baptism from the *Second London Confession of Faith* almost word for word: "Immersion or dipping of the person in water in the name of the Father, Son, and Holy Ghost, by such who are duly qualified by Christ."[56] Having answered the question of mode with this definition, this answer begs the question: "Who are the proper subjects of this ordinance?"

The response, once again, comes from the *Second London Confession*: "Those who do actually profess repentance towards God, faith in, and obedience to our Lord Jesus Christ."[57] Collins continues his treatment of baptism by denying the validity of the baptism of infants based upon the fact that Scripture nowhere commands it.[58] This is followed by a series of questions providing an extended four and a half page rebuttal of arguments for infant baptism from a theology of the covenants.[59] From this point on, Collins resumes following the *Heidelberg Catechism* in its treatment of the meaning of baptism. The discussion of the mode and proper recipients of baptism constitutes the main area of divergence between the two catechisms.

Additions to the *Heidelberg Catechism* in the *Orthodox Catechism*

There are four notable additions to the *Heidelberg Catechism* which Hercules Collins makes in his *Orthodox Catechism*. For the most part, these do not reflect a disagreement with the framers of the *Heidelberg Catechism*, but a special emphasis which Collins wanted to add for his edition. To the section on baptism is added a question regarding the "Laying On of Hands" upon the baptized. To the section on the Lord's Supper is added a question regarding the "Singing of a Hymn" after the Supper. Between the Lord's Prayer and its exposition is added a question on whether Christians are tied to using a form in prayer. At the very end of the catechism, follow-

---

[56] Ibid., 26. Cf. *The Second London Confession of Faith*, 29.1.

[57] Collins, *An Orthodox Catechism*, 26. Cf. *The Second London Confession of Faith*, 29.2.

[58] Collins, *An Orthodox Catechism*, 26–27.

[59] Ibid., 27–31.

ing the Apostles' Creed are added the Nicene and Athanasian creeds. The significance of these additions will be treated below.

Laying On of Hands

In his insistence that the laying on of hands upon the baptized was commanded by Scripture, Hercules Collins represents a minority position among seventeenth-century Particular Baptists. This was a commonly held belief among the General Baptists of the period, being included in their *Orthodox Creed* of 1678 as a major article of faith.[60] The other notable exception in the belief of this doctrine among Particular Baptists of the period was Benjamin Keach.[61] Collins believed it was "the duty of every Christian to be under this practice" which he defined as:

> Christ's ministers laying their hands solemnly upon the head of the baptized, with prayer to Almighty God for an increase of the graces and gifts of the Holy Ghost, to enable us to hold fast the faith which we now visibly own, having entered into the church by holy Baptism, and also be helped thereby to maintain constant war against the world, flesh and Devil.[62]

Singing of Hymns

Just as the laying on of hands was an ordinance to be added to the sacrament of baptism, so too was the singing of a hymn to be added to the sacrament of the Lord's Supper. This was a matter of no small controversy among the Baptists of the day.[63] Collins makes a beautiful, but succinct argument for the practice in these words:

> In singing praises to God vocally and audibly for his great benefits and blessings to his church in the shedding of the most precious blood of his

---

[60] See Article XXXII in *The Orthodox Creed* located in Lumpkin, *Baptist Confessions of Faith*, 295–334.

[61] Interestingly, this practice was brought over to America by Elias Keach, son of Benjamin, who persuaded the Philadelphia Baptists to include an article in their confession on the laying on of hands of the baptized. See Article XXXI in *The Philadelphia Confession* located in Lumpkin, *Baptist Confessions of Faith*, 351.

[62] Collins, *An Orthodox Catechism*, 34.

[63] On the hymn-singing controversy, see Murdina D. MacDonald, "London Calvinistic Baptists, 1689–1727: Tensions Within a Dissenting Community Under Toleration" (DPhil thesis, Regent's Park College, University of Oxford, 1982), 44–82; and Walker, *The Excellent Benjamin Keach*, 275–303.

Son to take away their sin; which blessings are pointed out in this sacrament. Also we find our Lord and his disciples did close up this ordinance in singing an hymn or psalm; and if Christ did sing, who was going to die, what cause have we to sing for whom he died, that we might not eternally die, but live a spiritual and eternal life with Father, Son, and Spirit in inexpressible glory.[64]

In addition to this section in the catechism, there is attached to this document "An Appendix Concerning the Ordinance of Singing"[65] in which the author sets forth the arguments for singing praise to God, as well as the proper attitude to accompany such singing. "Singing," says Collins, "is a moral duty"[66] and it must be accompanied with "faith," "spiritual joy" and "grace."[67]

Set Forms of Prayer

In between the Lord's Prayer and its exposition in the catechism, Collins inserts a question which raises a matter of particular concern to Baptists, as well as other Separatists. "Christians are tied to this very form of prayer."[68] This was a very important question considering that the Puritans had been ejected from their positions in the Church of England in 1662, largely because they would not use set forms of liturgy, including prayer, in their worship. Collins rightly asserts that the Lord's Prayer is:

… a brief sum of those things which we are to ask of God, but yet Christ will have us also to descend unto specials, and to ask particular benefits: for this form prescribed is nothing else but a set or course of certain heads or generals, whereunto all benefits both corporal and spiritual may be referred.[69]

This section again reflects the pastoral wisdom of Hercules Collins as he anticipates the needs and questions of his congregation regarding prayer.

---

[64] Collins, *An Orthodox Catechism*, 44–45.
[65] Ibid., 75–86. Excerpts found in Haykin and Weaver, *Devoted to the Service of the Temple*, 79–84.
[66] Collins, *An Orthodox Catechism*, 76.
[67] Ibid., 85.
[68] Ibid., 65–66.
[69] Ibid., 65.

The Creeds

At the very end of his catechism, Collins adds to the *Heidelberg's* already included Apostles' Creed, two more: the Nicene and Athanasian creeds. Together, these three creeds contain, in the words of Philip Schaff,

> ... in brief popular outline, the fundamental articles of the Christian faith, as necessary and sufficient for salvation. They embody the results of the great doctrinal controversies of the Nicene and post-Nicene ages. They are a profession of faith in the only true and living God, Father, Son, and Holy Ghost, who made us, redeemed us, and sanctifies us. They follow the order of God's own revelation, beginning with God and the creation, and ending with the resurrection of the body and the life everlasting. They set forth the articles of faith in the form of facts rather than dogmas, and are well suited ... for catechetical and liturgical use.[70]

The significance of the addition of the Nicene and Athanasian creeds to the Apostles' Creed in light of the doctrinal aberrations of Thomas Collier on the issue of the Trinity should be obvious. These creeds address many of the issues on which Collier had equivocated. Collins is here taking a position of orthodoxy that is unimpeachable. As he wrote in the Preface: "I have not undertaken to present you with new notions or principles, hoping an Athenian spirit is in none of you, but do believe that an old gospel (to you that have tasted the sweetness of it) will be more acceptable than a new, though published by an angel from Heaven."[71] This truly is an orthodox catechism, but is it thoroughly Protestant?

The Regulative Principle as the Basis for Collins' Edits

Having surveyed the historical origins of both the *Heidelberg* and *Orthodox* catechisms, the motivations of Hercules Collins for producing the catechism, and the way in which Collins edited the contents of his catechism; perhaps we are now prepared to make an assessment as to the basis upon which Collins has edited the *Heidelberg Catechism*. In all the decisions which Collins made regarding the content of his catechism, there is one recurring theme: the authority of Scripture to govern our worship. This principle is stated succinctly in the catechism in answer to the question of what the second commandment requires. The answer: "That we should not express or represent God by any image or shape and figure, or worship him any otherwise than he hath commanded himself in his Word

---

[70] Schaff, *Creeds of Christendom*, 1:13.
[71] Collins, *An Orthodox Catechism*, Preface.

to be worshiped."[72] This is nothing other than the regulative principle[73] in a nutshell. This principle can be traced back to the Genevan reformer John Calvin who stated in his tract on *The Necessity of Reforming the Church* that "God disapproves of all modes of worship not expressly sanctioned by His Word."[74] And even more forcefully, that: "God rejects, condemns, abominates all fictitious worship, and employs his Word as a bridle to keep us in unqualified obedience."[75]

What logic explains why Hercules Collins, though desirous to show unity with the wider Protestant Orthodox divines, nevertheless rejects their understanding of baptism? He denies the validity of infant baptism with these words: "We have neither precept nor example for that practice in all the Book of God."[76] To the question, "Doth the Scripture any where expressly forbid the baptizing of infants?" Collins replies: "It is sufficient that the Divine Oracle commands the baptizing of believers, unless we will make ourselves wiser than what is written. Nadab and Abihu were not forbidden to offer strange fire, yet for so doing they incurred God's wrath, because they were commanded to take fire from the altar." This logic by Collins mirrors that of Calvin who said, "it ought to be sufficient for the rejection of any mode of worship, that it is not sanctioned by the command of God."[77] For Collins, it was the Reformation's regulative principle of worship which required the rejection of infant baptism. This was also his argument in his treatise on baptism titled *Believer's Baptism from Heaven*. There Collins wrote that his intention in publishing this book was:

> … to display this Sacrament in its apostolic primitive purity, free from the adulterations of men, a sin which God charged upon the learned Jews, that they made void the commands of God by their traditions. O that none of the learned among the Gentiles, especially those of the

---

[72] Ibid., 52.

[73] The regulative principle's definitive treatment in a work first published in 1648 written by the Puritan Jeremiah Burroughs (1599–1646). *Gospel Worship* (Morgan, PA: Soli Deo Gloria Publications, 1990). Interestingly, the early English Baptist historian Thomas Crosby uses Burrough's (a paedo-baptist) own words to argue for Baptist principles in the Preface to his *The History of the English Baptists* (London, 1738), 1:xi-xiii.

[74] John Calvin, "The Necessity of Reforming the Church," in *Tracts Related to the Reformation*, trans. Henry Beveridge (Edinburgh: The Calvin Translation Society, 1844), 1:128.

[75] Ibid., 133.

[76] Collins, *An Orthodox Catechism*, 26–27.

[77] Calvin, "The Necessity of Reforming the Church," 1:133.

Reformed churches, may be charged with setting up men's inventions in the room of Christ's institutions.[78]

This helps explain why Collins would retain so much of a Reformed document, while rejecting its teaching on infant baptism. He believed that the catechism's teaching elsewhere was justified by Scripture, but where it was not, Collins was bound to follow Scripture.

Conclusion

Hercules Collins' commitment to the Reformation's regulative principle is perhaps most clearly seen in the Preface to his catechism where, in the midst of an appeal for Christian unity based on a common commitment to the "fundamental principles and articles of the Christian faith," he explains his "differing in some things about Church-constitution." He expresses his hope that his zeal for "the true form of God's house" will not be misunderstood. So he explains:

> That God whom we serve is very jealous of his worship; and forasmuch as by his providence the law of his house hath been preserved and continued to us, we look upon it as our duty in our generation to be searching out the mind of God in his holy oracle, as Ezra and Nehemiah did the Feast of Tabernacles, and to reform what is amiss; As Hezekiah, who took a great deal of pains to cleanse the House of God, and set all things in order, that were out of order, particularly caused the people to keep the Passover according to the Institution: for it had not, saith the text, been of a long time kept in such sort as it was written; and albeit the pure institutions of Christ were not for some hundreds of years practiced according to the due order, or very little, through the innovations of antichrist; and as circumcision for about forty years was unpracticed in the wilderness, yet as Joshua puts this duty in practice as soon as God signified his mind in that particular, so we having our judgments informed about the true way of worship, do not dare to stifle the light God hath given us.[79]

Though baptism may have been largely lost for centuries, it had now been recovered as a direct result of a recovered emphasis on the authority and sufficiency of the Word of God in the Protestant Reformation. Collins' zeal for worship regulated by God's Word drove him to reject the human innovation of infant baptism. In so doing, he was never more true to the spirit of Protestantism.

[78] Hercules Collins, *Believers Baptism from Heaven, and of Divine Institution. Infants-Baptism from Earth, and Human Invention* (London, 1691), 7.
[79] Collins, *An Orthodox Catechism*, Preface.

A N
Orthodox Catechifm:

Being the Sum of

Chriftian Religion,

Contained in the Law and Gofpel.

Publifhed

For preventing the Canker and
Poifon of 𝔥𝔢𝔯𝔢𝔰𝔶 and 𝔈𝔯𝔯𝔬𝔯.

By H. COLLINS.

Search the Scriptures. John 14. 39.

*The Words that I have fpoken, the fame
fhall judge you in the laft day.* John 12.48.

LONDON,

Printed in the Year, 1680.

An
Orthodox Catechism:
Being the Sum of
Christian Religion,
Contained in the Law and Gospel.

Published

For Preventing the Canker and
Poison of Heresy and Error.

by H. COLLINS.

Search the Scriptures. John 5.39.

The Words that I have spoken, the same
shall judge you in the Last day. John 12.48.

London,
Printed in the Year, 1680.

The Preface.

Unto the Church of Christ, who upon Confession of Faith have been Baptized, Meeting in Old-Gravil-Lane London, Grace Mercy and Peace be multiplied unto you, and the good will of him which dwelt in the Bush be with your Spirits, Amen.

Dearly Beloved,

Forasmuch as there is but a small time allotted unto any of us in this World, and not knowing but my Staff standeth next the Door ready to depart, I am desirous in this respect so to bestow my precious and present time in my Lord's business, as I may not return to him with my Talent wrapt up in a Napkin, but may leave behind me some poor token and testimony of my Love and Duty towards him, and his blessed Spouse the Church.

And forasmuch as the day we live in is very gloomy and dark, full of Error and Heresy, which spreads more and more (through the indefatigable indeavours of the maintainers of it) like an overflowing Leprosy, and eateth as doth a Canker.

Also considering it is a day of great declension in love to God and one to another also, from those Gospel Truths, the least of which is more worth then our lives: all which may give God just cause to say to England's Professors, as once to Israel, What iniquity have your Fathers found in me that they are gone away far from me? As if God should say, Am I not the same as ever in Power, Goodness, Faithfulness? is not my Word and Ordinances the same, yea my Promises and Heaven the same now as ever?

Now that you may not be shaken, shattered and carried away with every wind and blast, every puff and breath of Error, and Heresy; also that you may be the better established, strengthened, and settled on that sure Rock and Foundation of Salvation, Christ's Merits, in opposition to the poor imperfect works of an impotent Creature; also settled on the foundation of Church-constitution, on which you are already built, through the Grace of God which stirred you up to search the divine Oracle, and Rule of Divine Service, as Ezra and Nehemiah searched into the particular parts of Gods Worship, by which means they came to the practice of that almost lost Ordinance of God, the Feast of Tabernacles, which for many years was not practised after the due order, though a general notion was retained about it; I say, under these Considerations, I have in charitable regard to your Souls, presented you with this small (but I am bold to say) sound piece of Divinity, which may not unfitly be stiled an Abridgment, or Epitome of Law and Gospel, suited to every ones capacity in God's House: here is Milk for Babes, and Meat for strong Men. It may not unfitly be compared to the Waters of the Sanctuary, where some may go up to the Ancles, others to the Knees, others to the Loins, and they are deep enough for others to swim in. Here you are not only taught to be good Christians, but good Moralists; the wane of which among them that have the Leaves and Lamps of Profession (as 'tis to be feared such have little more) is of a heart-breaking Consideration to many that desire to walk wit God.

Now albeit here may be many things which some of you may know already, yet unto such those things I hope will be acceptable as St. Peter's Epistles were to the scattered Saints, though they knew much of the matter before, yet I dare say here is some things which may be for information as well as establishment to the most knowing among you.

I have not undertaken to present you with new Notions or Principles, hoping an Athenian Spirit is in none of you, but do believe that an old Gospel (to you that have tasted the sweetness of it) will be more acceptable than a new, though published by an Angel from Heaven.

In what I have written you will see I concenter with the most Orthodox Divines in the Fundamental Principles and Articles of the Christian Faith, and also have industriously expressed them in the same words,
which have on the like occasion been spoken, only differing in some things
about Church-constitution, wherein I have taken a little pains to show
you the true form of God's House, with the coming in thereof, and the
going out thereof: but I hope my Zeal in this will not be misinterpreted
by any that truly fear God. That God whom we serve is very jealous of his
Worship; and forasmuch as by his Providence the Law of his House hath
been preserved and continued to us, we look upon it as our Duty in our
generation to be searching out the mind of God in his holy Oracle, as Ezra
and Nehemiah did the Feast of Tabernacles, and to reform what is amiss,
As Hezekiah, who took a great deal of pains to cleanse the House of God,
and set all things in order, that were out of order, particularly caused the
People to keep the Passover according to the Institution: for it had not,
saith the Text, been of a long time kept in such sort as it was written; and
albeit the pure Institutions of Christ were not for some hundred of years
practiced according to the due order, or very little, through the Innovations
of Antichrist; and as Circumcision for about forty years was unpracticed
in the Wilderness, yet as Joshua puts this duty in practice as soon as God
signified his mind in that particular; so we having our judgments informed
about the true way of Worship, do not dare to stifle the Light God hath
given us.

Now albeit there are some differences between many Godly Divines
and us in Church-Constitution, yet inasmuch as those things are not the
Essence of Christianity, but that we do agree in the fundamental Doctrine
thereof, there is sufficient ground to lay aside all bitterness and prejudice,
and labour to maintain a spirit of Love each to other, knowing we shall
never see all alike here. We find in the primitive times that the Baptism of
Christ was not universally known, witness the ignorance of Apollos that
eminent Disciple and Minister, which know only the Baptism of John.
And if God shall enlighten any into any Truth, which they shall stifle for
base and unwarrantable ends, know that 'tis God must judge, and not Man.
And wherein we cannot concur, let us leave that to the coming of Christ
Jesus, as they did their difficult cases in the Church of old until there did
arise a Priest with Urim and Thummin, that might certainly inform them
of the mind of God there-about.

I have proposed three Creeds to your consideration, which ought thoroughly to be believed and embraced by all those that would be accounted
Christians, viz. the Nicene Creed, Athanasius His Creed, and the Creed
commonly called the Apostles; the last of which contains the sum of the

Gospel; which is industriously opened and explained; and I beseech you do not slight it because of its Form, nor Antiquity, nor because supposed to be composed by Men; neither because some that hold it maintain some Errors, or whose Conversation may not be correspondent to such fundamental Principles of Salvation; but take this for a perpetual Rule, That whatever is good in any, owned by any, whatever Error or Vice it may be mixed withal, the Good must not be rejected for the Error or Vice sake, but owned, commended, and accepted. Here is also in the close of the Book a brief, but full Exposition of that Prayer Christ taught his Disciples. Also the Decalogue, or ten Commandments unfolded.

Now forasmuch as I have taken a great deal of pains in gathering these broken fragments together for your utility and profit, I hope you will take a little pains to read it, and more to live it; and I pray do it seriously and observingly. Read it humbly and frequently, read it with prayer and meditation, then am I sure thou who art a true Christian wilt love it more & more. And as you love your own Souls, love your Children, and declare it in praying for them, as Job did for his, and instructing them as Abraham did his, also winning them to good by a good Example. And that this Book may be of advantage to Youth as well as others, it is catechistically handled for their more easy learning the Principles of Christian Religion, that so they being seasoned with the true Articles of Christian Faith, may not so easily be tainted with the sentiments of Men of corrupt minds in time of Temptation. And it is heartily desired that Parents, especially professing ones, were more concerned for the everlasting welfare of their Children, as David was for Solomon, when he charged him near his death to keep the Commandments and Judgments of God above all. And if Parents would but conscientiously read those Divine Oracles which hold forth their Duty to their Children, it would doubtless be to them of great advantage.

As for this that I have presented to public view, I beg the Readers kind indulgence as to the faults escaped therein: And for those whom the Lord hath committed to my Charge, that the Eternal God may be your Refuge, and underneath you everlasting Arms; that Grace may be opened to your Hearts, and your Hearts to Grace; that the blessing of the God of Abraham, Isaac and Jacob may be upon you, and the eternal Spirit may be with you, shall be the Prayer of your unworthy Brother, but more unworthy Pastor,

H. C.

A Catechism Containing the Sum of Christian Religion

Q. 1.   What is your only comfort in life and death?

A.   That both in soul and body (a), whether I live or die (b), I am
          not my own, but belong wholly unto my most faithful Lord
          and Savior Jesus Christ (c). By His most precious blood fully
          satisfying for all my sins (d), He has delivered me from all the
          power of the devil (e), and so preserves me (f), that without
          the will of my heavenly Father not so much as a hair may fall
          from my head (g). Yes, all things must serve for my safety (h)
          and by His Spirit, also He assures me of everlasting life (i), and
          makes me ready and prepared (j), that from now on I may live
          to Him.

> (a) 1 Corinthians 6:19; 1 Thessalonians 5:10. (b) Romans 14:8.
> (c) 1 Corinthians 3:23. (d) 1 Peter 1:18–19; 1 John 1:7; 2:2.
> (e) 1 John 3:8; Hebrews 2:14–15. (f) John 6:39. (g) Matthew
> 10:30; Luke 21:18. (h) Romans 8:28. (i) 2 Corinthians 1:12; 5:5;
> Ephesians 1:13–14. (j) Romans 8:24–25.

Q. 2.   How many things are necessary for you to know that, enjoy-
          ing this comfort, you may live and die happily?

A.   Three. The first, what is the greatness of my sin and misery (a).
          The second, how I am delivered from all sin and misery (b).
          The third, what thanks I owe to God for this delivery (c).

> (a) Luke 24:47; Romans 3:23. (b) Romans 8:15; 1 Corinthians
> 6:11; Titus 3:3–8. (c) Matthew 5:16; Romans 6:11–13; Ephesians
> 5:10; Titus 2:11–12; 1 Peter 2:9; 3:10–12.

THE FIRST PART
Of Man's Misery

Q. 3.   From what source do you know your misery?

A.   From the law of God (a).

> (a) Romans 3:20; 5:20; 7:5, 13.

Q. 4.   What does the law of God require of us?

A.   That which Christ summarily teaches us, Matthew 22:37–40.
          You shall love the Lord your God with all your heart, with all
          your soul, and with all your mind, and with all your strength
          (a). This is the first and the great commandment; and the sec-

ond is like it, You shall love your neighbor as yourself. On these two commandments hang the whole Law and the Prophets.

(a) Luke 10:27.

Q. 5. **Are you able to keep all these things perfectly?**

A. No (a). By nature I am prone to the hatred of God and of my neighbors (b).

(a) Romans 3:10, 23; 1 John 1:8. (b) Romans 8:7; Ephesians 2:3; Titus 3:3.

Q. 6. **Did God then make man so wicked and perverse?**

A. Not so (a). He made him good, and in His own image (b), endowing him with true righteousness and holiness (c), that he might rightly know God his Creator, and heartily love Him, and live with Him blessed forever, and that to laud and magnify Him (d).

(a) Genesis 1:31. (b) Genesis 1:26–27. (c) Ephesians 4:24; Colossians 3:10. (d) 2 Corinthians 3:18.

Q. 7. **From what source does the wickedness of man's nature arise?**

A. From the fall and disobedience of our first parents, Adam and Eve (a). For this reason our nature is so corrupt and we are all conceived and born in sin (b).

(a) Romans 5:12, 18–19. (b) Genesis 5:3; Psalm 51:5.

Q. 8. **Are we so corrupt that we are not at all able to do well and are prone to all vice?**

A. Indeed we are, except we are regenerated by the Holy Spirit (a).

(a) Genesis 6:5; Job 14:4; 15:16; Isaiah 53:6; John 3:5.

Q. 9. **Does not God, then, do injury to man who in the law requires that of him which he is not able to perform?**

A. No. God made man such a one as he might perform it (a), but man, by the impulsion of the devil (b) and his own stubbornness bereaved himself and all his posterity of those divine graces (c).

(a) Ecclesiastes 7:29. (b) Genesis 3. (c) Romans 5:12–21.

Q. 10.   Does God leave this stubbornness and falling away of man unpunished?

A.   No. He is angry in a most dreadful manner (a), for the sins wherein we are born and which we ourselves commit. In a most just judgment, He punishes them with present and everlasting punishments as He pronounces: "Cursed is he that does not confirm all the words of this law to do them" (b).

          (a) Romans 5:12. (b) Deuteronomy 27:26; Galatians 3:10.

Q. 11.   Is not God therefore merciful?

A.   Yes, very much so! He is merciful (a), but He is also just (b), wherefore His justice requires that the same which is committed against the divine majesty of God should also be recompensed with extreme, that is, everlasting punishment both in body and soul.

          (a) Exodus 34:6; Psalm 5:4–6. (b) Exodus 20:5.

THE SECOND PART
Of Man's Redemption

Q. 12.   Seeing, then, by the just judgment of God we are subject both to temporal and eternal punishments, is there yet any way or means remaining whereby we may be delivered from these punishments and be reconciled to God?

A.   God will have His justice satisfied (a). Therefore, it is necessary that we satisfy it either by ourselves or by another (b).

          (a) Exodus 20:5, 7; 23:7. (b) Romans 8:3.

Q. 13.   Are we able to satisfy God's justice by ourselves?

A.   Not one bit. Instead, we increase our debt every day (a).

          (a) Job 9:2–3; 15:15; Matthew 6:12.

Q. 14.   Is there any creature in heaven or in earth, which is only a creature, able to satisfy for us?

A.   None. For first, God will not punish that sin which man has committed in any other creature; and second, neither can that which is nothing but a creature sustain the wrath of God against sin and deliver others from it (a).

          (a) Job 4:18; 25:5; Psalm 130:3; Hebrew 2:14–18; 10:5–10.

Q. 15. What manner of mediator and deliverer, then, must we seek for?

A. Such a one as is very man and perfectly just, and yet in power above all creatures, that is, one who also is very God (a).

> (a) Isaiah 7:14; 53:11; Jeremiah 23:6; Romans 8:3; 1 Corinthians 15:25; 2 Corinthians 5:14; Hebrew 7:16.

Q. 16. Why is it necessary that the mediator be very man and perfectly just as well?

A. Because the justice of God requires that the same human nature which has sinned do itself likewise make recompense for sin (a); but he that is himself a sinner, cannot make recompense for others (b).

> (a) Romans 5:12, 17. (b) 1 Peter 3:18; Hebrew 7:26.

Q. 17. Why must he also be very God?

A. That He might by the power of His Godhead sustain in His flesh the burden of God's wrath (a) and might recover and restore to us that righteousness and life which we lost (b).

> (a) Isaiah 55:3, 8; Acts 2:24; 1 Peter 3:18.
> (b) John 3:16; Acts 20:28; 1 John 1:2; 4:9–10.

Q. 18. And who is that mediator which is together both very God and very perfectly a just man?

A. Even our Lord Jesus Christ (a) who is made to us of God's wisdom, righteousness, sanctification and redemption (b).

> (a) Matthew 1:23; Luke 2:11; John 14:16; 1 Timothy 2:5; 3:16.
> (b) 1 Corinthians 1:30.

Q. 19. From what source do you know this?

A. Out of the gospel which God first made known in paradise (a), and afterwards did spread it abroad by the patriarchs and prophets (b), shadowed it by sacrifices and other ceremonies of the law (c), and lastly accomplished it by His only begotten Son, Christ our Lord (d).

> (a) Genesis 3:15. (b) Genesis 22:18; 49:10–11; Acts 3:22; 10:43; Romans 1:2; Hebrews 1:1. (c) John 5:46; Hebrews 10:7ff.
> (d) Romans 10:4; Galatians 3:24; 4:4; Hebrews 13:8.

Q. 20.   Is, then, salvation restored by Christ to all men who perished in Adam?

A.   Not at all, but to those only who by a true faith are ingrafted into or untied with Him (a).

> (a) Psalm 2:12; Isaiah 53:11; John 1:12; 3:36; Romans 11:20; Hebrews 4:2; 10:39.

Q. 21.   What is faith?

A.   It is not only a knowledge, whereby I surely assent to all things which God has revealed to us in His Word (a), but also an assured trust (b) kindled in my heart by the Holy Spirit (c), through the gospel (d), whereby I make my repose in God being assuredly resolved that remission of sins, everlasting righteousness, and life is given not to others only, but to me also and that freely through the mercy of God for the merits of Christ alone (e).

> (a) Hebrews 11:1–3; Galatians 2:20; James 2:19. (b) Romans 4:16; 5:1; 10:10. (c) Matthew 16:17; John 3:5; Acts 10:45; Galatians 5:22; Philippians 1:19. (d) Mark 16:16; Acts 16:14; Romans 1:16; 10:17; 1 Corinthians 1:21. (e) Acts 10:42–43; Romans 3:24–25.

Q. 22.   What are those things which are necessary for a Christian man to believe?

A.   All things which are promised us in the gospel. The sum of this is briefly comprised in the articles of the catholic and undoubted faith of all true Christians, commonly called the Apostles' Creed.

I believe in God the Father Almighty, Maker of heaven and earth, and in Jesus Christ His only Son, our Lord, who was conceived by the Holy Spirit, born of the virgin Mary, suffered under Pontius Pilate, was crucified, dead and buried, He descended into *hell, the third day He rose from the dead, and ascended into heaven, from where He shall come to judge both the living and the dead. I believe in the Holy Spirit, the holy +catholic Church, the communion of saints, the forgiveness of sins, the resurrection of the body, and the life everlasting. Amen.

> *Not that He, (that is, Christ), went into the place of the damned, but that He went absolutely into the state of the dead. See Dr. Ussher of Christ, in his Body of Divinity, page 174. and Mr. Perkins on the Creed.

+Not that we are to believe in, but that there is a catholic Church, and by catholic, we mean no more than the universal Church, which is a company chosen out of the whole of mankind to everlasting life, by the Word and Spirit of God.

Q. 23. **Into how many parts is this Creed divided?**

A. Into three: the first of the eternal Father, and our creation; the second of the Son, and our redemption; and the third of the Holy Spirit, and our sanctification.

Q. 24. **Seeing there is but one only substance of God (a), why do you name those three, the Father, the Son, and the Holy Spirit?**

A. Because God has manifested Himself in His Word that these three distinct persons are that one true everlasting God (b).

> (a) Deuteronomy 6:4; Isaiah 44:6; 1 Corinthians 8:4; Ephesians 4:6. (b) Psalm 110:1; Isaiah 61:1; Matthew 3:16–17; 28:19; Luke 4:18; John 14:26; 15:26; 2 Corinthians 13:14; Galatians 4:6; Ephesians 2:18; Titus 3:5–6; 1 John 5:7.

God the Father

Q. 25. **What do you believe when you say, "I believe in God the Father Almighty, Maker of heaven and earth"?**

A. I believe in the everlasting Father of our Lord Jesus Christ, who made of nothing heaven and earth (a), with all that are in them, who likewise upholds and governs the same by His eternal counsel (b) and providence. This God I believe to be my God and Father for Christ's sake (c), and therefore to trust in Him, and rely on Him (d), that I do not doubt that He will provide all things necessary both for my soul and body (e). But also, whatever evils He sends on me in this troublesome life, He will turn out to my safety (f), because both He is able to do it, being God Almighty, and willing to do it, being a bountiful Father (g).

> (a) Genesis 1:1–2; Job 33:4; Psalm 33:6; Isaiah 45:7; Acts 4:24; 14:15. (b) Psalm 104:3; 115:3; Matthew 10:29; Romans 11:36; Hebrews 1:3. (c) John 1:12; Romans 8:15; Galatians 4:5–6; Ephesians 1:5. (d) Psalm 55:23. (e) Matthew 6:26; Luke 12:22.
> (f) Romans 8:28. (g) Isaiah 46:4; Romans 8:38–39; 10:12.

Q. 26.   **What is the providence of God?**

A.   The almighty power of God, everywhere present (a), whereby
          He does, as it were, by His hand uphold and govern heaven
          and earth (b), with all creatures therein, so that those things
          which grow in the earth, as likewise rain and drought, fruit-
          fulness and barrenness, meat and drink, health and sickness,
          riches and poverty, in a word, all things come not rashly and
          by chance, but by His fatherly counsel and will (c).

          (a) Psalm 94:9; Isaiah 29:15; Ezekiel 8:12; Acts 17:25.
          (b) Hebrews 1:2–3. (c) Proverbs 22:2; Jeremiah 5:24;
          John 9:3; Acts 14:17.

Q. 27.   **What does this knowledge of the creation and providence of
          God profit us?**

A.   That in adversity we may be patient (a), and thankful in pros-
          perity (b), and have hereafter our chief hope (c) reposed in
          God our most faithful Father. We can be sure that there is
          nothing which may withdraw us from His love (d), forasmuch
          as all creatures are so in His power, that without His will they
          are not able not only to do anything, but not so much as once
          to move (e).

          (a) Job 1:21; Romans 5:3. (b) Deuteronomy 8:10; 1 Thessalonians
          5:18. (c) Romans 5:4–5. (d) Romans 8:19, 38. (e) Job 1:12; 2:6;
          Proverbs 21:1; Acts 17:27.

God the Son

Q. 28.   **Why is the Son of God called Jesus, that is, a Savior?**

A.   Because He saves us from our sins (a); neither ought any safety
          to be sought from any other (b), nor can it be found elsewhere.

          (a) Matthew 1:21. (b) Acts 4:12; Hebrews 7:25.

Q. 29.   **Do they then who seek for happiness and safety of the saints,
          or of themselves, or elsewhere believe in the only Savior Jesus?**

A.   No. For although in word they boast themselves of Him as
          their only Savior, yet indeed they deny the only Savior Jesus
          (a). For either Jesus is not a perfect Savior, or that those who
          embrace Him as their Savior with a true faith, possess all
          things in Him (b) which are required unto salvation.

(a) 1 Corinthians 1:13, 30. (b) Isaiah 9:6; 43:11, 25; John 1:16; Colossians 1:19–20; 2:10; Hebrews 12:2.

Q. 30. Why is He called Christ, that is, Anointed?

A. Because He was ordained of the Father and anointed of the Holy Ghost (a) the chief Prophet and Teacher (b), who has opened unto us the secret counsel and all the will of His Father concerning our redemption (c). He was ordained and anointed the high Priest (d), who with that one only sacrifice of His body has redeemed us (e) and continually makes intercession to His Father for us (f). He was also ordained and anointed a King (g), who rules us by His Word and Spirit, and defends and maintains that salvation which He has purchased for us (h).

> (a) Psalm 45:7; Hebrews 1:9. (b) Deuteronomy 18:15; Acts 3:22.
> (c) Matthew 11:27; John 1:18; 15:15. (d) Hebrews 7:21.
> (e) Romans 3:24; 5:9–10; Hebrews 10:12. (f) Hebrews 7:25.
> (g) Psalm 2:6; Luke 1:33. (h) Matthew 28:18.

Q. 31. But why are you called a Christian?

A. Because through faith I am a member of Jesus Christ (a), and partaker of His anointing (b), that both I may confess His name (c), and present myself unto Him a living sacrifice of thankfulness (d), and also may in this life fight against sin and Satan with a free and good conscience (e), and afterwards enjoy an everlasting kingdom with Christ (f).

> (a) Acts 11:26; 1 Corinthians 6:15. (b) 1 John 2:27. (c) Matthew 10:32. (d) Romans 12:1; Hebrews 13:15; 1 Peter 2:5; Revelation 5:8. (e) Romans 6:12–13; 1 Timothy 1:18–19. (f) 2 Timothy 2:12; Revelation 1:6.

Q. 32. For what cause is Christ called the only begotten Son of God, when we also are the sons of God?

A. Because Christ alone is the eternal and natural Son of the eternal Father (a), and we are but sons adopted of the Father by grace for His sake (b).

> (a) John 3:16; Romans 8:3; Hebrews 1:2–3.
> (b) John 1:12; Galatians 4:5; Ephesians 1:6; 1 John 3:1.

Q. 33.   Why do we call Him our Lord?

A.   Because He, redeeming and ransoming both our body and
          soul from sin, not with gold or silver, but with His precious
          blood, and delivering us from all the power of the devil, has set
          us free to serve Him (a).

          (a) Romans 14:9; 1 Corinthians 6:20; Ephesians 1:7; 1 Timothy
          2:5–6; 1 Peter 1:18.

Q. 34.   What do you believe when you say He was conceived by the
          Holy Spirit, and born of the virgin Mary?

A.   That the Son of God, who is and continues true and everlast-
          ing God (a), took the very nature of man (b), of the flesh and
          blood of the virgin Mary (c), through the working of the Holy
          Spirit (d), that He might be the true Seed of David (e), like
          unto His brethren in all things, sin excepted (f).

          (a) John 20:28; Romans 9:5; 1 John 5:20. (b) Isaiah 7:14; 9:6;
          John 1:14. (c) Galatians 4:4. (d) Matthew 1:20. (e) Romans 1:3.
          (f) Philippians 2:7; Hebrews 4:15; 7:26.

Q. 35.   What profit do you take by Christ's holy conception and na-
          tivity?

A.   That He is our Mediator, and does cover with His innocence
          and perfect holiness my sins (a), in which I was conceived, that
          they may not come in the sight of God (b).

          (a) Hebrews 2:16–17; 4:15. (b) Psalm 32:1; Romans 8:3–4;
          1 Corinthians 1:30; Romans 8:3–4.

Q. 36.   What do you believe when you say He suffered?

A.   That He all the time of His life which He led on the earth,
          but especially at the end of it, sustained the wrath of God,
          both in body and soul (a), against the sin of all mankind, that
          He might by His passion, as the only propitiatory sacrifice
          (b), deliver our body and soul from everlasting damnation and
          purchase for us the favor of God, righteousness, and eternal
          life.

          (a) Isaiah 53:12; 1 Peter 2:4; 3:18. (b) 1 John 2:2; 4:10.

Q. 37.   For what cause should He suffer under Pilate, as being His
          judge?

A.   That He being innocent (a) and condemned before a civil
            judge (b), might deliver us from the severe judgment of God
            which remained for all men (c).

> (a) Luke 23:14; John 19:4. (b) Psalm 69:4; John 15:25.
> (c) Isaiah 53:4–5; 2 Corinthians 5:21; Galatians 3:13.

Q. 38.   **But is there any more in it, that He was fastened to the cross,
            than if He had suffered any other kind of death?**

A.   There is more. By this I am assured that He took upon Him-
            self the curse which did lie on me, for the death of the cross
            was cursed of God (a).

> (a) Deuteronomy 21:23; Galatians 3:13.

Q. 39.   **Why was it necessary for Christ to humble Himself unto
            death?**

A.   Because the justice and truth of God could by no other means
            be satisfied for our sins (a), but by the very death of the Son of
            God (b).

> (a) Genesis 2:17. (b) Philippians 2:8; Hebrews 2:9, 14–18.

Q. 40.   **To what end was He buried?**

A.   That by it He might manifest that He was dead indeed (a).

> (a) Matthew 27:59– 60; Luke 23:53; John 19:38; Acts 13:29.

Q. 41.   **But since Christ died for us, why must we also die?**

A.   Our death is not a satisfaction for our sins, but the abolishing
            of sin and our passage into everlasting life (a).

> (a) John 5:24; Romans 7:24; Philippians 1:23.

Q. 42.   **What other benefit do we receive by the death of Christ?**

A.   That by virtue of His death our old man is crucified, slain, and
            buried together with Him (a), figured out in holy baptism, that
            henceforth evil lusts and desires may not reign in us (b), but
            we may offer ourselves unto Him a sacrifice of thanksgiving
            (c).

> (a) Romans 6:6. (b) Romans 6:12. (c) Romans 12:1.

Q. 43.   **Why is there added, "He descended into hell"?**

A.   That in my greatest pains and most grievous temptations I may support myself with this comfort, that my Lord Jesus Christ has delivered me (by the unspeakable distresses, torments, and terrors of His soul, into which He was plunged both before and then especially when He hung on the cross) from the straits and torments of hell (a).

> (a) Isaiah 53:10; Matthew 27:46. Not that He (that is, Christ) went into the place of the damned, but that He went absolutely into the place of the dead. See Dr. Ussher in his *Body of Divinity*, 174 and Mr. Perkins on the Creed.

Q. 44.   **What does the resurrection of Christ profit us?**

A.   First, by His resurrection, He vanquished death (a), that He might make us partakers of that righteousness which He had gotten us by His death. Second, we are now also stirred up by His power to a new life (b). Lastly, the resurrection of our head, Christ, is a pledge to us of our glorious resurrection (c).

> (a) Romans 4:25; 1 Peter 1:3–4, 21. (b) Romans 6:4; Colossians 3:1. (c) Romans 8:11; 1 Corinthians 15:22–23.

Q. 45.   **How do you understand that He ascended into heaven?**

A.   That Christ, His disciples looking on, was taken up from the earth into heaven (a), and yet still is there for our sakes (b), and will be until He comes again to judge the living and the dead (c).

> (a) Mark 16:19; Luke 24:51; Acts 1:9. (b) Romans 8:34; Ephesians 4:10; Colossians 3:1; Hebrews 4:14; 7:25; 9:11. (c) Matthew 24:30; Acts 1:11.

Q. 46.   Is not Christ with us then until the end of the world, as He has promised?

A.   Christ is true God, and true man, and so according to His manhood is not now on earth (a), but according to His Godhead, His majesty, His grace and Spirit is at no time apart from us (b).

> (a) Matthew 26:11; John 16:18; 17:11; Acts 3:21. (b) Matthew 28:20; John 14:17; 16:13; Ephesians 4:8.

Q. 47. Are not by this means the two natures in Christ pulled apart, if His humanity be not wherever His divinity is?

A. No. Seeing His divinity is incomprehensible, and everywhere present (a), it follows necessarily that the same is without the bounds of His human nature which He took to Himself, and yet is nevertheless in it, and abides personally united to it (b).

> (a) Jeremiah 23:23–24; Acts 7:48–49; 17:27. (b) Matthew 28:6; Colossians 2:9.

Q. 48. What fruit does the ascension of Christ into heaven bring to us?

A. First, that He makes intercession to His Father in heaven for us (a). Second, that we have our flesh in heaven, that we may be confirmed thereby, as by a sure pledge, that He who is our head will lift us up (b), His members, unto Him. Third, that He sends us His Spirit as a pledge between Him and us (c), by whose power we seek after not earthly but heavenly things (d), where He Himself is sitting at the right hand of God (e).

> (a) Romans 8:34; 1 John 2:1–2. (b) John 14:2; 20:17; Ephesians 2:6. (c) John 14:16; 16:7; 2 Corinthians 5:5; Ephesians 1:13–14. (d) Philippians 3:14; Colossians 3:1. (e) Ephesians 1:20; Philippians 3:20.

Q. 49. Why is it further said, "He sits at the right hand of God"?

A. Because Christ is ascended into heaven, to show there that He is the head of His Church (a), by whom the Father governs all things (b).

> (a) Ephesians 1:20–23; 5:23; Colossians 1:18. (b) Matthew 28:18; John 5:22.

Q. 50. What profit is this glory of our head Christ to us?

A. First, that through His Holy Spirit, He pours upon us, His members, heavenly graces (a), and that He shields and defends us by His power against all our enemies (b).

> (a) Ephesians 4:16. (b) Psalm 2:9; 110:2; John 10:28; Ephesians 4:8.

Q. 51. What comfort do you have by the coming of Christ again to judge the living and the dead?

A.   That in all my miseries and persecutions, I look with my head
        lifted up (a), for the very same who before yielded Himself to
        the judgment of God for me, and took away all malediction
        from me, will come as judge from heaven to throw all His and
        my enemies into everlasting pains (b). He will also translate
        me with all His chosen to Himself, into celestial joys, and ev-
        erlasting glory (c).

> (a) Luke 21:28; Romans 8:23; Philippians 3:20; Titus 2:13.
> (b) Matthew 25:41; 2 Thessalonians 1:6–10. (c) Matthew 25:34;
> 1 Thessalonians 4:16–18; Jude 24–25.

God the Holy Spirit

Q. 52.   **What do you believe concerning the Holy Spirit?**

A.   First, that He is true and coeternal God, with the eternal Fa-
        ther and the Son (a). Second, that He is also given unto me (b),
        to make me partaker of Christ and all His benefits through a
        true faith (c), to comfort me (d), and to abide with me forever
        (e).

> (a) Genesis 1:2; Isaiah 48:16; Matthew 28:19; Acts 5:3–4;
> 1 Corinthians 3:16; 6:19. (b) John 14:16. (c) 1 Corinthians 6:17;
> 1 Peter 1:2; 4. (d) Acts 9:31. (e) John 14:16; 1 Peter 4:14.

Q. 53.   **What do you believe concerning the holy and catholic Church
        of Christ?**

A.   I believe that the Son of God does (a), from the beginning to
        the end of the world (b), gather, defend, and preserve for Him-
        self, by His Spirit and Word (c), out of the whole of mankind
        (d), a company chosen to everlasting life (e), and agreeing in
        true faith (f); and that I am a lively member of that company
        (g), and so shall remain forever (h).

> (a) Ephesians 1:10–13. (b) John 10:10; Romans 3:25.
> (c) Isaiah 59:21; Matthew 16:18; Romans 1:16; 10:14–17;
> Ephesians 5:26. (d) Genesis 26:4. (e) Romans 8:29–30.
> (f) Matthew 16:16–18; Ephesians 4:3–6.
> (g) 2 Corinthians 13:5; 1 John 3:21. (h) 1 John 5:20.

Q. 54.   **What do these words mean, the communion of saints?**

A.   First, that all and everyone who believes are in common par-
        takers of Christ and all His graces (a), as being His members,
        and then that everyone ought readily and cheerfully to bestow

the gifts and graces which they have received to the common commodity and safety of all (b).

> (a) Romans 8:32; 1 Corinthians 1:2; 6:17; 12:21; 1 John 1:3.
> (b) 1 Corinthians 12:21; Philippians 2:4–6.

Q. 55. **What do you believe concerning remission of sins?**

A. That God, for the satisfaction made by Christ (a), has put out all the remembrance of my sins (b), and also of that corruption within me which I must fight all my lifetime, and does freely endow me the righteousness of Christ, that I come not at any time into judgment (c).

> (a) 2 Corinthians 5:19, 21; 1 John 2:2. (b) Psalm 103:3–4; 10–12; Jeremiah 31:34; Romans 7:24–25. (c) John 3:18; Romans 8:1–3.

Q. 56. **What comfort do you have by the resurrection of the flesh?**

A. That not only my soul, after it shall depart out of my body, shall presently be taken up to Christ (a), but that this my flesh also, being raised up by the power of Christ, shall again be united to my soul, and made like the glorious body of Christ (b).

> (a) Luke 23:43; Philippians 1:23.
> (b) Job 19:25–26; 1 Corinthians 15:53; Philippians 3:21; 1 John 3:2.

Q. 57. **What comfort do you take from the article of everlasting life?**

A. That forasmuch as I feel already in my heart the beginning of everlasting life (a), it shall at length come to pass that after this life I shall enjoy full and perfect bliss (b), wherein I may magnify God forever, which blessedness surely neither eye has seen, nor ear heard, neither has any man in thought conceived it (c).

> (a) 2 Corinthians 5:1–3. (b) John 17:3; Jude 24–25.
> (c) 1 Corinthians 2:9.

Q. 58. **What profit is there to you when you believe all these things?**

A. That I am righteous in Christ before God, and an heir of eternal life (a).

> (a) John 3:36; Romans 1:17; 3:22, 24, 25, 28; 5:1; Galatians 2:16; Ephesians 2:8–9.

Q. 59.   How are you righteous before God?

A.   Only by faith in Christ Jesus. Although my conscience accuse
          me that I have grievously trespassed against all the command-
          ments of God, and have not kept one of them (a), and further
          am as yet prone to all evil (b), yet nevertheless, if I embrace
          these benefits of Christ with a true confidence and persua-
          sion of mind (c), the full and perfect satisfaction, righteous-
          ness, and holiness of Christ (d), without any merit of mine (e),
          of the mere mercy of God (f) is imputed and given to me (g),
          and that so, as if neither I had committed any sin, neither any
          corruption did stick to me, yes as if I myself had perfectly ac-
          complished that obedience which Christ accomplished for me
          (h).

          (a) Romans 3:9. (b) Romans 7:23. (c) John 3:18; Romans 3:22.
          (d) 1 John 2:1. (e) Romans 3:24; Ephesians 2:8–9; 1 John 2:2.
          (f) Titus 3:5. (g) Romans 4:4–5; 2 Corinthians 5:19.
          (h) 2 Corinthians 5:21.

Q. 60.   Why do you affirm that you are made righteous by faith only?

A.   Not because I please God through the worthiness of mere
          faith, but because only the satisfaction, righteousness, and ho-
          liness of Christ is my righteousness before God (a), and I
          cannot take hold of it, or apply it to myself any other way than
          by faith (b).

          (a) 1 Corinthians 1:30; 2:2. (b) 1 John 5:10.

Q. 61.   Why can't our good works be righteousness, or some part of
          righteousness, before God?

A.   Because the righteousness which must stand fast before the
          judgment of God, must be in all points perfect and agreeable
          to the law of God (a). Now our works, even the best of them,
          are imperfect in this life, and defiled with sin (b).

          (a) Deuteronomy 27:26; Galatians 3:10. (b) Isaiah 64:6.

Q. 62.   How is it that our good works merit nothing, seeing God
          promises that He will give a reward for them both in this life
          and in the life to come?

A.   That reward is not given of merit, but of grace (a).

          (a) Luke 17:10.

Q. 63. But does not this doctrine make men careless and profane?

A. No. Those who are incorporated into Christ through faith, necessarily bring forth the fruits of thankfulness (a).

> (a) Matthew 7:18; John 15:5.

The Sacraments

Q. 64. Since faith alone makes us partakers of Christ and His benefits, from where does this faith come?

A. From the Holy Spirit (a), who kindles it in our hearts by the preaching of the gospel (b), and other ordinances (c), and confirms it by the use of the sacraments (d).

> (a) John 3:5; Ephesians 2:8; 3:16–17; Philippians1:29.
> (b) Romans 10:17. (c) Ephesians 3:16–17; Hebrews 4:16.
> (d) 1 Corinthians 10:16; 1 Peter 3:21.

Q. 65. What are the sacraments?

A. They are sacred signs and seals set before our eyes and ordained of God for this purpose, that He may declare and confirm by them the promise of His gospel unto us, to this, that He gives freely remission of sins and life everlasting to everyone in particular who believes in the sacrifice of Christ which He accomplished once for all upon the cross (a).

> (a) Matthew 28:19–20; 1 Corinthians 10:16; Romans 6:3–6;
> Hebrews 10:10.

Q. 66. Do not then both the Word and sacraments tend to that end, to lead our faith to the sacrifice of Christ finished on the cross as the only ground of our salvation?

A. It is even so. The Holy Spirit teaches us by the gospel, and assures us by the sacraments that the salvation of all of us stands in the once for all sacrifice of Christ offered for us upon the cross (a).

> (a) Romans 6:3; 1 Corinthians 11:23–26; Galatians 3:27.

Q. 67. How many sacraments has Christ ordained in the New Testament?

A. Two. Baptism and the Lord's Supper.

Baptism

Q. 68.   What is baptism?

A.   Immersion or dipping of the person in water in the name of
          the Father, Son, and Holy Spirit, by such who are duly quali-
          fied by Christ (a).

          (a) Matthew 3:16; 28:19–20; John 3:23; Acts 8:38–39;
          Romans 6:4.

Q. 69.   Who are the proper subjects of this ordinance?

A.   Those who do actually profess repentance towards God, and
          faith in and obedience to our Lord Jesus Christ (a).

          (a) Acts 2:38; 8:36–37.

Q. 70.   Are infants to be baptized?

A.   None by no means, for we have neither precept nor example
          for that practice in all the book of God.

Q. 71.   Do the Scriptures anywhere expressly forbid the baptism of
          infants?

A.   It is sufficient that the divine oracle commands the baptiz-
          ing of believers (a), unless we will make ourselves wiser than
          what is written. Nadab and Abihu were not forbidden to offer
          strange fire, yet for so doing they incurred God's wrath, be-
          cause they were commanded to take fire from the altar (b).

          (a) Matthew 28:18–19; Mark 16:16. (b) Leviticus 9:24; 10:1–3.

Q. 72.   May the infant seed of believers under the gospel be baptized
          just as the infant seed of Abraham under the law was circum-
          cised?

A.   No. Abraham had a command then from God to circumcise
          his infant seed, but believers have no command to baptize
          their infant seed under the gospel.

          (a) Genesis 17:9–12.

Q. 73.   Since some say that the infants of believers are in the covenant
          of grace with their parents, why may they not be baptized un-
          der the gospel, just as Abraham's infant seed was circumcised
          under the law?

A.   By asserting that the infants of believers are in the covenant of grace, they must either mean of the covenant of grace absolutely considered, and if so, then there is no total and final apostasy of any infant seed of believers from the covenant, but all must be saved then (a).

(a) Jeremiah 32:38–40; John 10:28.

Or, they must mean conditionally, that when they come to years of maturity, they by true faith, love, and holiness of life, taking hold of God's covenant of grace, shall have the privileges of it. If this is their meaning, then what spiritual privilege does the infant seed of believers have more than the infant seed of unbelievers, if they live also to years of maturity, and by true faith and love take hold God's covenant? Furthermore, would not the seal of the covenant belong as much to the children of unbelievers as to the children of believers? Yes, since the infant seed of the unbeliever sometimes comes to embrace God's covenant, and the infant seed of the believer does not; as often this is seen to the sorrow of many godly parents (b).

(b) Isaiah 56:3–8; John 3:16; Acts 10:34–35.

Suppose all the infant seed of believers are absolutely in the covenant of grace; yet believers under the gospel ought no more to baptize their infant seed than Lot to circumcise himself or his infant seed, if he had males as well as females, although he was related to Abraham, a believer, and in the covenant of grace, since circumcision was limited to Abraham and his immediate family. If the infant seed of believers are absolutely in the covenant of grace, we may bring infants to the Lord's Table because the same qualifications are required to the due performance of baptism as for the Lord's Supper (c).

(c) Acts 2:41–42.

The covenant made with Abraham had two parts:

First, a spiritual component, which consisted in God's promising to be a God to Abraham and all his spiritual seed in a peculiar manner (d), whether they were circumcised or uncircumcised, who believed as Abraham the father of the faithful did (e). And this was signified in God's accepting such as His people which were not of Abraham's seed, but bought with his money, and this promise was sealed to Abraham by circumcision, that through Jesus Christ (whom Isaac typified) the Gentiles, the uncircumcision which believed (f), should have their faith counted for righteousness, as Abraham's was before he was circumcised (g).

(d) Genesis 17:19, 21; 21:10; Galatians 4:30. (e) Acts 2:39; Romans 9:7–8. (f) Galatians 3:16, 28–29. (g) Romans 4:9–14.

Second, this promise consisted of a temporal component. Thus, God promised Abraham's seed should enjoy the land of Canaan, and have plenty of outward blessings (h), so He sealed this promise by circumcision (i). Circumcision also distinguished the Jews as being God's people from all the nations of the Gentiles, which as yet were not the seed of Abraham. But when the Gentiles came to believe and by faith became the people of God as well as the Jews, then circumcision, that distinguishing mark, ceased. The distinguishing mark of being the children of God now is faith in Christ and circumcision of the heart (j). Therefore, whatever pretence there may be to baptize the infants of believers avails nothing, whether their being the seed of believers, their being in the covenant, or that the infant seed of Abraham, a believer, was circumcised. Circumcision was limited also to the family of Abraham, all others, though believers, being excluded. Circumcision was limited also to the eighth day, and whatever pretence might be made, it was not to be done before nor after. It was limited to males, which if baptism came in the room of circumcision and is the seal of the covenant under the gospel, as circumcision was under the law, none but males must be baptized. Just as under the law circumcision had peculiar regulations, so it is under the gospel concerning baptism. These regulations concerning baptism depend purely upon the will of the Lawgiver, that Prophet to whom we would do well to listen (k). He determines upon whom, when, and how baptism is to be administered.

(h) Genesis 12:6–7; 13:15–17; 15:16, 18. (i) Genesis 17:8–11.
(j) John 1:12; Romans 2:28–29; Galatians 3:26–28;
Philippians 3:3. (k) Acts 3:22.

Q. 74. How are you admonished and assured in baptism that you are a partaker of the only sacrifice of Christ?

A. Because Christ commanded the outward washing of water (a), joining this promise to it, that I am no less assuredly washed by His blood and Spirit from all uncleanness of my soul, that is, from all my sins (b), than I am washed outwardly from the filthiness of the body with water.

(a) Matthew 28:19; Acts 2:38.
(b) Matthew 3:11; Mark 1:4; 16:16; Luke 3:3; Romans 6:3.

Q. 75. **What is it to be washed with the blood and Spirit of Christ?**

A. It is to receive of God forgiveness of sins freely, for the blood of Christ which He shed for us in His sacrifice upon the cross (a) and also to be renewed by the Holy Spirit, and through His sanctifying of us to become members of Christ, that we may more and more die to sin, and live holy and without blame (b).

(a) Ezekiel 36:25; Zechariah 13:1; Hebrews 12:24; 1 Peter 1:2; Revelation 1:5. (b) John 1:33; 3:5; Romans 6:4; 1 Corinthians 6:11; 12:13; Colossians 2:12.

Q. 76. **Where does Christ promise us that He will as certainly wash us with His blood and Spirit as we are washed with the water of baptism?**

A. In the institution of baptism, the words of which are these, go, teach all nations, baptizing them in the name of the Father, the Son, and the Holy Ghost (a); he that shall believe, and be baptized, shall be saved, but he that will not believe shall be damned (b). This promise is repeated again when the Scripture calls baptism the washing of the new birth (c), and forgiveness of sins (d).

(a) Matthew 28:19. (b) Mark 16:16. (c) Titus 3:5. (d) Acts 22:16.

Q. 77. **Is then the outward baptism in water the washing away of sins?**

A. It is not (a). The blood of Christ alone cleanses us from all sin (b).

(a) Ephesians 5:25–26; 1 Peter 3:21. (b) 1 Corinthians 6:11; 1 John 1:7.

Q. 78. **Why then does the Holy Spirit call baptism the washing of the new birth and forgiveness of sins?**

A. God speaks so not without great cause, to this, not only to teach us that as the filth of our body is purged by water, so our sins also are purged by the blood and Spirit of Christ (a), but much more to assure us by this divine token and pledge that we are as surely washed from our sins with the inward washing as we are washed by the outward and visible water (b).

(a) 1 Corinthians 6:11; Revelation 1:5; 7:14.
(b) Mark 16:16; Galatians 3:27.

Q. 79. What principle of Christ's doctrine in the Holy Scripture follows baptism in order?

A. Laying on of hands, as in Hebrews 6:1–2.

Q. 80. What is the form and end of this ordinance?

A. Christ's ministers laying their hands solemnly upon the head of the baptized with prayer to Almighty God for an increase of the graces (a) and gifts of the Holy Spirit (b), to enable us to hold fast the faith which we now visibly own, having entered into the church by Holy Baptism, and also be helped thereby to maintain a constant war against the world, flesh, and the devil (c).

(a) 2 Timothy 1:6; Acts 2:38–39. (b) John 14:16–18, 26; 16:7.
(c) Ephesians 1:13–14.

Q. 81. Is it the duty of every Christian to be under this practice?

A. It is so and appears plainly if we do first consider the practice of the primitive saints. We may read in Acts 8:12–19 of men and women that were baptized by Philip in Samaria, which when the church at Jerusalem heard thereof, they sent down St. Peter and St. John (two apostles) to them, who when they came there laid their hands on them and they received the Holy Spirit. "What, them?" some may say. Were these they that were baptized which were men and women? So likewise in Acts 19:6–7, when Paul came to Ephesus he found certain disciples there who were baptized but had not heard whether there was any Holy Spirit, nor I conceive of the promise of the Holy Spirit mentioned in Acts 1:4. Then the Apostle laid his hands on them and they received the Holy Ghost, and it is said the number of them was about twelve. And reason shows us from this place, and Acts 8 where St. Peter and St. John laid hands on men and women, that had here been twelve score, he would have laid his hands on them all. And whereas it is objected we do not find the three thousand in Acts 2 under this ordinance, nor many others which were baptized—as to the three thousand it is plain enough they had been taught it, and doubtless so practiced this ordinance, if we consider the Apostle writing to the Jews in Hebrews 5 telling them they had need be taught again the first principles of the oracles of God, which oracles, laying on of hands was one. And as for others which were baptized, where mention is not made of their being under this ordinance, we may also say many hundreds were baptized which we have no mention of. Shall we conclude many of the Apostles were not baptized because it is not particularly mentioned? So we must conclude the primitive saints were not short in this point, although it be not always specified. Forasmuch as it is called one of God's oracles, as we all know the moral law was, which is perpetually binding and universally obliging, also called a principle of Christ's doctrine, yea one of the first principles, and that is not all, but called a foundation principle, this with the other five must be laid first in that foundation on which the superstructure of Christianity must be built. And would it not have been very unbecoming the Jews when God gave them Ten Commandments for them to have excluded, the fourth? Is it not also as unbecoming for any to exclude the fourth principle of laying on of hands, a practical principle of the doctrine of Christ, and so practiced by the primitive Christians? (a)

(a) Hebrews 5:12; Acts 7:38; Hebrews 6:2.

Q. 82.   **Did not the extraordinary gifts of the Spirit follow upon laying on of hands in the Apostles' time?**

A.   It did so, but not simply as the end of that ordinance. For that ordinance was appointed for the ordinary gifts of the Spirit to the world's end. Though it is true God honored and crowned that ordinance with signs and wonders in the primitive time as he did others of his appointment. For instance in Acts 4, the place was shaken as the effect of the church's prayer. So preaching was extraordinarily crowned when St. Peter converted three thousand at one sermon and in God's giving the Holy Spirit to the house of Cornelius while Peter was preaching so that they spoke with tongues, Acts 10. Also God crowned the holy ordinance of baptism extraordinarily when the Spirit came in the likeness of a dove and sat upon our Savior Christ as He came out of the water (Matthew 3) and a voice was heard from heaven, saying, "This is my beloved Son, in whom I am well pleased." Also the eunuch's baptism was wonderfully confirmed to him in God's taking away Philip as soon as he came up out of the water, insomuch that he went away rejoicing. Now, beloved, as prayer, baptism, and preaching does not cease, though it be not so miraculously owned as in the primitive times, neither does laying on of hands cease from the same parity of reason though it be not so crowned now as in the apostles' days. Moreover, our brethren generally do hold, that five of those principles in Hebrews 6 are the duty of every individual member to believe and practice, namely every member (say they) ought to repent, believe, be baptized, believe the resurrection of the dead, and eternal judgment. Why this principle of laying on of hands should be excluded from being the practice of every Christian, since being a practical ordinance the bare belief of it not being enough and it being among the universal principles of Christ's doctrine, I never yet did nor cannot see any good reason.

The Lord's Supper

Q. 83.   How are you in the Lord's Supper admonished and warranted that you are a partaker of that only sacrifice of Christ offered on the cross and of all His benefits?

A.   Because Christ has commanded me and all the faithful to eat of this bread broken and to drink of this cup distributed in remembrance of Him. With this He has joined the promise that His body was as certainly broken and offered for me upon the cross and His blood shed for me as I behold with my eyes the bread of the Lord broken unto me and the cup communicated unto me. Further, my soul is no less assuredly fed to everlasting life with His body, which was crucified for me, and His blood, which was shed for me, than I receive and taste by the mouth of my body the bread and wine, the signs of the body and blood of the Lord, received at the hand of the minister (a).

        (a) Matthew 26:27–28; Mark 14:22–24; Luke 22:16, 20;
        1 Corinthians 10:16–17; 11:23–25; 12:13.

Q. 84. What is it to eat of the body of Christ?

A.   It is not only to embrace, by an assured confidence of mind, the whole passion and death of Christ and thereby to obtain forgiveness of sins and everlasting life (a), but also by the Holy Spirit, who dwells both in Christ and us, so more and more to be united to His sacred body (b), that though He be in heaven and we on earth (c), yet nevertheless we are flesh of His flesh and bone of His bones (d). As all the members of the body are quickened by one soul, so are we also quickened and guided by one and the same Spirit (e).

(a) John 6:35, 40, 47, 48, 50, 51, 53, 54. (b) John 6:56.
(c) Acts 1:9; 3:21; 1 Corinthians 11:26. (d) John 14:23;
1 Corinthians 6:15, 17, 19; Ephesians 5:29, 30, 32; 1 John 3:24;
4.13. (e) John 6:56–58; 15:1–6; Ephesians 4:15–16.

Q. 85. **Where has Christ promised that He will as certainly give His body and blood to be eaten and drank as they eat this bread broken and drink this cup?**

A. In the institution of the Supper, the words of which are these:

Our Lord Jesus Christ in the night that He was betrayed, took bread, and when He had given thanks, He broke it, and said, take, eat, this is My body which is broken for you. This do in remembrance of Me. Likewise also He took the cup, when He had eaten, and said, this cup is the New Covenant in My blood. This do as often as you shall drink it in remembrance of Me. For as often as you shall eat this bread and drink this cup you show the Lord's death until He comes (a).

(a) Matthew 26:26ff.; Mark 14:22ff.; Luke 22:19;
1 Corinthians 11:23ff.

This promise is repeated by St. Paul, where he says, the cup of blessing which we bless, is it not the communion of the blood of Christ? The bread which we break, is it not the communion of the body of Christ? For we that are many are one bread and one body, because we are all partakers of one bread (b).

(b) 1 Corinthians 10:16–17.

Q. 86. **Are then the bread and wine made the very body and blood of Christ?**

A. No. As the water of baptism is not turned into the blood of Christ, but is only a sign and pledge of those things that are sealed to us in baptism, so neither is the bread of the Lord's Supper the very body of Christ, although according to the manner of sacraments and that form of speaking of them which is usual to the Holy Spirit, the bread is called the body of Christ (a).

(a) Matthew 26:28; Mark 14:24; 1 Corinthians 10:16–17.

Q. 87.   **Why then does Christ call bread His body and the cup His blood, or the New Testament in His blood; and St. Paul calls bread and wine the communion of the body and blood of Christ?**

A.   Christ not without great consideration speaks in this manner, not only to teach us that as the bread and wine sustain the life of the body, so also His crucified body and shed blood are indeed the meat and drink of our souls, whereby they are nourished to eternal life (a). But more than that, by this visible sign and pledge, He may assure us that we are as surely partakers of His body and blood (b), through the working of the Holy Spirit as we do perceive by the mouth of our body these holy signs in remembrance of Him, and further also, that His sufferings and obedience is so certainly ours, as though we ourselves had suffered punishments for our sins, and had satisfied God.

(a) John 6:51, 55, 56. (b) 1 Corinthians 10:16–17.

Q. 88.   **What difference is there between the Supper of the Lord and the Popish mass?**

A.   The Supper of the Lord testifies to us that we have perfect forgiveness of all our sins, on account of the only sacrifice of Christ, which He once fully wrought on the cross (a). It also testifies that we, by faith, are grafted into Christ (b), who now according to His human nature is only in heaven at the right hand of His Father (c), and there will be worshipped by us (d). But in the mass it is denied that the living and the dead have remission of sins by the only passion of Christ, except He also be daily offered for them by their sacrifices. Further, it is taught that Christ is bodily under the forms of bread and wine, and therefore is to be worshipped in them and so the very foundation of the mass is nothing else but an utter denial of that only sacrifice and passion of Christ Jesus, and an accursed idolatry.

(a) Matthew 26:28; Luke 22:19–20; John 19:30; Hebrews 7:27; 9:12, 26, 28; 10:10, 12, 14. (b) 1 Corinthians 6:17; 10:16–17; 12:13. (c) Luke 24:5; John 20:17; Acts 7:55–56; Philippians 3:20;

Colossians 3:1; 1 Thessalonians 1:9–10; Hebrews 1:3.
(d) John 4:21–24; Hebrews 1:6, 8.

Q. 89. **Who are to come to the table of the Lord?**

A. They only who are truly sorrowful they have offended God by their sins, and yet trust that those sins are pardoned them for Christ's sake, and what other infirmities they have, that those are covered by His passion and death, who also desire more and more to go forward in faith and integrity of life. But hypocrites, and those who do not truly repent, do eat and drink damnation to themselves (a).

(a) 1 Corinthians 10:21–22; 11:27ff.

Q. 90. **Are they also to be admitted to the Lord's Supper who in confession and life declare themselves to be infidels, profane, and ungodly?**

A. No. By that means the ordinance of God is profaned and the wrath of God is stirred up against the whole assembly (a), wherefore the church by the commandment of Christ and His Apostles, inspired by the Holy Spirit, using the keys of the kingdom of heaven, ought to drive them from this Supper till they shall repent and change their manners.

(a) 1 Corinthians 11:20–22, 34; Cf. Psalm 50:1ff; Isaiah 1:11ff; 66:3; Jeremiah 7:21ff.

Q. 91. **How ought this ordinance of the Lord's Supper to be closed?**

A. In singing praises to God vocally and audibly for His great benefits and blessings to His Church in the shedding of the most precious blood of His Son to take away their sin, which blessings are pointed out in this sacrament. Also, we find our Lord and His disciples concluded this ordinance in singing a hymn or psalm (a). If Christ sang, who was going to die, how much more cause to sing have we for whom He died. He died that we might not eternally die, but live a spiritual and eternal life with Father, Son, and Spirit in inexpressible glory.

(a) Matthew 26:30.

Q. 92. **You told us but now, that those who in confession and life declare themselves to be infidels, profane and ungodly, should**

by the keys of the kingdom of heaven be driven from this Supper. What are the keys of the kingdom of heaven?

A.   The preaching of the gospel and ecclesiastical discipline, by which heaven is opened to the believers, and is shut against the unbelievers (a).

(a) Matthew 16:19; 18:18.

Q. 93.   How is the kingdom of heaven opened and shut by the preaching of the gospel?

A.   The kingdom of heaven is opened when, by the commandment of Christ, it is publicly declared to everyone who believes that all their sins are pardoned by God due to the merit of Christ, as they embrace by a lively faith the promise of the gospel. But to the contrary, the kingdom of heaven is shut when it is announced to all infidels and hypocrites that as long as the wrath of God abides upon them, they perish in their wickedness, according to which testimony of the gospel God will judge them in this life and also in the life to come (a).

(a) Job 20:21–23; Matthew 16:19; John 12:48.

Q. 94.   How is the kingdom of heaven opened and shut by ecclesiastical discipline?

A.   The kingdom of heaven is shut when, according to the commandments of Christ, those who profess to be Christians, but who, in their doctrine and life, show themselves aliens from Christ, and after being admonished, will not depart from their error, heresies, or wickedness, are made known to the church. If they do not obey the church's admonition, they are by the same church to be kept from the sacrament and shut out of the congregation by authority received from Christ, and by God Himself shut out of the kingdom of heaven (a).

(a) Matthew 18:15–17; 1 Corinthians 5:3–5; 2 Thessalonians 3:14–15.

The kingdom of heaven is opened if such persons as above profess and declare an amendment of life, nothing to the contrary being able to be proved upon strict scrutiny and search. These are to be received again in love and tenderness as members of Christ and His church (b).

(b) 2 Corinthians 2:6–7, 10, 11.

THE THIRD PART
Of Mans' Thankfulness

Q. 95.　Whereas we are delivered from all our sins and miseries without any merit of ours, by the mercy of God, only for Christ's sake, for what cause are we to do good works?

A.　Because, after Christ has redeemed us with His blood, He renews us also by His Spirit to the image of Himself, that we, receiving so great benefits, should show ourselves all our lifetime thankful to God, and honor Him (a); secondly that every one of us be assured of his faith by his fruit (b); and lastly, that by our good conversation we may win others to Christ (c).

　　(a) Romans 6:1–4; 12:1–2; 1 Corinthians 6:20; 1 Peter 2:5, 9, 12.
　　(b) Matthew 7:17–18; Galatians 5:22; 2 Peter 1:10.
　　(c) Matthew 5:16; 1 Peter 3:1–2.

Q. 96.　Can they be saved who are unthankful, and remain still careless in their sins, and are not converted from their wickedness to God?

A.　By no means; for as the Scripture bears witness, neither unchaste persons, nor idolaters, nor adulterers, nor thieves, nor covetous, nor drunkards, nor slanderers, nor robbers, shall enter into the kingdom of God (a).

　　(a) 1 Corinthians 6:9–10; Ephesians 5:5–6; 1 John 3:14–15.

Q. 97.　In how many things does true repentance toward or conversion to God consist?

A.　It consists of the dying or mortifying of the old man and the renewing or quickening of the new man (a).

　　(a) Romans 6:4–6; 1 Corinthians 5:7; 2 Corinthians 7:11; Ephesians 4:22–24; Colossians 3:5–10.

Q. 98.　What is the dying or mortifying of the old man?

A.　To be truly and heartily sorry that you have offended God by your sins, and daily more and more hate and avoid them (a).

　　(a) Joel 2:13; Romans 8:13.

Q. 99.　What is the renewing or quickening of the new man?

A.　True joy in God through Christ (a), and an earnest desire to order your life according to God's will and to do all good works (b).

> (a) Romans 5:1; 14:17. (b) Romans 6:10–11; 12:1–2; Galatians 2:20.

Q. 100. What are good works?

A. Those only which are done by a true faith (a), according to God's law (b), and are referred only to His glory (c), and not those which are imagined by us as seeming to be right and good (d), or which are delivered and commanded by men (e).

> (a) Romans 14:23. (b) 1 Samuel 15:22. (c) 1 Corinthians 10:31. (d) Ephesians 2:10. (e) Deuteronomy 11:32; Isaiah 29:13; Ezekiel 20:18–19; Matthew 15:9.

The Law of God

Q. 101. What is the law of God?

A. The Decalogue, or Ten Commandments (a).

> (a) Exodus 20; Deuteronomy 5.

Q. 102. How are these commandments divided?

A. Into two tables (a), whereof the former delivered in four commandments, how we ought to behave ourselves towards God; the latter delivered in six commandments, what duties we owe to our neighbors (b).

> (a) Exodus 34:28; Deuteronomy 4:13; 10:3–4.
> (b) Matthew 22:37–39.

Q. 103. What is the preface to the Ten Commandments?

A. I am Jehovah, the Lord your God, which brought you out of the land of Egypt, out of the house of bondage.

Q. 104. What do we learn from the preface?

A. Three things: first, He shows to whom the right of all rule belongs, that is, to God Himself for I am (says He) Jehovah; secondly, He says, He is the God of His people, that through the promise of His bountifulness He might allure them to obey Him; and thirdly, He says, which brought you out of the land of Egypt, as if He should say, I am He who has manifested Myself to you and bestowed all those blessings upon you, therefore you are bound to show thankfulness and obedience to Me (a).

(a) Exodus 20:2.

Q. 105. Do these things belong to us?

A. They do so, because they do figuratively comprehend and imply all the deliverances of the Church; and further, this was a type of our wonderful deliverance achieved by Christ.

Q. 106. What is the first commandment?

A. You shall have no other Gods before Me.

Q. 107. What does God require in the first commandment?

A. That as dearly as I render the salvation of my own soul, so earnestly should I shun and flee all idolatry (a), sorcery (b), enchantments, superstition, praying to saints, or any other creatures (c), and should rightly acknowledge the only and true God (d), trust in Him alone (e), submit and subject myself to Him with all humility (f) and patience (g), look for all good things from Him alone (h), and lastly with the entire affection of my heart love, reverence, and worship Him (i), so that I am ready to renounce and forsake all creatures rather than to commit the least thing that may be against His will (j).

(a) 1 Corinthians 6:9–10; 10:7, 14. (b) Leviticus 19:31; Deuteronomy 18:11. (c) Matthew 4:10; Revelation 19:10; 22:8–9. (d) John 17:3. (e) Jeremiah 17:5. (f) 1 Peter 5:5–6. (g) Romans 5:3–4; 1 Corinthians 10:10; Philippians 2:14; Colossians 1:11; Hebrews 10:36. (h) Isaiah 45:7; James 1:17. (i) Deuteronomy 6:5; Psalm 10:4; Matthew 22:37. (j) Deuteronomy 6:2; Psalm 111:10; Matthew 4:20; 5:29; 10:37–38.

Q. 108. What is idolatry?

A. It is in place of that one God, or besides that one true God who has manifested Himself in His word and works, to make or imagine, and account any other thing in which you rest your hope and confidence (a).

(a) John 5:23; Galatians 4:8; Philippians 3:19; Ephesians 2:12; 5:5; 1 John 2:23.

Q. 109.   **What is the second commandment?**

A.   You shall not make any graven image, nor the likeness of any-thing which is in heaven above, or in the earth beneath, nor in the waters under the earth: you shall not bow down to them, nor worship them, for I the Lord your God and a jealous God, and visit the sins of the fathers upon the children, to the third and fourth generation of them that hate me, and show mercy to thousands of them who love me, and keep My command-ments.

Q. 110.   **What does the second commandment require?**

A.   That we should not express or represent God by any image or shape and figure (a), or worship Him any other way than He has commanded in His word to be worshipped (b).

> (a) Deuteronomy 4:15ff.; Isaiah 40:18ff.; Acts 17:29;
> Romans 1:23ff. (b) Deuteronomy 12:30ff.; 1 Samuel 15:23;
> Matthew 15:9.

Q. 111.   **May there be made any images or resemblances of God at all?**

A.   God neither ought, nor can be represented by any means. As for things created, although it is lawful to depict them, God nevertheless forbids their images to be made or possessed in order to worship or honor either them or God by them (a).

> (a) Exodus 23:24; 34:13–14, 17; Numbers 33:52; Deuteronomy
> 7:5; 12:13; 16:22; 2 Kings 18:4.

Q. 112.   **But may not images be tolerated in churches, which may serve as books to the common people?**

A.   No, for that would make us wiser than God, who will have His church to be taught by the lively preaching of His word (a), and not with speechless images (b).

> (a) 2 Timothy 3:16–17; 2 Peter 1:19.
> (b) Jeremiah 10:8ff.; Habakkuk 2:18–19.

Q. 113.   **What is the third commandment?**

A.   You shall not take the name of the Lord your God in vain, for the Lord will not hold him guiltless that takes His name in vain.

Q. 114. **What does God decree in the third commandment?**

A. We must not use His name despitefully or irreverently, not only by cursing or false swearing (a), but also by unnecessary oaths (b). We must not be partakers of these horrible sins in others either by silence or consent. We must always use the sacred and holy name of God with great devotion and reverence (c), that He may be worshipped and honored by us with a true and steadfast confession and invocation of His name (d). This should be the case in all our words and actions (e).

> (a) Leviticus 19:12; 24:11ff. (b) Matthew 5:37; James 5:12.
> (c) 1 Timothy 2:8. (d) Matthew 10:32.
> (e) Romans 2:24; Colossians 3:17; 1 Timothy 6:1.

Q. 115. **Is taking God's name in vain by swearing or cursing so grievous a sin that God is also angry with those who do not forbid or hinder it with all their ability?**

A. Surely it is most grievous (a). There is no sin greater or more offending to God than the despising of His sacred name, wherefore He even commanded this sin to be punished with death (b).

> (a) Leviticus 5:1. (b) Leviticus 24:15–16.

Q. 116. **May a man swear reverently by the name of God?**

A. Yes, he may when lawful magistrates or necessity require it. By this means the faith and truth of any man, or thing to be ratified and established, both the glory of God may be advanced and the safety of others procured. This kind of swearing is ordained by God's word (a), and therefore was well–used by the fathers both in the Old and New Testament (b).

> (a) Deuteronomy 6:13; 10:20; Isaiah 48:1; Hebrews 6:16.
> (b) Genesis 21:24, 31; Joshua 9:15, 19; 2 Samuel 3:35;
> 1 Kings 1:29; Romans 1:9.

Q. 117. **Is it lawful to swear by saints or other creatures?**

A. No. A lawful oath is an invocation of God, whereby we desire that He, as the only searcher of hearts, bear witness to the truth and punish the swearer if he knowingly swears falsely (a). No creature deserves this honor (b).

> (a) 2 Corinthians 1:23. (b) Matthew 5:34–36; James 5:12.

Q. 118.   What is the fourth commandment?

A.   Remember that you keep holy the Sabbath Day. You shall labor
            six days, and do all your work, but the seventh day is the Sab-
            bath of the Lord your God. In it you should do no manner of
            work, you, nor your son, nor your daughter, your man-servant,
            nor your maid-servant, nor your cattle, nor the stranger that is
            within your gates. For in six days the Lord made heaven, and
            earth, the sea, and all that is in them, and rested the seventh
            day, and hallowed it.

Q. 119.   What are we taught by the fourth commandment?

A.   That one day in seven be kept in the worship of God. Under
            the Old Testament this was the last day of the week, but under
            the gospel changed to the first day of the week. The Lord's
            Day is to be spent in private and public devotion, hearing
            the Word diligently, practicing the gospel-sacraments zeal-
            ously, doing deeds of charity conscionably, and resting from
            servile works, except for cases of necessity. This was the laud-
            able practice of the holy Apostles, who best knew the mind of
            Christ as to the time of worship. We do not find in all the New
            Testament that any gospel church in the Apostle's time set any
            other day apart solemnly to worship God but the first day. This
            they were right to do. For if Israel, the natural seed of Abra-
            ham, was to keep the seventh day to keep up the remembrance
            of their deliverance out of temporal bondage, how much more
            are we bound to keep the first day in remembrance of Christ's
            deliverance of us from eternal bondage (a).

            (a) Deuteronomy 5:15; Psalm 40:9–10; Isaiah 66:23; John 20:19–
            20; Acts 2:42, 46; 20:7; 1 Corinthians 11:33; 14:16, 19, 29, 31;
            16:1–2; 1 Timothy 2:1–3, 8–9; Revelation 1:10.

Q. 120.   What is the fifth commandment?

A.   Honor your father and mother that your days may be long in
            the land which the Lord your God gives you.

Q. 121.   What does God require of us in the fifth commandment?

A.   That we yield due honor, love, and faithfulness to our parents,
            and to all who have authority over us, and submit ourselves
            with such obedience as is fitting to their faithful command-
            ments and chastisements (a). And that by our patience, we

endure their mannerisms (b), thinking within ourselves that God will govern and guide us by them (c).

(a) Exodus 21:17; Proverbs 1:8; 4:1; 15:20; 20:20; Romans 13:1; Ephesians 5:22; 6:1–2, 5; Colossians 3:20, 22–24.
(b) Proverbs 23:22; 1 Peter 2:18.
(c) Matthew 22:21; Romans 13:1; Colossians 3:18–25.

Q. 122. What is the sixth commandment?

A.   You shall do no murder.

Q. 123. What does God require in the sixth commandment?

A.   That neither in thought or in gesture, much less in deed, I reproach, or hate, or harm, or kill my neighbor, either by myself, or by another and that I cast away all desire of revenge (a). Furthermore, that I do not hurt myself or knowingly cast myself into any danger (b). God has armed the magistrate with the sword as a deterrent to murder (c).

(a) Matthew 5:21–22; 18:35; 26:52; Romans 12:19; Ephesians 4:26. (b) Matthew 4:7; Romans 13:14; Colossians 2:23.
(c) Genesis 9:6; Exodus 21:14; Matthew 26:52; Romans 13:4.

Q. 124. But does this commandment forbid murder only?

A.   No. In forbidding murder, God further teaches that He hates the root, namely, anger (a), envy (b), hatred (c), and desire for revenge, accounting them all as murder (d).

(a) Galatians 5:20–21; James 1:20. (b) Romans 1:29.
(c) 1 John 2:9, 11. (d) Matthew 5:21–22; 1 John 3:15.

Q. 125. Does this commandment only require that we harm no one?

A.   No. When God condemns anger, envy, and hatred, He requires that we love our neighbor as ourselves (a). We must use tenderness, courtesy, patience, and mercy towards him (b). We must also protect him from whatever may be hurtful to him, as much as we are able (c). Indeed, we must be so affected in mind that we do not hesitate to do good even to our enemies (d).

(a) Matthew 7:12; 22:39. (b) Matthew 5:5, 7; Luke 6:36; Romans 12:10, 18; Galatians 6:1–2; Ephesians 4:2.
(c) Exodus 23:5. (d) Matthew 5:43–45; Romans 12:20.

Q. 126. **What is the seventh commandment?**

A.   You shall not commit adultery.

Q. 127. **What is the meaning of the seventh commandment?**

A.   That God hates and abominates all sexual vileness and filthi-
            ness (a). Therefore, we must hate and detest the same (b).
            This also means that we must live temperately, modestly, and
            chastely, whether we are married or single (c).

> (a) Leviticus 18. (b) Jude 22–23.
> (c) 1 Corinthians 7:1–5; 1 Thessalonians 4:3–4; Hebrews 13:4.

Q. 128. **Does God forbid nothing else in this commandment but ac-
            tual adultery and other external acts of sexual sin?**

A.   No. Since our bodies and souls are the temples of the Holy
            Spirit, God will have us keep both in purity and holiness (a).
            Therefore, deeds, gestures, words, thoughts, filthy lusts (b), and
            whatever entices us to these, are all forbidden (c).

> (a) 1 Corinthians 6:18–20. (b) Matthew 5:27–28.
> (c) Job 31:1; Psalm 39:1; Ephesians 5:18.

Q. 129. **What is the eighth commandment?**

A.   You shall not steal.

Q. 130. **What does God forbid in the eighth commandment?**

A.   Not only those thefts (a) and robberies, which the magistrate
            ought to punish, but whatever evil tricks and devices where we
            seek after the goods of others and endeavor with force (b) or
            with some form of deceit to convey them to ourselves. These
            include false weights, false or uneven measurements, false ad-
            vertisement, counterfeit money, exorbitant interest (c), or any
            other way or means of benefitting ourselves, which God has
            forbidden (d). To these we may add all covetousness (e) and
            the manifold waste and abusing of God's gifts.

> (a) 1 Corinthians 6:10. (b) Ezekiel 45:9.
> (c) Psalm 15:5; Luke 6:35. (d) Deuteronomy 25:13–15;
> Proverbs 11:1; 16:11; 1 Corinthians 5:10–13; 6:10;
> 1 Thessalonians 4:6. (e) Proverbs 5:15; Luke 3:14.

Q. 131.   What are those things which God here commands?

A.   That with my power, I help and further the commodities and profit of my neighbor, and that I so deal with him as I would desire to be dealt with myself (a). I am required to do my own work plainly and faithfully, that I may thereby help others who are distressed with any need or calamity (b).

(a) Matthew 7:12. (b) Ephesians 4:28.

Q. 132.   What is the ninth commandment?

A.   You shall not bear false witness against your neighbor.

Q. 133.   What does the ninth commandment require?

A.   That I bear no false witness against any man (a), neither falsify any man's words, nor backbite (b), nor reproach any man, nor condemn any rashly or unheard (c). I must avoid and shun with all carefulness all kinds of lies and deceits, as the proper works of the Devil (d), lest I stir up against me the most grievous wrath of God (e). In judgments and other affairs, I must follow the truth, and freely and constantly profess the matter as it indeed is, as well as defend and increase, as much as in me lies, the good name and estimation of others (f).

(a) Proverbs 19:5, 9; 21:28. (b) Psalm 15:3; Romans 1:29, 30. (c) Matthew 7:1; Luke 6:37. (d) John 8:44. (e) Proverbs 12:22; 13:5. (f) Ephesians 4:24–25; 1 Peter 4:8.

Q. 134.   What is the tenth commandment?

A.   You shall not covet your neighbor's house, nor his wife, nor his servant, nor his maid, nor anything that is his (a).

(a) Exodus 20:17.

Q. 135.   What does the tenth commandment forbid?

A.   That our hearts be not moved by the least desire or cogitation against any commandment of God, but that we continually, from our heart, detest all sin and delight in all righteousness (a).

(a) Romans 7:7.

Q. 136.   **Can they who are converted to God observe and keep these commandments perfectly?**

A.   No. Even the holiest men, as long as they live, have only small beginnings in obedience (a). Yet they begin with an unfeigned and earnest desire and endeavor to live not according to some, but all the commandments of God (b).

> (a) Ecclesiastes 7:22; Romans 7:14–15; James 2:10.
> (b) Romans 7:22.

Q. 137.   **Why does God require His law to be preached exactly and severely, knowing that there is no man in this life able to keep it?**

A.   First, that we increasingly acknowledge the great proneness of our nature to sin and heartily desire forgiveness and righteousness in Christ (a). Second, that we do this always and so implore and crave form the Father the grace of His Holy Spirit (b). It is by this grace that we may be renewed, day by day, to the image and likeness of God (c). Once we depart out of this life, we will attain to that joyful perfection which is promised to us (3).

> (a) Romans 7:24; 1 John 1:9. (b) Psalm 22:5; Luke 11:13;
> Ephesians 3:16. (c) 1 Corinthians 9:24–27; Ephesians 4:17–24;
> Philippians 3:12–14; Colossians 3:5–14. (d) Philippians 3:20–21;
> 1 John 3:2; Jude 24–25.

Prayer

Q. 138.   **Why is prayer necessary for Christians?**

A.   Because it is the chief part of thankfulness which God requires of us, and also because God gives His grace and Holy Spirit to those who with sincere groanings ask them continually of Him, and give Him thanks for them (a).

> (a) Psalm 50:15; Matthew 7:7–8; Luke 11:9–13.

Q. 139.   **What is required for our prayers to please God and be heard by Him?**

A.   That we ask of the only true God, who has manifested Himself in His Word (a), all things which He has commanded to be asked of Him (b). This is to be done with a true affection and desire of our heart (c). As well, we are, through an inward feeling of our need and misery, to cast ourselves prostrate in the presence of His divine majesty (d), and build ourselves on the sure foundation that we, though unworthy, yet for Christ's sake, are certainly heard by God (e), even as He has promised us in His Word (f).

(a) John 4:22–24. (b) Romans 8:26; 1 John 5:14. (c) Psalm 145:18. (d) Psalm 2:11; 34:19; Isaiah 66:2. (e) Psalm 143:1; Romans 8:15–16; 10:13–17; James 1:6ff. (f) Daniel 9:17–19; John 14:13; 15:16; 16:23.

Q. 140. **What are those things which God commands us to ask of Him?**

A. All things necessary both for soul and body, which our Lord Jesus Christ has comprised in the prayer He taught us (a).

(a) Matthew 6:9–13; James 1:17.

Q. 141. **What prayer is that?**

A. Our Father who is in heaven, hallowed be Your name. Your kingdom come. Your will be done on earth, as it is in heaven. Give us this day our daily bread. And forgive us our trespasses, as we forgive those who trespass against us. And lead us not into temptation, but deliver us from evil. For Yours is the kingdom, the power, and the glory, forever and ever. Amen.

Q. 142. **Are Christians tied to this very form of prayer?**

A. We are not. Our Lord here delivers to His Church a brief summary of those things which we are to ask of God. Christ will have us also to ask for special things or particular benefits. The form prescribed is nothing else but a set of headings or general categories, wherein all benefits both bodily and spiritual are implied. But all particulars of prayer must agree and correspond with this general form. We are not tied to this form, as appears from James 1:5, where the Apostle exhorts the saints, if anyone lacks wisdom they should ask of God who gives to all liberally. Though these words are not in the form of prayer particularly expressed in the Lord's prayer, they are implied. Besides, we have examples of prayer both in the Old and New Testament, which are not in the form here expressed, though all they asked was comprehended in this prayer. Therefore, the form of prayer delivered to us by Christ is a thing indifferent.

Q. 143.   **Why does Christ teach us to call God our Father at the beginning of this prayer?**

A.   That He might stir up in us such a reverence and confidence in God as is proper for the sons of God. This must be the ground and foundation of our prayer; that is, that God through Christ is made our Father and will much less deny us these things which we ask of Him with a true faith, than our earthly parents deny us earthly things (a).

> (a) Matthew 7:9–11; Luke 11:11–13.

Q. 144.   **Why are the words "who is in heaven" added?**

A.   That we conceive not basely nor mundanely of God's heavenly majesty, and also that we look for and expect from His omnipotence whatever things are necessary for our soul and body (a).

> (a) Jeremiah 23:24; Acts 17:24–27; Romans 10:12.

Q. 145.   **What is the first petition?**

A.   Hallowed be Your name. In this we are asking that You would grant us, first to know You rightly (a) and worship, praise, and magnify Your almighty goodness, justice, mercy, and truth, which shine in all Your works (b). Also, we are asking You to direct our whole life, thoughts, words, and works to the end that Your most holy name be not reproached by us, but rather renowned with honor and praises (c).

> (a) Psalm 119:105; Jeremiah 9:23–24; 31:33–34; Matthew 16:17; John 17:3; James 1:5. (b) Exodus 34:5–7; Psalm 119:137–138; 143:1–2, 5, 10–12; 145:8–9, 17; Jeremiah 31:3; 32:18–19, 40–41; 33:11, 20–21; Matthew 19:17; Luke 1:45–55, 68–79; Romans 3:3–4; 11:22–23; 2 Timothy 2:19. (c) Psalm 115:1; 71:8.

Q. 146. **What is the second petition?**

A.   Your kingdom come. In this we are asking that You would rule us by Your Word and Spirit, that we may humble and submit ourselves more and more to You (a). Also, we ask that You would preserve and increase Your Church (b), destroy the works of the Devil (c), and all power that lifts up itself against Your majesty. Make all those councils frustrated and void which are taken against Your Word, until finally You reign fully and perfectly (d), when You shall be all in all (e).

> (a) Psalm 119:5; 143:10; Matthew 6:33. (b) Psalm 51:18; 122:6–7.
> (c) Romans 16:20; 1 John 3:8. (d) Romans 8:22–23;
> Revelation 22:17, 20. (e) 1 Corinthians 15:28.

Q. 147.　What is the third petition?

A.　　　Your will be done in earth, as it is in heaven. We are asking that You grant that we, and all men, renouncing and forsaking our own will (a), may readily and without any grudging (b), obey Your most holy will. This we pray that every one of us may faithfully perform that duty and charge which You have committed to us (c), even as the blessed angels do in heaven (d).

> (a) Matthew 16:24; Titus 2:12. (b) Luke 22:42.
> (c) 1 Corinthians 7:24. (d) Psalm 103:20–21.

Q. 148.　What is the fourth petition?

A.　　　Give us this day our daily bread. We ask that You give to us everything which is needful for this life, that by these things we may acknowledge and confess You to be the only fountain from where all good things flow (a). We also confess that all our care and industry, and even Your own gifts, are unfavorable and harmful to us unless You bless them (b). Grant that turning our trust away from all creatures, we place and rest it in You alone (c).

> (a) Psalm 10:4; 145:15–16; Matthew 6:25–34. (b) Acts 14:16–17.
> (c) Deuteronomy 8:3; Psalm 27:13; 62:11.

Q. 149.　Which is the fifth petition?

A.　　　Forgive us our trespasses, as we forgive those who trespass against us. On the basis of the blood of Christ, do not impute unto us, most miserable and wretched sinners, any of our offences or the corruption which still cleaves to us (a). By Your grace in our hearts, we sincerely purpose to pardon and forgive all those who have offended us (b).

> (a) Psalm 32:1–2; 143:2. (b) Matthew 6:14.

Q. 150.　What is the sixth petition?

A.　　　Lead us not into temptation, but deliver us from evil. We are feeble and weak by nature (a) and cannot stand one moment without our most deadly enemies, Satan (b), the world (c), and our own flesh (d), incessantly attacking and assaulting us. Therefore, uphold, establish, and strengthen us by the might of Your Spirit that we may not in this spiritual combat yield as conquered, but withstand our enemies both stoutly and consistently (e), until we get the full and perfect victory (f).

(a) Psalm 103:14; John 15:5. (b) Ephesians 6:12; 1 Peter 5:8.
(c) John 15:19. (d) Romans 7:23; Galatians 5:17.
(e) Matthew 26:41; Mark 13:33. (f) 1 Thessalonians 3:13; 5:23.

Q. 151.   How should you conclude this prayer?

A.   For Yours is the kingdom, the power, and the glory forever. We ask and crave all these things of You because You are our King and almighty and are, therefore, both willing and able to give them to us (a). We ask these things that Your holy name alone may receive glory (b).

(a) Romans 8:32; 10:11–12; 2 Peter 2:9.
(b) Psalm 115:1; Jeremiah 33:8–9.

Q. 152.   What does the final word, "Amen," mean?

A.   That the thing is sure and not to be doubted. This is so because my prayer is much more certainly heard by God than I feel in my heart that I desire things from Him.

(a) 2 Corinthians 1:20; 2 Timothy 2:13.

The Nicene Creed, A.D. 325

We believe in one God, the Father Almighty, Maker of all things, visible and invisible. We believe in one Lord Jesus Christ, the Son of God, the only begotten Son of the Father, that is, of the substance of the Father, God of God, Light of Light, very God of very God, begotten, not made, being of one substance with the Father, by whom all things were made, both the things in heaven and the things in earth, who for us men and for our salvation came down and was incarnate. He was made man. He suffered and arose the third day. He ascended into heaven. He shall come to judge both the living and the dead. And we believe in the Holy Spirit. Those who say there was a time when the Son was not, therefore He was begotten, or He had His beginning of nothing, or that He is of another substance, or essence, or that affirm Him to be made, or to be changeable or mutable, these the catholic and apostolic churches of God pronounce accursed.

The Athanasian Creed

Whoever will be saved before all things, it is necessary that he hold the catholic faith, which faith unless everyone do keep undefiled, without doubt he shall perish everlastingly.

And the catholic faith is this, that we worship one God in Trinity, and Trinity in unity, neither confounding the persons, nor dividing the substance.

For there is one person of the Father, another of the Son, and another of the Holy Spirit, but the Godhead of the Father, of the Son, of the Holy Spirit is all one, the glory equal, the majesty coeternal.

Such as the Father is, such is the Son, such is the Holy Spirit.

The Father uncreated, the Son uncreated, the Holy Spirit uncreated. The Father incomprehensible, the Son incomprehensible, the Holy Spirit incomprehensible.

The Father eternal, the Son eternal, the Holy Spirit eternal; yet are they not three eternals, but one eternal.

Also there is not three incomprehensibles, nor three uncreated, but one uncreated, and one incomprehensible.

So likewise the Father is almighty, the Son almighty, the Holy Spirit almighty, yet they are not three almighties, but one almighty.

So likewise the Father is Lord, the Son Lord, the Holy Spirit is Lord; yet are they not three Lords, but one Lord.

For like as we are compelled by the Christian verity to acknowledge every person by Himself to be God and Lord, so are we forbidden by the catholic religion to say there be three Gods, or three Lords.

The Father is made of none, neither created, nor begotten. The Son is of the Father alone, not made, nor created, but begotten. The Holy Spirit is of the Father and the Son, neither made nor created, nor begotten, but proceeding.

So there is one Father, not three Fathers; one Son, not three Sons; one Holy Spirit, not three Holy Spirits.

And in this Trinity none are before or after another, none is greater or less than another, but the whole three persons are coeternal and coequal. So that in all things, as is aforesaid, the unity in Trinity, and the Trinity in unity is to be worshipped.

He therefore that will be saved, must thus think of the Trinity.

Furthermore it is necessary to everlasting life, that we also rightly believe the incarnation of our Lord Jesus Christ.

For the right faith is, that we believe and confess, that our Lord Jesus Christ the Son of God is God and man, God of the substance of the Father, begotten before the world, and man of the substance of His mother born in the world; perfect God, perfect man, of a reasonable soul and human flesh subsisting; equal to the Father as touching His Godhead, inferior to the Father as touching His manhood; who although He be God and man, yet is not two, but one Christ; one, not by conversion of the Godhead into flesh, but by taking of the manhood into God; one altogether not by confusion of substance, but by unity of Person. For as the reasonable soul, and flesh is one man, so God and man is one Christ, who suffered for our salvation, descended into hell, rose again the third day from the dead, He ascended into heaven, sits on the right hand of God the Father almighty, from whence He shall come to judge the living and the dead. At whose coming all men shall rise again with their bodies, and give an account for their own works: and them that have done good, shall go into life everlasting; and them that have done evil, into everlasting fire.

This is the catholic faith, which everyone should believe faithfully.

An Appendix Concerning the Ordinance of Singing

My dearly beloved, whether churches in general, or Christians in particular, wherever this appendix may come:

Forasmuch as singing is generally owned to be a gospel-ordinance; but there is great doubt with many regarding what ought to be the matter of the songs and what manner and mode we ought to sing in. Also knowing that it is heartily desired by many officers and other particular members of some churches of Christ that they could agree together to perform this ordinance of God, especially at the Lord's Supper, as Christ himself, and his Apostles, did. And that the churches may return to the practice of this ordinance (singing after the Lord's Supper), which for many years has been lost in many Churches (as the Feast of Tabernacles was for a long time). This is my great design to them that do not practice it (although it is very clear that this ordinance was practiced at other times by the church in general and the saints in particular), which I hope all Churches will further practice as God shall enlighten them into it upon their diligent search.

That singing vocally and audibly, has been and still is God's ordinance, is proved:

Argument I: From the Command of God.

Ephesians 5:19 "Speaking to yourselves in psalms, hymns, and spiritual songs; singing, and making melody in your hearts to the Lord."

Colossians 3:16 "Teaching and admonishing one another in psalms, and hymns, and spiritual songs, singing with grace in your hearts to the Lord."

That the Apostle presses this as an ordinance, is clear:

1. Because he speaks to the whole church, and as a public duty, not appropriated to any office, but as a command universally on all.

2. The Apostle distinguishes this ordinance from that of preaching, or teaching doctrinally, which belongs to the officers, or occasionally, to a gifted brother. For he does not say, as in other places, teach and admonish; but gives us the modification of this admonition in psalms, and hymns, and spiritual songs.

Argument II: As praising God is a moral duty, so singing is often linked with that moral duty, which is universally obliging and perpetually binding, namely, prayer.

James 5:13 "Is any among you afflicted? Let him pray. Is any merry? Let him sing psalms." That this duty may particularly be done, this proves. That it must be generally done, the former proves. So in Acts 16:25 Paul and Silas join the two duties together. They "hymned God," or celebrated his praises with an hymn, or, as Beza said, "with singing." And Justin Martyr tells us in "hymning" they sang, and sent up praises to God. See also Psalm 95:1, 2, and 6.

Prayer, we all grant, is a moral duty, and is always obliging. We ought to acknowledge God as the giver of all good things in praying unto him for them. And surely to praise God for the mercies received is as great a duty. And to sing praise to God with the heart is one of the best ways of praising God. Although we do grant God may be praised after another manner.

Argument III: This is further confirmed by Scriptural pattern.

1. Christ and his Apostles sung an hymn together, Matthew 26:30.

2. Godly princes have honored God this way, as Hezekiah in 2 Chronicles 29:30. So also Jehoshaphat in 2 Chronicles 20:21–22.

3. Worthy governors, as Nehemiah, took care to bless God this way, Nehemiah 7:1. So also Moses in Exodus 15.

4. The holy Apostles and churches in the New Testament have honored God thus, 1 Corinthians 14:15. See also Ephesians 5:19 and Colossians 3:16.

5. Godly prophets were much in this practice. 2 Samuel 22 is a song of holy David, a little before his death, to bless God for many mercies. So also Moses in Deuteronomy 32 closes up his life with a song.

6. As singing has not been too low for kings and princes, so not too good for subjects. The body of the people sang. Numbers 21:17 "Then Israel sang this song, 'Spring up, O well, sing to it! See also Psalm 149:1–2.

7. All sexes have practiced this work, women as well as men. Miriam, the sister of Moses and Aaron, sings a song to God, Exodus 15:21. So also Deborah, as well as Barak, in Judges 5:1.

8. Primitive Christians were much in this work. Tertullian said, "When we come to a feast, we sit not down before there is prayer; and after meal is past, one cometh forth with a Psalm, either from the holy Scriptures, or else some spiritual song of his own composure."

9. Eminent Fathers practiced it. Basil called singing, "sweet incense." Augustine was highly in commendation of this and assures us that Ambrose and Athanasius were in agreement with him in this thing.

10. This duty is further confirmed by Scripture-prophecy. Divines observe the 100th Psalm is prophetical of Christ's kingdom

wherein there will be great cause of rejoicing. So also Isaiah 52:7–8. Musculus said, "Those watchmen shall jubilee when they consider the great joy approaching by Christ's redemption."

Argument IV: Let us further consider,

1. That singing is the music of nature, and shall not the saints sing? The valleys sing, Psalm 65:13. The mountains and trees are said to sing, 1 Chronicles 16:32–33.

2. Singing is the music of ordinances. Augustine reports of himself, that when he came to Milan and heard the people sing, he wept for joy. Beza confesses that when he entered into the congregation and heard the people sing the 19th Psalm, he was greatly comforted. The Rabbis tell us that the Jews, after the Feast of the Passover was celebrated, sung the 111th Psalm and the five following. And Christ and his Apostles sung an hymn after the Lord's Supper.

3. This is the music of angels, Job 38:7. The heavenly host, when they proclaimed the birth of Christ, declared it in this raised way of singing. Luke 2:13. Revelation 5.11.

4. This is the music of saints in their triumphant state in the bride-chamber where will be eternal hallelujahs, Revelation 15:3; 19:7–9; 5:9–12, etc.; and Psalm 30:5. Shall we not begin that work on earth which will be continued in glory?

Argument V: Also it is worth our consideration,

1. That this duty has been performed in the greatest numbers. Numbers 21:17; Psalm 149:1–2; and Exodus 15.

2. In the greatest difficulties. In Acts 16:25, Paul and Silas sang in prison. This may serve to rectify the judgment of some which ask how they can sing when in trouble. When some persuaded Luther of the dangers of the church and what a black cloud did hang over the church's head, he then called for the 46th Psalm to be sung as a charm against slavish fear, since called "Luther's Psalm."

3. In the greatest deliverances this duty has also been performed. In Exodus 15 when Israel was delivered from Pharaoh's host. See also Psalm 126. So also 2 Samuel 22 is a song for mercies

and great deliverances. So shall the gospel-church sing after a better manner when it is out of the wilderness and led into the celestial Canaan, Revelation 5:9–12.

Argument VI: Such has been the constant observation of this duty, that it has been performed in all places.

1. Moses praises God by singing in the wilderness, Exodus 15.

2. David praises God in the Tabernacle, Psalm 27:4, 6.

3. Solomon and Hezekiah in the Temple, extol Jehovah, 2 Chronicles 29:30.

4. Jehoshaphat in the camp, 2 Chronicles 20:20–21.

5. Christ and His Apostles in a private room, Matthew 26:30.

6. Paul and Silas in a prison, Acts 16:25.

7. The primitive saints in public assemblies, 1 Corinthians 14:5; Ephesians 5:19; and Colossians 3:16.

Argument VII: Consider how this ordinance has been crowned,

1. With his own glorious appearance, 2 Chronicles 20:17, 20–21.

2. Crowned with eminent miracles, Acts 16:25–26. As they were praising God "there was a great earthquake,…the foundations of the prison were shaken,…the doors were opened, and every one's bands were loosed."

3. Honored with eminent victories, 2 Chronicles 20:21–22.

Consider also:

1. This ordinance is of great benefit to the church. It is for admonition and teaching, Colossians 3:16.

2. It can sweeten a prison, so it did for Paul and Silas, Acts 16.

3. It can prepare the soul for suffering, so Christ sings before He dies, Matthew 26:30.

4. It enlivens and exhilarates the soul in trouble.

Objection: How can a serious Christian sing, where there is a mixt multitude?

Answer: By the same rule as we may pray and hear with them, for we ought to be as pure in praying as singing. Besides, singing may be sanctified to the conviction of sinners, as well as praying and preaching is. Though singing and praying properly belong to the saints and is best done by them, yet forasmuch as prayer and praises are natural duties as well as a part of instituted worship and all men are bound by the law of their creation to seek unto God for what they want and praise him for what they have, we dare not, when we are about that work, shut them out and say, "Stand by yourselves," Isaiah 65:5. For praise is the natural duty of all, the proper duty of saints, and the perfect act of angels.

Question: But what may be the right mode and way of singing?

Answer: To sing is not only meant the inward frame of the heart, but also of the voice, is apparent:

1. Because the Word says they should be speaking to one another and admonishing one another in psalms, hymns, and spiritual songs (Ephesians 5:19 and Colossians 3:16). But we cannot admonish one another by silent speakings and inward rejoicings.

2. As the Apostle says there must be melody in the heart, so he says as well, we must sing. One contains the inward frame, the other the outward act. Sing with the voice, as well as with the heart.

3. Singing in Scripture is ever put in distinction from reading, praying, and speaking, and commonly signifies a modulation of the tongue or expressing anything musically. And so it is a musical speaking. None will say when they hear a man speak or pray that that man is singing. This would make the greatest confusion in ordinances imaginable. Hence it is said Christ and His disciples sung an hymn, or praised God by singing. And that Paul and Silas sung vocally and audibly is plain for it is said the prisoners heard them, Acts 16:25.

Objection: If singing be with the voice, why not with lute, harp, organs, and other instruments?

Answer: In the New Testament the voice and heart are only God's instruments. The voice is still required because it is the immediate interpreter of the heart, and though artificial instruments are laid aside from God's worship, yet not natural ones.

2. The union of heart, tongue, and voice make the spiritual way of worship under the gospel complete. We have not anything as typical now to look at as the lute and harp were in the law, as also those ceremonies which typed out Christ's sacrifice. But when the substance came, the shadow ceased. So the Spirit being more abundantly poured out, we have no need of those instruments. But there always needs to be a soul and body to sing forth the high praises of God.

Objection: If any has a special spiritual gift of singing in the church, it may be lawful, but we cannot allow of set forms.

Answer: Every man that preaches profitably has a set form in his head and heart how he will deliver his message, and yet that man may be said to preach by the assistance of the spirit. Also it is lawful for a man to consider what he wants before he goes to God by prayer. For order is necessary in prayer, as well as in preaching, as Christ has directed us in that form of prayer, Matthew 6. And yet, notwithstanding this consideration and order in his mind, he may be said to pray with the Spirit's assistance. So in like manner it is as lawful to compose a hymn, grounded on the Word of God, in a set form and deliver it to the people either by strength of memory or as written, as well as to deliver a sermon in a set form by notes or strength of memory, which is alike grounded on the Word of God.

2. Moreover, to speak of an extraordinary gift to sing in the church, is the ready way to weaken the authority of the Scripture. For how came so many so much to slight the Scriptures, but by pretending to extraordinary gifts and new revelations?

3. It is the ready way to make hypocrites and impose a deceit upon the whole church. For how easy is it for a man to compose by strength of parts an excellent hymn, and deliver it by strength of memory, and pretend he is immediately inspired? How many such cheats have been in our days?

4. God never made any such promise of giving an extraordinary gift of singing. Of prayer, supplication, and preaching He has. If there had been such a gift promised, it would have been made by Christ, as the gift of tongues and miracles were. And then no doubt but the saints would have been instructed to seek for it, and such as had it would

have been commanded to wait on it, as God does exhort his to wait on teaching and ruling, Romans 12.

5. To be sure Christ would not ordain an ordinance of that consequence as singing is of, which most of the churches in the world must lack the use of, for the lack of a pretended gift. That Christ has appointed this ordinance in his church we have showed. That he never promised any extraordinary gift of singing, is clear. Therefore we may conclude, as God ordinarily gives every Christian a spirit of prayer, so he also has ordinarily given them a gift to sing praises to God. And as many might pray better if they used it more, so many may lack a gift of singing for lack of use.

6. As for that in 1 Corinthians 14:26, "One has a psalm, and another a doctrine, etc.," it does not concern us to expect that gift as they had because they had a doctrine, a tongue, a revelation, an interpretation, a psalm after an extraordinary manner. Yet we say, though we have not the spirit of prayer as the church had to make the place shake (Acts 4) as the effect of it; nor cannot preach extraordinarily, as Peter did to the 3,000 and to the house of Cornelius; yet we say not, preaching and prayer is ceased. So though none should have an extraordinary gift to sing now, as they might have in the church of Corinth, yet the duty remains still in the church as a standing ordinance as well as prayer and preaching.

Objection: But what psalms must we sing? David's or a composure of our own from the holy Scriptures?

Answer: As for singing the holy psalms of holy David as they are in meter; as long as they retain the sense and meaning of the reading psalms, which I think they generally do, I have nothing against the thing or those which shall do it.

But yet also I do think, that we are at our liberty to compose other parts or portions of God's Word to that end, provided our hymns are founded directly on God's Word. These very hymns may be called the Word of God, or spiritual hymns. For, as a learned man says the sense and meaning is the Word of God, whether in prose or in meter; and further says we may as well be said to sing God's Word, as to read it; it is only orderly composed and disposed for that action. Every duty must be performed according to the analogy of faith and founded on God's Word. All prayer or preaching that does not correspond with sacred writ, notwithstanding any pretense of an extraordinary inspiration, I am to explode out of God's worship. And as prayer and preaching must correspond with the sacred record, so must singing. And as we count them the best prayers and sermons that are fullest of Scripture, so those hymns that are founded on the sacred Scriptures can no more be denied to be of the Spirit than a man's preaching or prayer which is full of the Word of God.

But how must we sing?

1. With understanding, 1 Corinthians 14:15. As we must pray, so we must sing. We must not only be guided by the tune, but words of the psalm, the matter more than the manner, else this would be more the work of a chorister than a Christian. Upon this Davenant cries out, Adieu to the bellowing of the papists who sing in an unknown tongue. God will not understand us in this service, which we understand not ourselves.

2. We must sing with zeal and affection. Love is the fulfilling of the law. It is a notable saying of Augustine, it is not crying, but loving sounds in the ears of God that makes the music, Isaiah 5:1.

3. We must sing with grace, Colossians 3:16. It is grace, not nature, sweetens the music. One well notes that grace is the root of true devotion. God will not hear sinners when they pray, no, nor when they sing. They make a noise like a cracked string of a lute or violin. The raven only croaks, it is the nightingale that sings. The singing of wicked men is but disturbance, not obedience. The saints above sing their hallelujahs in glory, the saints below must sing their psalms with grace.

4. We must sing with spiritual joy. Singing is the only triumphant gladness of a gracious heart. We must sing as David danced before the ark with shouting and rejoicing, 2 Samuel 6:12–15.

5. We must sing with faith. This grace only puts a pleasantness upon every duty, Hebrews 4:2. We must bring faith always to Christ's table, or else, as Augustin says, if faith be asleep, Christ is asleep. Faith carries on this ordinance of singing so as it may be accepted of God.

6. We must sing with excited grace, not only with grace habitual, but excited and actual. We must stir up the grace in us (1 Timothy 4:14) and cry out as David in Psalm 57:7–8. Awake love,

awake delight. The Clock must be pulled up before it can guide our time. God loves active grace in duty that the soul should be ready trimmed when it presents itself to Christ in any worship.

7. We must sing in the Spirit, as well as pray in the Spirit, 1 Corinthians 14:15–16; Jude 20. The Spirit must breathe as well as grace acts. Davenant says they are called spiritual songs, in point of their origin. The Spirit excites and completes the soul to this holy service. Thus Ephesians in 5:18 he exhorts to be filled with the Spirit and so calls us to sing spiritual songs as the effect of this fullness. This wind must fill our organs before we can make any music, it is so called in John 3:8.

8. We must take great care to keep our hearts while about this work. One observes, without this we may please men with the artificial suavity of the voice and displease God with the odious impurity of the heart.

9. Neglect not preparatory prayer for singing, as well as other duties. Jehovah is the great harmonist who must put every heart in tune, tighten up every peg of affection, and strain every string of meditation, Proverbs 16:1.

10. Labor to see thy interest in Christ clear when you go about this work. If we are not in Christ, we are certainly out of tune. It is Christ must put acceptance upon this service as well as others. Here the altar must sanctify the gift. Christ perfumes the prayers of saints (Revelation 5:8) and he must articulate their singing. Though we have Esau's garments, he can give us Jacob's voice. If we are in him, he can raise our hearts to a pleasing elevation.

11. Let us sometimes raise our hearts into holy contemplations. Let us think of the music of the bride-chamber, there shall be no cracked strings, displeasing sounds, harsh voices, nothing to abate our melody. There shall be no willows to hang our harps upon, Psalm 137:2. In the bride-chamber, there shall be no sorrow to interfere. When we sing the song of the Lamb, there shall be no grief to jar our harmony. For this day let us all pray.

FINIS.

2

The Baptist Catechism

also called Keach's Catechism

An Introduction

Perhaps more than all others combined, this catechism defined what it was to be a Baptist throughout the eighteenth century and for some years into the nineteenth. Beyond that, its father, the *Westminster Shorter Catechism*, molded the thought of evangelicalism for more than two-hundred years after its completion and adoption in 1648 by the "Churches of Christ in the kingdoms of Scotland, England, and Ireland." When Baptists adopted it in 1693, they affirmed their "near agreement with many other christians, of whom we have great esteem." In the same spirit which prompted them to adopt a confession of faith "almost in all points" the same as the *Westminster* (Presbyterian) and the *Savoy* (Congregational), they produced a "short account of christian principles" for instructing families "in most things agreeing with the Shorter Catechism of the Assembly." Because they had "commonly made use of that catechism" in their families and the difference in the two "being not much" they felt it would be more easily committed to memory.

Its Broad Evangelical Usefulness

It is not surprising then, that when the New England Congregationalist, Luther Rice, adopted Baptist principles while travelling to the mission field under Congregational sponsorship, Baptist churches received him warmly without any sense of theological incongruity. When he became a Christian, Luther Rice recognized his total dependence on God for salvation and, according to his testimony "the whole of that luminous system of divinity drawn out in the *Westminster Catechism*, opened on my view with light, and beauty and power." He had been taught to repeat it as a child and all of his life remained "glad that I had been so taught." From the books read prior to his conversion, from the Bible and from the Catechism, Rice said, "the incipient outline of my religious sentiments was formed; my exercises of experience modified and characterized; and my hope developed, shaped, and established; Glory to God!" [1]

Rice's theological training was little different from that received by children in Baptist households growing up in churches where the catechism was used regularly. Richard Furman, long-time pastor of First Baptist Church, Charleston, SC, valued the catechism as a tool of education and evangelism. It was printed by the Charleston Association in 1813 and recommended to the churches for use. Furman, aggressive with the education of young people, took the charge seriously (in fact, probably led the charge) and engaged the entire church in the responsibility of catechising. In 1913, the Foreign Mission Board published a work on women in missions which included a commendation of Furman's work in mission education. The testimony of one of the youth he catechised was included. Though this incident has been described in the introduction to this book, it is worth repeating.

> We had no Sabbath school then, but we had the Baptist Catechism, with which we were as familiar as with the Lord's Prayer. At our quarterly seasons, we children of the congregation repeated the Baptist Catechism standing, in a circle round the font. ... We had to memorize the whole book, for none knew which question would fall to them. I think I hear at this very moment the dear voice of our pastor saying, 'A little louder, my child,' and then a trembling, sweet voice would be raised a little too loud. ... This practice was of incalculable benefit, for when it pleased God to change our hearts, and when offering ourselves to the church for membership, we knew what the church doctrines meant and were quite familiar with answering questions before the whole congregation, and did not quake when pastor or deacon or anyone else asked what we understood by Baptism, the Lord's Supper, Justification, Adoption, Sanctification. Oh, no; we had been well taught. ... What a pity that such a course of instruction has been abandoned.[2]

[1] James B. Taylor, *Memoir of Rev. Luther Rice* (Baltimore: Armstrong & Berry, 1840), 26, 27.

[2] Fannie E. S. Heck, *In Royal Service* (Richmond: Education Department, Foreign Mission Board, 1926 [originally copyrighted 1913]), 26, 27.

Benjamin Keach and William Collins

The present catechism was prepared about 1693. In June of that year the General Assembly of Particular Baptists in England passed the following resolution:

> That a catechism be drawn up, containing the substance of the Christian religion, for the instruction of children and servants; and that Brother William Collins be desired to draw it up.

The catechism has popularly been assigned to Benjamin Keach, and it is called Keach's catechism. In light of the resolution of 1693, however, it appears that William Collins had, at least, as much to do with the catechism as Keach did. Collins served as pastor of the Petty France church from 1673 until his death in 1702. He was noted as a "learned and judicious minister." He, along with Nehemiah Cox, was responsible for the publication of the confession of faith in 1677 which was eventually adopted in 1689 by more than 100 churches and is known as the *Second London Confession*.[3] It served as the theological backdrop for the catechism of 1693.

Benjamin Keach was born in 1640, baptized in 1655, and began to preach in 1658. After a brief stint as a General (Arminian) Baptist, he became a Particular Baptist. Cathcart's *Baptist Encyclopedia* characterizes this change in theology in the following words:

> At first he was an Arminian about the extent of the atonement and free-will, but the reading of the Scriptures and the conversation of those who knew the will of God more perfectly relieved him from both errors.

At age 28, he became pastor of the Baptist church in Horsleydown, London. A virtual roll call of Baptist fame served the pulpit of this church: Benjamin Stinton, John Gill, John Rippon, and Charles Spurgeon.

When he was 24 years old, Keach discovered that catechisms not only were effective, but were dangerous. In 1664, he wrote, printed, and published a catechism entitled *The Child's Instructor or A New and Easy Primer*. Arrested for violation of the Act of Uniformity and the Conventicle Act, Keach found himself indicted as a "seditious, schismatic person, evily and maliciously disposed and disaffected to his majesty's government and the

---

[3] The text of the *Second London Confession* may be found in *Baptist Confessions of Faith*, ed. William L. Lumpkin (Valley Forge: The Judson Press, 1959 [rev. ed., 1969]), 235–295.

government of the church of England." The jury, intimidated and brow-beaten by a judge hostile to dissenters, found Keach guilty of the accusation. Keach was placed in the pillory on two separate occasions in two separate towns, Aylesbury and Winslow, and saw his book burnt under his nose. The indictment described the book as containing "by way of questions and answers, these damnable positions, contrary to the book of common prayer and the Liturgy of the Church of England:" the rejection of infant baptism, the affirmation that laymen (those not ordained and educated according to the rites of the church of England) may have a calling and God-given abilities to preach the Gospel, and Christ shall reign personally upon the earth for a thousand years. Excerpts from this scandalously un-lawful catechism appear in Joseph Ivimey's *History of the English Baptists*.

Q. **Who are the right subjects of *baptism*?**

A. *Believers*, or godly men and women only, who can make confession of their faith and repentance....

Q. **How shall it go with the Saints?**

A. O very well, it is the day that they have longed for; then shall they hear that sentence, *Come ye blessed of my Father, inherit the kingdom prepared for you*; and so shall they reign with Christ on the earth a thousand years, even on Mount *Sion*, in the new *Jerusalem*, for there will Christ's throne be, on which they must sit down with him.

Q. **When shall the rest of the wicked and the fallen angels, which be the devils, be judged?**

A. When the thousand years shall be expired, then shall all the rest of the dead be raised and then shall be the general and last judgment; then shall all the rest of the dead, and devils be judged by Christ, and his glorified Saints, and they being arraigned and judged, the wicked shall be condemned, cast by the angels into the lake of fire, there to be burned for ever and ever....

Q. **Why may not *Infants* be received into the church now, as they were under the law?**

A. Because the fleshly seed is cast out, tho' God under that dispensation did receive *Infants* in a lineal way by generation; yet he that hath the key of *David, that openeth and no man shutteth, that shutteth, and no man openeth*, hath shut up that way into the church, and hath opened the door of regeneration, receiving in none now but true *believers*.

Q. What then is the case of *Infants*?

A. *Infants* that die are members of the kingdom of glory, tho' they be not members of the visible church.

Q. Do they then that bring in *Infants* in a lineal way by generation, err from the way of truth?

A. Yea, they do; for they make not God's holy word their rule, but do presume to open a door, that Christ hath shut, and none ought to open.[4]

When Keach died in July 1704, he had attained a position of prominence not only among the Baptists but among all the evangelical dissenters and evangelical churchmen as well. Though often polemical in writing and given to debate, Keach's Christian allegories and his books of doctrine and biblical interpretation [especially his book on the parables and one on Scripture metaphors] were received with appreciation by the entire Christian community. Though Spurgeon commented that Keach's metaphors run on as "many legs as a centipede," he maintained that they were not to be sneered at. Keach's impact on Baptist life gained gained for him the epithet, the "Famous Mr. Keach."

Charles Spurgeon

E. B. Underhill's contention that this catechism "continues to be the only catechism of value among Baptists" would be difficult to dispute. If the claim, however, is hyperbolic, one must recognize that the catechism's influence was extended exponentially by C. H. Spurgeon's utilization of it.

Born in 1834, converted in 1850, baptized in 1851, Spurgeon became pastor of Waterbeach church in Cambridgeshire in 1852. One year later he was invited to preach at the ancient church in Southwark, London, where Benjamin Keach, John Gill, and John Rippon had formerly served. On April 28, 1854, he accepted a unanimous call to the church.

The crowds flocking to hear the young Spurgeon preach grew so rapidly that the capacity of the chapel was quickly overrun. A new tabernacle

---

[4] Joseph Ivimey, *A History of the English Baptists*, 4 Vols. (London: for the Author [vols. 1 & 2], for B. J. Holdsworth [vol. 3], and Isaac Taylor Hinton [vol. 4], 1811–1830) 1: 341, 342.

begun in 1859 was completed in 1861 at a cost of $150,000. The tabernacle would seat over 5,500 people with standing room for another 1,000. He always preached to overflow crowds.

Several major controversies punctuated the glorious ministry of Spurgeon. Early in his London days his espousal of Calvinism brought controversy and rebuff from the latitudinarian and Arminian ministers of London,, but he remained undaunted. In the middle years the baptismal regeneration controversy lost him friends among the evangelical Anglicans. In his later years the Downgrade controversy brought about his severance from the Baptist Union. Throughout his ministry, his earnest appeals for the salvation of the unconverted brought opposition and often ridicule from a staunch group of hyper-Calvinists.

The fine line of truth sometimes is difficult to walk, especially when temptation both to compromise and exaggeration would make one's course more friendly and profitable. In 1887, at the beginning of the Downgrade Controversy, Spurgeon wrote his brother co-pastor of the tabernacle and his deacons concerning this temptation. He had been warned that his stance would cost him popularity, friends, money, and health. All of these predictions were right. But he reminded himself and his co-laborers that theirs was a heritage of truth which could not be sold at any price.

> My eminent predecessor, Dr. Gill, was told by a certain member of his congregation who ought to have known better, that, if he published his book, *The Cause of God and Truth*, he would lose some of his best friends and his income would fall off. The doctor said, "I can afford to be poor, but I cannot afford to injure my conscience;" and he has left his mantle as well as his chair in our vestry.[5]

The same commitment to the defense and propagation of truth led Spurgeon to give prominence to both *The Baptist Confession of Faith* and *The Baptist Catechism* in his pastoral teaching ministry. When the confession was reprinted in 1855 under his sponsorship, he commended it as an aid to the "cause of the glorious gospel" by which the younger members would have a "Body of Divinity in small compass" which, in conjunction with the Scripture proofs, would prepare them to "be ready to give a reason for the hope that is in them."[6]

Complementary to the confession's usefulness, Spurgeon used an edited version of the catechism. He shortened the catechism by omitting portions of the expositions of the Ten Commandments and the Lord's

---

[5] C. H. Spurgeon, *Autobiography* 2 Vols. (Edinburgh: The Banner of Truth Trust, 1973 rev. ed), 2:477.

[6] Ibid., 1:398.

Prayer. As a hedge against heresy and a wedge to open the mind to truth, the catechism serves as a valuable spiritual tool. Spurgeon often thought about the long-term benefits of projects he initiated. This was true of his commendation of *The Baptist Catechism*.

> In matters of doctrine you will find orthodox congregations frequently changed to heterodoxy in the course of thirty or forty years, and that is because, too often, there has been no catechising of the children in the essential doctrines of the Gospel. For my part, I am more and more persuaded that the study of a good Scriptural catechism is of infinite value to our children. ... Even if the youngsters do not understand all the questions and answers ... yet, abiding in their memories, it will be infinite service when the time of understanding comes, to have known these very excellent, wise and judicious definitions of the things of God. ... It will be a blessing to them—the greatest of all blessing ... a blessing in life and death, in time and eternity, the best of blessings God Himself can give.

The Philadelphia Association

In America, Keach's catechism also became influential. Its formative place in Baptist life was guaranteed when the Philadelphia Association employed it for the instruction of its youth. The date of the catechism's first use is not ascertained, but the association had used the *Second London Confession* at least since 1724. In that year the association answered a doctrinal query by pointing to the confession's exposition of the fourth commandment. A reference to the catechism appears in 1738 when the Association sought to raise money to have it reprinted.

> Agreed, that since the catechisms are expended, and few or none to be had, and our youth thereby not likely to be instructed in the fundamentals of saving knowledge, that the several congregations we represent should consult amongst themselves what they can raise for so good a design ... (*Minutes*, p. 39).

Clearly for some years prior to this (1738) instruction of youth was identified with teaching the catechism. In 1761 the Association again considered reprinting the catechism. In order "to know whether there would be proper encouragement to have them reprinted" (p. 83), the churches were encouraged to notify Morgan Edwards what number of catechisms each was willing to take. "A call for the catechisms from divers places" prompted a similar appeal to the churches in 1779.

The Association often encouraged the churches to pursue the catechising of their young people. In 1774 some churches had become lax in the practice, and since it was so "plain and important a duty," the Association "thought it expedient to recommend to the churches, seriously to consider and promote the same" (p. 141). In 1794 a resolution passed that it be recommended to the different churches in the Association "to institute the catechising of children in their respective congregations" (p. 297).

On at least three occasions, alterations in the catechism were considered. In 1761 the Association considered a suggested alteration in question 10 of the catechism. Instead of "whatsoever comes to pass" the alteration would read "Whatsoever he brings to pass." It appears some were nervous about the fulness of God's providence as taught in the catechism. The majority, however, remained unflappable in their affirmation of the pervasiveness of God's decrees and decided not to entertain a change in the catechism.

> Resolved: God worketh all things after the council [sic] of his own will. Whatsoever comes to pass is either by his agency or permission; and, though he permit sin to be is not therefore, the author of it; neither is the said answer in the catechism expressive or productive of the inference and conclusions the adversaries of God's sovereignty would fain charge upon it (p. 83).

Again, in 1794, an alteration was considered. The word "offered" was eliminated in favor of the words "held forth" in response 34 concerning *effectual calling*. This change reflects a theological discussion being agitated in England due to the publication of Andrew Fuller's *The Gospel Worthy of All Acceptation* in 1785 and William Carey's *Enquiry into the Obligations of Christians to Use Means for the Conversion of the Heathen*. Ironically, the Philadelphia Association practiced evangelism and missions in the spirit of Fuller and Carey but favored the vocabulary of their opponents.

The following year, 1795, a committee brought a report on the catechism recommending several changes. Linguistic clarity fueled the change to number 5 and response 6 was reworded in light of the evangelical commitment to the scriptural motif of Law and Gospel. This matter had been the subject of discussion in the circular letters of 1794 and 1795. The following response has a distinct advantage over the one in the original text.

A. The Holy Scriptures chiefly contain what man ought to believe concerning God; they also teach what duty God requireth of man in his Law; and in his Gospel how men are reconciled unto God through a Mediator.

Numbers 10 and 12 were altered for the sake of greater clarity, eliminating some linguistic awkwardness while making no theological change. Numbers 15, 16, and 19 eliminate the idea of covenant and emphasize the positive command of God as an exercise of unilateral authority on the part of a Sovereign Judge. While not an intended meaning of covenant theology, some members of the Association viewed the concept as concealing an implicit Arminianism; they believed the change would avoid the possibility of misunderstanding. Compare the following response with number 15 in the catechism text.

> A.(15)   Man being created a subject of moral government, God was pleased to give him a positive command for the trial of his obedience, forbidding him to eat of the tree of knowledge of good and evil upon the pain of death.

The change in number 19 is the effect of changing number 15.

> A. (19)   Adam being made a public head, all mankind, descending from him by ordinary generation, sinned in him, and fell with him in his first transgression.

Numbers 30, 32, and 33 had slight verbal changes which unnecessarily diminished the vigor of the language but made no substantial theological change. For example, compare the amended response with number 30 in the text.

> A. (30)   Christ's humiliation consisted in his being born, and that in a low condition, made under the law, and in his enduring the penalty of the law as the sinner's substitute and surety; in the miseries of his life, and in the death of the cross, in being buried, and continuing under the power of death for a time.

The changes in response 30 contain some positive, some negative qualities. The addition of the phrase "in his enduring the penalty of the law as the sinner's substitute and surety" again adds clear precision and symmetry to the theological balance of the response. However, the removal of the phrase "the wrath of God," while possibly eliminating redundancy, removes unmistakable vigor and pathos; a like effect arises from erasing the word "cursed" before "death."

The most substantial and meaningful changes were made in responses 64, 90, 93, and 96.

> **Q. 64.** **Which day of the seven hath God appointed to be the weekly Sabbath?**
>
> **A.** Before the resurrection of Christ, God appointed the seventh day of the week to be the weekly Sabbath; but now the first day of the week is observed, both for rest and worship, in conformity to the example of Christ, and the practice of his holy apostles.

This change again adds precision and accuracy. The former wording implies a specific divine appointment of the first day in the same way as God appointed the seventh. The substituted statement appears more harmonious with the actual testimony of Scripture.

The response to 90 gives a more streamlined evangelical response.

> **Q. 90.** **How may we escape the wrath and curse of God due to us for sin?**
>
> **A.** We ought diligently to use the outward means, whereby Christ communicateth to us the benefits of redemption, that we may have faith in Jesus Christ, and repentance unto life; without which it is impossible to escape the wrath and curse of God due to us for sin.

The question itself is streamlined and the answer conforms more closely to an evangelical *ordo salutis*. The prior answer probably had no intention of error but is greatly improved theologically by the change. The confusion apparent in these articles results from the historical situation of Keach and Collins. They made only slight verbal changes in the *Westminster Shorter Catechism* in order to make the document Baptist while retaining as many of the original words as possible. Their changes, however, were not sufficient, especially in light of the Baptist distinctiveness in understanding the ordinances and church membership. It is easy to understand why they exercised minimal editorial power, but they created uncertainty in expression and implied a non-Baptistic sacramentalism. They were careful to drop the word "sacrament" but unintentionally retained something of its substance.

The helpful nature of the changes made in 1795 can be seen clearly in the following exchange.

Q. 93. **What are the outward means whereby Christ communicateth to us the benefits of redemption?**

A. The outward and ordinary means whereby Christ communicateth to us the benefits of redemption, are the reading, but especially the preaching of the word, which the Spirit of God maketh an effectual means of convincing and converting the sinner, and the ordinances as additional means of building up believers in holiness and comfort, through faith unto salvation.

The answer substituted in this exchange far excels the old answer. Formerly, the word, the ordinances, and prayer were treated as equal means through which Christ communicates the benefits of redemption. Indeed they were said to be "effectual to the elect for salvation." Such language is tantamount to sacramentalism. The change recognizes the erroneous tendency of that answer and spotlights the word, especially the preaching of it, as effectual means under the Spirit's control. The ordinances properly take their place as means of "building up believers."

The change in number 96 reflects this elimination of false sacramentalism.

Q. 96. **What is the use of Baptism and the Lord's Supper?**

A. Baptism and the Lord's Supper are ordinances of Jesus Christ, and are of use to set forth our faith and every grace in us, through the blessing of Christ and the operation of the Spirit.

In the South

The catechism was used widely in the South in the late eighteenth and through much of the nineteenth century. Richard Furman, as mentioned earlier, used it effectively in Charleston, South Carolina. Associational minutes and other documents of Baptist life in Georgia, Alabama, Mississippi, Louisiana, and Tennessee show the influence of the catechism on Baptist churches of those states.

It is from the edition as printed by the Charleston Association in 1813 that the following text is taken. Some questions and responses that do not apear in that edition but do appear in present day versions of the catechism have been added in brackets. Scripture references are placed with their respective articles, some proof texts have been added, and the Roman numerals used for chapters have been changed to Arabic numerals.

THE

BAPTIST CATECHISM;

COMMONLY CALLED

KEACH'S CATECHISM:

OR,

A BRIEF INSTRUCTION

IN

THE PRINCIPLES OF THE CHRISTIAN RELIGION.

AGREEABLY TO THE CONFESSION OF FAITH, PUT FORTH BY UPWARDS OF
AN HUNDRED CONGREGATIONS IN GREAT BRITAIN, JULY 3, 1689,
AND ADOPTED BY THE PHILADELPHIA BAPTIST ASSO-
CIATION, SEPTEMBER 22, 1742.

NEW EDITION, WITH REFERENCES.

"And these words, which I command thee this day, SHALL BE IN
THINE HEART: And THOU SHALT TEACH THEM DILIGENTLY UNTO THY
CHILDREN, and shalt talk of them when thou sittest in thine house,
and when thou walkest by the way, and when thou liest down, and
when thou risest up."—DEUT. vi. 6, 7.

Philadelphia:

AMERICAN BAPTIST PUBLICATION SOCIETY,

118 ARCH STREET.

The

Baptist Catechism

Commonly Called

Keach's Catechism

or,

A Brieif Instruction

in

The Principles of the Christian Religion

Q. 1.   **Who is the first and chiefest being?**

A.   God is the first and chiefest being (Isaiah 44:6; 48:12; Psalm 97:9).

Q. 2.   **Ought everyone to believe there is a God?**

A.   Everyone ought to believe there is a God (Hebrews 11:6); and it is their great sin and folly who do not (Psalm 14:1).

Q. 3.   **How may we know there is a God?**

A.   The light of nature in man and the works of God plainly declare there is a God (Romans 1:19, 20; Psalm 19:1, 2, 3; Acts 17:24); but His Word and Spirit only do it fully and effectually for the salvation of sinners (1 Corinthians 2:10; 2 Timothy 3:15, 16).

Q. 4.   **What is the Word of God?**

A.   The Holy Scriptures of the Old and New Testament are the Word of God, and the only certain rule of faith and obedience (2 Timothy 3:16; Ephesians 2:20).

Q. 5.   **May all men make use of the Holy Scriptures?**

A.   All men are not only permitted, but commanded and exhorted to read, hear, and understand the Holy Scriptures (John 5:38; John 17:17–19; Revelation 1:3; Acts 8:30).

Q. 6.   What things are chiefly contained in the Holy Scriptures?

A.   The Holy Scriptures chiefly contain what man ought to believe concerning God, and what duty God requireth of man (2 Timothy 1:13; 3:15, 16).

Q. 7.   What is God?

A.   God is a Spirit (John 4:24), infinite (Job 11:7, 8, 9), eternal (Psalm 110:2), and unchangeable (James 1:17) in His being (Exodus 3:14), wisdom (Psalm 147:5), power (Revelation 4:8), holiness (Revelation 15:4), justice, goodness, and truth (Exodus 34:6).

Q. 8.   Are there more gods than one?

A.   There is but one only, the living and true God (Deuteronomy 6:4; Jeremiah 10:10).

Q. 9.   How many persons are there in the Godhead?

A.   There are three persons in the godhead, the Father, the Son, and the Holy Spirit; and these three are one God, the same in essence, equal in power and glory (1 John 5:7; Matthew 28:19).

Q. 10.   What are the decrees of God?

A.   The decrees of God are His eternal purpose according to the counsel of His will, whereby, for His own glory, He hath foreordained whatsoever comes to pass (Ephesians 1:4, 11; Romans 9:22–23; Isaiah 46:10; Lamentations 3:37).

Q. 11.   How doth God execute His decrees?

A.   God executeth His decrees in the works of creation and providence.

Q. 12.   What is the work of creation?

A.   The work of creation is God's making all things of nothing, by the word of His power, in the space of six days, and all very good (Genesis 1 throughout; Hebrews 11:3).

Q. 13. How did God create man?

A. God created man, male and female, after His own image, in knowledge, righteousness, and holiness, with dominion over the creatures (Genesis 1:26, 27, 28; Colossians 3:10, Ephesians 4:24).

Q. 14. What are God's works of providence?

A. God's works of providence are His most holy (Psalm 145:17), wise (Isaiah 28:29, Psalm 104:24), and powerful preserving (Hebrews 1:3) and governing all His creatures, and all their actions (Psalm 103:19; Matthew 10:29, 30, 31).

Q. 15. What special act of providence did God exercise towards man in the estate wherein He was created?

A. When God had created man, He entered into a covenant of life with him upon condition of perfect obedience: forbidding him to eat of the tree of the knowledge of good and evil, upon pain of death (Galatians 3:12; Genesis 2:17).

Q. 16. Did our first parents continue in the estate wherein they were created?

A. Our first parents being left to the freedom of their own will, fell from the estate wherein they were created, by sinning against God (Genesis 3:6, 7, 8, 13; Ecclesiastes 7:29).

Q. 17. What is sin?

A. Sin is any want of conformity unto, or transgression of, the law of God (1 John 3:4).

Q. 18. What was the sin whereby our first parents fell from the estate wherein they were created?

A. The sin whereby our first parents fell from the estate wherein they were created, was their eating the forbidden fruit (Genesis 3:6, 12, 16, 17).

Q. 19. Did all mankind fall in Adam's first transgression?

A. The covenant being made with Adam, not only for himself but for his posterity, all mankind descending from him by ordinary generation sinned in him, and fell with him in his first transgression (Genesis 2:16, 17; Romans 5:12; 1 Corinthians 15:21, 22).

Q. 20.   Into what estate did the fall bring mankind?

A.   The fall brought mankind into an estate of sin and misery (Romans 5:12).

Q. 21.   Wherein consists the sinfulness of that estate whereinto man fell?

A.   The sinfulness of that estate whereinto man fell, consists in the guilt of Adam's first sin, the want of original righteousness, and the corruption of his whole nature, which is commonly called original sin; together with all actual transgressions which proceed from it (Romans 5:12, to the end; Ephesians 2:1, 2, 3; James 1:14, 15; Matthew 15:19).

Q. 22.   What is the misery of that estate whereinto man fell?

A.   All mankind by their fall lost communion with God (Genesis 3:8, 10, 24), are under His wrath and curse (Ephesians 2:2, 3; Galatians 3:10), and so made liable to all miseries in this life, to death itself, and to the pains of hell for ever (Lamentations 3:39; Romans 6:23; Matthew 25:41, 46).

Q. 23.   Did God leave all mankind to perish in the estate of sin and misery?

A.   God having out of His mere good pleasure, from all eternity, elected some to everlasting life (Ephesians 1:4, 5), did enter into a covenant of grace, to deliver them out of the estate of sin and misery, and to bring them into an estate of salvation by a Redeemer (Romans 3:20–22; Galatians 3:21, 22).

Q. 24.   Who is the Redeemer of God's elect?

A.   The only Redeemer of God's elect is the Lord Jesus Christ (1 Timothy 2:5, 6); who, being the eternal Son of God, became man (John 1:14; Galatians 4:4), and so was and continueth to be God and man in two distinct natures, and one person for ever (Romans 9:5; Luke 1:35; Colossians 2:9; Hebrews 7:24, 25).

Q. 25.   How did Christ, being the Son of God become man?

A.   Christ the Son of God became man by taking to Himself a true body (Hebrews 2:14, 17; 10:5), and a reasonable soul (Matthew 26:38); being conceived by the power of the Holy Spirit in the womb of the Virgin Mary, and born of her (Luke 1:27, 31, 34, 35, 42; Galatians 4:4), yet without sin (Hebrews 4:15; 7:26).

Q. 26.   What offices doth Christ execute as our Redeemer?

A.   Christ as our Redeemer executeth the offices of a prophet, of a priest, and of king, both in His estate of humiliation and exaltation (Acts 3:22; Hebrews 12:25; 2 Corinthians 13:3; Hebrews 5:5, 6, 7; 7:25; Psalm 2:6; Isaiah 9:6, 7; Matthew 21:5; Psalm 2:8–11).

Q. 27.   How doth Christ execute the office of a prophet?

A.   Christ executeth the office of prophet in revealing to us, by His Word and Spirit, the will of God for our salvation (John 1:18; 1 Peter 1:10,11, 12; John 15:15; and 20:31).

Q. 28.   How doth Christ execute the office of a priest?

A.   Christ executeth the office of priest in His once offering up Himself a sacrifice to satisfy divine justice (Hebrews 9:14, 28) and reconcile us to God (Hebrews 2:17), and in making continual intercession for us (Hebrews 7:24, 25).

Q. 29.   How doth Christ execute the office of king?

A.   Christ executeth the office of a king, in subduing us to Himself (Acts 15:14, 15, 16), in ruling (Isaiah 33:22), and defending us (Isaiah 32:1, 2), and in restraining and conquering all His and our enemies (1 Corinthians 15:25; Psalm 110 throughout).

Q. 30.   Wherein did Christ's humiliation consist?

A.   Christ's humiliation consisted in His being born, and that in a low condition (Luke 2:7), made under the law (Galatians 4:4), undergoing the miseries of this life (Hebrews 12:2, 3; Isaiah 53:2, 3), the wrath of God (Luke 22:44; Matthew 27:46), and the cursed death of the cross (Philippians 2:8); in being buried (1 Corinthians 15:3,4), and continuing under the power of death for a time (Acts 2:24, 25, 26, 27, 31; Matthew 12:40).

Q. 31.   **Wherein consisteth Christ's exaltation?**

A.   Christ's exaltation consisteth in His rising again from the dead on the third day (1 Corinthians 15:4), in ascending up into heaven (Mark 16:19), in sitting at the right hand of God the Father (Ephesians 1:20), and in coming to judge the world at the last day (Acts 1: 11; 17:31).

Q. 32.   **How are we made partakers of the redemption purchased by Christ?**

A.   We are made partakers of the redemption purchased by Christ, by the effectual application of it to us (John 1:11,12) by His Holy Spirit (Titus 3:5,6).

Q. 33.   **How doth the Spirit apply to us the redemption purchased by Christ?**

A.   The Spirit applieth to us the redemption purchased by Christ, by working faith in us (Ephesians 1:13, 14; John 6:37, 39; Ephesians 2:8), and thereby uniting us to Christ, in our effectual calling (Ephesians 3:17; 1 Corinthians 1:9).

Q. 34.   **What is effectual calling?**

A.   Effectual calling is the work of God's Spirit (2 Timothy 1:9; 2 Thessalonians 2:13, 14), whereby convincing us of our sin and misery (Acts 2:37), enlightening our minds in the knowledge of Christ (Acts 26:18), and renewing our wills (Ezekiel 36:26, 27), He doth persuade and enable us to embrace Jesus Christ freely offered to us in the gospel (John 6:44, 45; Philippians 2:13).

Q. 35.   **What benefits do they that are effectually called partake of in this life?**

A.   They that are effectually called do in this life partake of justification (Romans 8:30), adoption (Ephesians 1:5), sanctification, and the several benefits which in this life do either accompany or flow from them (1 Corinthians 1:30).

Q. 36.   What is justification?

A.   Justification is an act of God's free grace, wherein He pardoneth all our sins (Romans 3:24, 25; and 4:6, 7, 8), and accepteth us as righteous in His sight (2 Corinthians 5:19, 21), only for the righteousness of Christ imputed to us (Romans 5:17–19), and received by faith alone (Galatians 2:16; Philippians 3:9).

Q. 37.   What is adoption?

A.   Adoption is an act of God's free grace (1 John 3:1), whereby we are received into the number and have a right to all the privileges of the sons of God (John 1:12; Romans 8:14–17).

Q. 38.   What is sanctification?

A.   Sanctification is the work of God's free grace (2 Thessalonians 2:13), whereby we are renewed in the whole man after the image of God (Ephesians 4:23, 24), and are enabled more and more to die unto sin, and live unto righteousness (Romans 6:4, 6; 8:1).

Q. 39.   What are the benefits which in this life do accompany or flow from justification, adoption, and sanctification?

A.   The benefits which in this life do accompany or flow from justification, adoption, and sanctification, are assurance of God's love, peace of conscience (Romans 5:1, 2, 5), joy in the Holy Spirit (Romans 5:5, 17), increase of grace (Proverbs 4:18), and perseverance therein to the end (1 John 5:13; 1 Peter 1:5).

Q. 40.   What benefits do believers receive from Christ at their death?

A.   The souls of believers are at their death made perfect in holiness (Hebrews 12:23), and do immediately pass into glory (2 Corinthians 5:1, 6, 8; Philippians 1:23; Luke 23:43); and their bodies being still united to Christ (1 Thessalonians 4:14), do rest in their graves (Isaiah 57:2) till the resurrection (Job 19:26, 27).

Q. 41.   What benefits do believers receive from Christ at the resurrection?

A.   At the resurrection believers, being raised up in glory (1 Corinthians 15:43), shall be openly acknowledged, and acquitted in the day of judgment (Matthew 25:23; Matthew 10:32), and made perfectly blessed, both in soul and body, in the full enjoyment of God (1 John 3:2; 1 Corinthians 13:12) to all eternity (1 Thessalonians 4:17, 18).

Q. 42.   **But what shall be done to the wicked at their death?**

A.   The souls of the wicked shall, at their death, be cast into the torments of hell, and their bodies lie in their graves, till the resurrection and judgment of the great day (Luke 16:23, 24; Acts 2:24; Jude 5, 7; 1 Peter 3:19; Psalm 49:14).

Q. 43.   **What shall be done to the wicked, at the day of judgment?**

A.   At the day of judgment the bodies of the wicked, being raised out of their graves, shall be sentenced, together with their souls, to unspeakable torments with the devil and his angels forever (John 5:28, 29; Matthew 25:41, 46; 2 Thessalonians 1:8, 9).

Q. 44.   **What is the duty which God requireth of man?**

A.   The duty which God requireth of man is, obedience to His revealed will (Micah 6:8; 1 Samuel 15:22).

Q. 45.   **What did God at first reveal to man for the rule of his obedience?**

A.   The rule which God at first revealed to man for his obedience, was the moral law (Romans 2:14, 15, and 10:5).

Q. 46.   **Where is the moral law summarily comprehended?**

A.   The moral law is summarily comprehended in the Ten Commandments (Deuteronomy 10:4; Matthew 19:17).

Q. 47.   **What is the sum of the Ten Commandments?**

A.   The sum of the Ten Commandments is, to love the Lord our God, with all our heart, with all our soul, with all our strength, and with all our mind; and our neighbor as ourselves (Matthew 22:37–40).

Q. 48.   What is the preface to the Ten Commandments?

A.   The preface to the Ten Commandments is in these words; I am the Lord thy God which have brought thee out of the land of Egypt, out of the house of bondage (Exodus 20:2).

Q. 49.   What doth the preface to the Ten Commandments teach us?

A.   The preface to the Ten Commandments teacheth us that because God is the Lord, and our God and redeemer, therefore we are bound to keep all His commandments (Luke 1:74, 75; 1 Peter 1:15–19).

Q. 50.   Which is the first commandment?

A.   The first commandment is, Thou shalt have no other gods before Me (Exodus 20:3).

Q. 51.   What is required in the first commandment?

A.   The first commandment requireth us to know and acknowledge God to be the only true God and our God (1 Chronicles 28:9; Deuteronomy 26:17), and to worship and glorify Him accordingly (Matthew 4:10; Psalm 29:2).

Q. 52.   What is forbidden in the first commandment?

A.   The first commandment forbiddeth the denying (Psalm 14: 1), or not worshipping and glorifying the true God (Romans 1:21), as God and our God (Psalm 81:10, 11), and the giving of that worship and glory to any other, which is due unto Him alone (Romans 1:25, 26).

Q. 53.   What are we especially taught by these words before Me, in the first commandment?

A.   These words before Me, in the first commandment teach us, that God, who seeth all things, taketh notice of and is much displeased with the sin of having any other god (Exodus 8:5, to the end).

Q. 54.   Which is the second commandment?

A.   The second commandment is, Thou shalt not make unto thee any graven image, or any likeness of anything that is in heaven above, or that is in the earth beneath, or that is in the water under the earth; thou shalt not bow down thyself to them, nor serve them: for I the Lord thy God am a jealous God, visiting the iniquity of the fathers upon the children unto the third and fourth generation of them that hate Me; and shewing mercy unto thousands of them that love Me, and keep My commandments (Exodus 20:4, 5, 6).

Q. 55.   What is required in the second commandment?

A.   The second commandment requireth the receiving, observing, and keeping pure and entire all such religious worship and ordinances, as God hath appointed in His Word (Deuteronomy 32:46; Matthew 23:20; Acts 2:42).

Q. 56.   What is forbidden in the second commandment?

A.   The second commandment forbiddeth the worshipping of God by images (Deuteronomy 4:15–19; Exodus 32:5, 8), or any other way not appointed in His Word (Deuteronomy 7:31, 32).

Q. 57.   What are the reasons annexed to the second commandment?

A.   The reasons annexed to the second commandment are, God's sovereignty over us (Psalm 45:2, 3, 6), His propriety in us (Psalm 45:11), and the zeal He hath to His own worship (Exodus 34:13, 14).

Q. 58.   Which is the third commandment?

A.   The third commandment is, Thou shalt not take the name of the Lord thy God in vain; for the Lord will not hold him guiltless that taketh His name in vain (Exodus 20:7).

Q. 59.   What is required in the third commandment?

A.   The third commandment requireth the holy and reverent use of God's names (Matthew 6:9; Deuteronomy 28:58), titles (Psalm 68:4), attributes (Revelation 15:3, 4), ordinances, (Malachi 1:11, 14), word (Psalm 136:1, 2) and works (Job 36:24).

Q. 60.   What is forbidden in the third commandment?

A.   The third commandment forbiddeth all profaning and abus-
           ing of anything whereby God makes Himself known (Malachi
           1:6, 7, 12; 2:2; 3:14).

Q. 61.   What is the reason annexed to the third commandment?

A.   The reason annexed to the third commandment is, that how-
           ever the breakers of this commandment may escape punish-
           ment from men, yet the Lord our God will not suffer them
           to escape His righteous judgment (1 Samuel 2:12, 17, 22, 29;
           3:13; Deuteronomy 28:58, 59).

Q. 62.   What is the fourth commandment?

A.   The fourth commandment is, Remember the Sabbath day to
           keep it holy: six days shalt thou labor and do all thy work; but
           the seventh day is the Sabbath of the Lord thy God, in it thou
           shalt not do any work, thou, nor thy son, nor thy daughter, nor
           thy man-servant, nor thy maid-servant, nor thy cattle, nor the
           stranger that is within thy gates: for in six days the Lord made
           heaven and earth, the sea, and all that in them is, and rested
           the seventh day; wherefore the Lord blessed the Sabbath day
           and hallowed it (Exodus 20:8–11).

Q. 63.   What is required in the fourth commandment?

A.   The fourth commandment requireth the keeping holy to God
           such set times as He hath appointed in His Word, expressly,
           one whole day in seven to be a holy sabbath to Himself (Exo-
           dus 20:8–11; Deuteronomy 5:12–14).

Q. 64.   Which day of the seven hath God appointed to be the weekly
           Sabbath?

A.   Before the resurrection of Christ, God appointed the seventh
           day of the week to be the weekly Sabbath (Exodus 20:8–11;
           Deuteronomy 5:12–14); and the first day of the week ever
           since, to continue to the end of the world, which is the Chris-
           tian Sabbath (Psalm 118:24; Matthew 28:1; Mark 2:27, 28;
           John 20:19, 20, 26; Revelation 1:10; Mark 16:2; Luke 24:1,
           30–36; John 20:1; Acts 1:3; 2:1, 2; 20:7; 1 Corinthians 16:1, 2).

Q. 65.   How is the Sabbath to be sanctified?

A.   The Sabbath is to be sanctified by a holy resting all that day
          (Exodus 20:8, 10), even from such worldly employments and
          recreations as are lawful on other days (Exodus 16:25–28; Ne-
          hemiah 13:15–22); and spending the whole time in the public
          and private exercises of God's worship (Luke 4:16; Acts 20:7;
          Psalm 92 title; Isaiah 66:23), except so much as is to be taken
          up in the works of necessity and mercy (Matthew 12:1–13).

Q. 66.   What is forbidden in the fourth commandment?

A.   The fourth commandment forbiddeth the omission or careless
          performance of the duties required (Ezekiel 22:26; Amos 8:5;
          Malachi 1:13), and the profaning the day by idleness (Acts
          20:7, 9), or doing that which is in itself sinful (Ezekiel 23:38),
          or by unnecessary thoughts, words, or works, about worldly
          employments or recreations (Jeremiah 17:24–27; Isaiah
          58:13).

Q. 67.   What are the reasons annexed to the fourth commandment?

A.   The reasons annexed to the fourth commandment, are God's
          allowing us six days of the week for our own lawful employ-
          ments (Exodus 20:9), His challenging a special propriety in a
          seventh, His own example, and His blessing the Sabbath day
          (Exodus 20:11).

Q. 68.   Which is the fifth commandment?

A.   The fifth commandment is, Honor thy father and thy mother;
          that thy days may be long in the land which the Lord thy God
          giveth thee (Exodus 20:12).

Q. 69.   What is required in the fifth commandment?

A.   The fifth commandment requireth the preserving the honor
          and performing the duties belonging to everyone in their sev-
          eral places and relations, as superiors (Ephesians 5:21), inferi-
          ors (1 Peter 2:17), or equals (Romans 12:10).

Q. 70.   What is forbidden in the fifth commandment?

A.   The fifth commandment forbiddeth the neglect of, or doing anything against the honor and duty which belongeth to everyone in their several places and relations (Matthew 15:4–6; Ezekiel 34:24; Romans 13:8).

Q. 71.   What is the reason annexed to the fifth commandment?

A.   The reason annexed to the fifth commandment is a promise of long life and prosperity (as far as it shall serve for God's glory, and their own good) to all such as keep this commandment (Deuteronomy 5:16; Ephesians 6:2, 3).

Q. 72.   What is the sixth commandment?

A.   The sixth commandment is, Thou shalt not kill (Exodus 20:13).

Q. 73.   What is required in the sixth commandment?

A.   The sixth commandment requireth all lawful endeavors to preserve our own life (Ephesians 5:28,29) and the life of others (1 Kings 18:4).

Q. 74.   What is forbidden in the sixth commandment?

A.   The sixth commandment absolutely forbiddeth the taking away of our own life, or the life of our neighbor unjustly, or whatsoever tendeth thereunto (Acts 26:28; Genesis 9:9).

Q. 75.   Which is the seventh commandment?

A.   The seventh commandment is, Thou shalt not commit adultery (Exodus 20:14).

Q. 76.   What is required in the seventh commandment?

A.   The seventh commandment requireth the preservation of our own and our neighbor's chastity, in heart, speech, and behavior (1 Corinthians 7:2, 3, 5, 34, 36; Colossians 4:6; 1 Peter 3:2).

Q. 77.   What is forbidden in the seventh commandment?

A.   The seventh commandment forbiddeth all unchaste thoughts, words, and actions (Matthew 15:19, 5:28; Ephesians 5:3, 4).

Q. 78.   Which is the eighth commandment?

A.   The eighth commandment is, Thou shalt not steal (Exodus 20:15).

Q. 79.   What is required in the eighth commandment?

A.   The eighth commandment requireth the lawful procuring and furthering the wealth and outward estate of ourselves and others (Genesis 30:30; 1 Timothy 5:8; Leviticus 25:35; Deuteronomy 22:1, 2, 3, 4, 5; Exodus 23:4, 5; Genesis 47:14, 20).

Q. 80.   What is forbidden in the eighth commandment?

A.   The eighth commandment forbiddeth whatsoever doth or may unjustly hinder our own (1 Timothy 5:8; Proverbs 28:19) or our neighbor's wealth or outward estate (Proverbs 21:17, and 23:20, 21; Ephesians 4:28).

Q. 81.   Which is the ninth commandment?

A.   The ninth commandment is, Thou shalt not bear false witness against thy neighbor (Exodus 20:16).

Q. 82.   What is required in the ninth commandment?

A.   The ninth commandment requireth the maintaining and promoting of truth between man and man (Zechariah 8:16), and of our own neighbor's good name (John 5:12), especially in witnessbearing (Proverbs 14:5, 25).

Q. 83.   What is forbidden in the ninth commandment?

A.   The ninth commandment forbiddeth whatsoever is prejudicial to the truth, or injurious to our own or our neighbor's good name (1 Samuel 17:28; Leviticus 19:16; Psalm 15:2, 3).

Q. 84.   Which is the tenth commandment?

A.   The tenth commandment is Thou shalt not covet thy neighbor's house, thou shalt not covet thy neighbor's wife, nor his man-servant, nor his maid-servant, nor his ox, nor his ass, nor anything that is thy neighbor's (Exodus 20:17).

Q. 85. What is required in the tenth commandment?

A. The tenth commandment requireth full contentment with our own condition (Hebrews 13:5; 1 Timothy 6:6), with a right and charitable frame of spirit toward our neighbor, and all that is his (Job 31:29; Romans 7:15; 1 Timothy 1:5; 1 Corinthians 8:4, 7).

Q. 86. What is forbidden in the tenth commandment?

A. The tenth commandment forbiddeth all discontentment with our own estate (1 Kings 21:4; Esther 5:13; 1 Corinthians 10:10), envying or grieving at the good of our neighbor (Galatians 5:26; James 3:14, 16), and all inordinate motions and affections to anything that is his (Romans 7:7, 8, 13:9; Deuteronomy 5:21).

Q. 87. Is. any man able perfectly to keep the commandments of God?

A. No mere man since the fall is able in this life perfectly to keep the commandments of God (Ecclesiastes 7:20; 1 John 1:8, 10; Galatians 5:17), but doth daily break them in thought, word, or deed (Genesis 4:5, and 7:21; Romans 3:9–21; James 3:2–13).

Q. 88. Are all transgressions of the law equally heinous?

A. Some sins in themselves, and by reason of several aggravations, are more heinous in the sight of God than others (Ezekiel 8:6, 13, 15; 1 John 5:16; Psalm 78:17, 32, 56).

Q. 89. What doth every sin deserve?

A. Every sin deserveth God's wrath and curse, both in this life and that which is to come (Ephesians 5:6; Galatians 3:10; Lamentations 3:39; Matthew 25:41; Romans 6:23).

Q. 90. What doth God require of us that we may escape His wrath and curse, due to us for sin?

A. To escape the wrath and curse of God due to us for sin, God requireth of us faith in Jesus Christ, repentance unto life (Acts 20:21), with the diligent use of all the outward means whereby

Christ communicateth to us the benefits of redemption (Proverbs 2:1–6, 8:33 to the end; Isaiah 55:2, 3).

Q. 91.   What is faith in Jesus Christ?

A.   Faith in Jesus Christ is a saving grace (Hebrews 10:39), whereby we receive and rest upon Him alone for salvation, as He is offered to us in the gospel (John 1:12; Isaiah 26:3, 4; Philippians 3:9; Galatians 2:16).

Q. 92.   What is repentance unto life?

A.   Repentance unto life is a saving grace (Acts 11:28), whereby a sinner, out of a true sense of his sin (Acts 2:37, 38), and apprehension of the mercy of God in Christ (Joel 2:12; Jeremiah 3:22), doth, with grief and hatred of his sin, turn from it unto God (Jeremiah 31:18, 19; Ezekiel 36:31), with full purpose of and endeavor after new obedience (2 Corinthians 7:11; Isaiah 1: 16, 17).

Q. 93.   What are the outward means whereby Christ communicateth to us the benefits of redemption?

A.   The outward and ordinary means whereby Christ communicateth to us the benefits of redemption are his ordinances, especially the Word, baptism, the Lord's supper, and prayer; all which means are made effectual to the elect for salvation (Matthew 28:19, 20; Acts 2:42, 46, 47).

Q. 94.   How is the Word made effectual to salvation?

A.   The Spirit of God maketh the reading, but especially the preaching of the Word, an effectual means of convincing and converting sinners, and of building them up in holiness and comfort through faith unto salvation (Nehemiah 8:8; Acts 26:18; Psalm 19:8; Acts 20:32; Romans 1: 15, 16, 10:13, 14, 15, 16, 17; 15:4; 1 Corinthians 14:24, 25; 2 Timothy 3:15, 16, 17).

Q. 95.   How is the Word to be read and heard, that it may become effectual to salvation?

A.   That the Word may become effectual to salvation, we must attend thereunto with diligence (Proverbs 8:34), preparation

(1 Peter 2:1, 2), and prayer (Psalm 119:18); receive it with faith and love (Hebrews 4:2; 2 Thessalonians 2:10), lay it up in our hearts (Psalm 119:18), and practice it in our lives (Luke 8:15; James 1:25).

Q. 96. How do baptism and the Lords supper become effectual means of salvation?

A. Baptism and the Lords supper become effectual means of salvation, not for any virtue in them, or in him that doth administer them, but only by the blessing of Christ (1 Peter 3:21; Matthew 3:11; 1 Corinthians 3:6, 7), and the working of the Spirit in those that by faith receive them (1 Corinthians 12:3; Matthew 28:19).

Q. 97. What is baptism?

A. Baptism is an ordinance of the New Testament instituted by Jesus Christ, to be unto the party baptized a sign of his fellowship with Him, in His death, burial, and resurrection; of his being ingrafted into Him (Romans 6:3, 4, 5; Colossians 2:12; Galatians 3:27); of remission of sins (Mark 1:4; Acts 2:38, and 22:16); and of his giving up himself unto God through Jesus Christ, to live and walk in newness of life (Romans 6:3, 4).

Q. 98. To whom is baptism to be administered?

A. Baptism is to be administered to all those who actually profess repentance towards God (Acts 2:38; Matthew 3:6), faith in and obedience to our Lord Jesus Christ, and to none other (Acts 8:12, 36, 37, 38; 10:47, 48).

Q. 99. Are the infants of such as are professing believers to be baptized?

A. The infants of such as are professing believers are not to be baptized, because there is neither command or example in the holy Scriptures, or certain consequence from them to baptize such (Exodus 23:13; Proverbs 30:6; Luke 3:7, 8).

Q. 100. How is Baptism rightly administered?

A. Baptism is rightly administered by immersion, or dipping the whole body of the party in water, into the name of the Father, and of the Son, and of the Holy Spirit, according to Christ's institution, and the practice of the apostles (Matthew 3:16; John 3:23; 4:1, 2; Matthew 28:19, 20; Acts 8:38; Romans 6:4; Colossians 2:12), and not by sprinkling or pouring of water, or dipping some part of the body, after the tradition of men.

Q. 101. **What is the duty of such who are rightly baptized?**

A. It is the duty of such who are rightly baptized to give up themselves to some particular and orderly church of Jesus Christ, that they may walk in all the commandments and ordinances of the Lord blameless (Acts 2:41, 42; 5:13, 14; 9:26; 1 Peter 2:5; Luke 1:6).

Q. 102. **What is the Lord's supper?**

A. The Lord's supper is an ordinance of the New Testament, instituted by Jesus Christ; wherein by giving and receiving bread and wine, according to His appointment, His death is shown forth, and the worthy receivers are, not after a corporal and carnal manner, but by faith, made partakers of His body and blood, with all His benefits, to their spiritual nourishment and growth in grace (Matthew 26:26, 27, 28; 1 Corinthians 11:23–26; 10:16).

Q. 103. **Who are the proper subjects of this ordinance?**

A. They who have been baptized upon a personal profession of their faith in Jesus Christ, and repentance from dead works (Acts 2:41, 42).

Q. 104. **What is required to the worthy receiving of the Lord's supper?**

A. It is required of them that would worthily partake of the Lord's supper, that they examine themselves of their knowledge to discern the Lord's body (1 Corinthians 11:28, 29), of their faith to feed upon Him (2 Corinthians 13:5), of their repentance (1 Corinthians 11:31), love (1 Corinthians 10:16, 17), and new obedience (1 Corinthians 5:7, 8), lest coming unworthily they eat and drink judgment to themselves (1 Corinthians 11:28, 29).

Q. 105.   What is prayer?

A.   Prayer is an offering up our desires to God (Psalm 62:8), by
          the assistance of the Holy Spirit (Romans 8:26), for things
          agreeable to His will (1 John 5:14; Romans 8:27), in the name
          of Christ (John 16:23), believing (Matthew 21:22; James 1:6),
          with confession of our sins (Psalm 32:5, 6; Daniel 9:4), and
          thankful acknowledgments of His mercies (Philippians 4:6).

Q. 106.   What rule hath God given for our direction in prayer?

A.   The whole Word of God is of use to direct us in prayer (1 John
          5:14); but the special rule of direction is that prayer which
          Christ taught His disciples, commonly called the Lord's prayer
          (Matthew 6:9–13; with Luke 11:2–4).

Q. 107.   What doth the preface of the Lord's prayer teach us?

A.   The preface of the Lord's prayer, which is Our Father which
          art in heaven (Matthew 6:9), teacheth us to draw near to God
          with all holy reverence and confidence, as children to a father,
          able and ready to help us (Romans 8:15; Luke 11:13; Isaiah
          24:8); and that we should pray with and for others (Acts 12:5;
          1 Timothy 2:1, 2).

Q. 108.   What do we pray for in the first petition?

A.   In the first petition, which is, Hallowed be Thy name (Mat-
          thew 6:9), we pray that God would enable us and others to
          glorify Him in all that whereby He maketh Himself known
          (Psalm 67:2, 3), and that He would dispose all things to His
          own glory (Psalm 83 throughout; Romans 11:36).

Q. 109.   What do we pray for in the second petition?

A.   In the second petition, which is, Thy kingdom come (Matthew
          6:10), we pray that Satan's kingdom may be destroyed (Psalm
          68:1, 18), and that the kingdom of grace may be advanced
          (Revelation 12:10, 11), ourselves and others brought into it
          and kept in it (2 Thessalonians 3: 1; Romans 10: 1; John 17:19,
          20), and that the kingdom of glory may be hastened (Revela-
          tion 22:10).

Q. 110.   What do we pray for in the third petition?

A.   In the third petition, which is, Thy will be done on earth as it is in heaven (Matthew 6:10), we pray that God by His grace would make us able and willing to know, obey, and submit to His will in all things (Psalm 67: throughout; Psalm 119:36; 2 Samuel 15:25; Job 1:21), as the angels do in heaven (Psalm 103:20, 21).

Q. 111.   What do we pray for in the fourth petition?

A.   In the fourth petition, which is, Give us this day our daily bread (Matthew 6:11), we pray that of God's free gift we may receive a competent portion of the good things of this life, and enjoy His blessing with them (Proverbs 30:8; Genesis 28:20; 1 Timothy 4:4, 5).

Q. 112.   What do we pray for in the fifth petition?

A.   In the fifth petition, which is, And forgive us our debts as we forgive our debtors (Matthew 6:12), we pray that God, for Christ's sake, would freely pardon all our sins (Psalm 51:1, 2, 7, 9; Daniel 9:17–19); which we are rather encouraged to ask because of His grace we are enabled from the heart to forgive others (Luke 11:4; Matthew 18:35).

Q. 113.   What do we pray for in the sixth petition?

A.   In the sixth petition, which is, And lead us not into temptation but deliver us from evil (Matthew 6:13), we pray that God would either keep us from being tempted to sin (Matthew 26:31), or support and deliver us when we are tempted (2 Corinthians 12:8).

Q. 114.   What doth the conclusion of the Lord's prayer teach?

A.   The conclusion of the Lord's prayer, which is, For Thine is the kingdom, and the power, and the glory, forever. Amen (Matthew 6:13), teacheth us to take our encouragement in prayer from God only (Daniel 9:4, 7–9, 16–19), and in our prayers to praise Him, ascribing kingdom, power, and glory, to Him (1 Chronicles 29:10–13). And in testimony of our desire and assurance to be heard, we say, Amen (1 Corinthians 4:16; Revelation 11:20; 22:20, 21).

3

Catechism for Girls and Boys

An Introduction

How does one educate children in gospel truth? This question has been a matter of practical interest for the people of God since the nation of Israel was called to bear the oracles of God. Deuteronomy 6 assumes the urgent importance of training the minds of children in both doctrine and worship and laying a reasonable foundation for both.

The Challenge

In 1798, Richard Cecil proposed a question for a group of his evangelical minister friends to discuss: "What may be done towards the interests of the children of a congregation?"[1] These leaders of two centuries ago seemed to have many modern problems. Richard Cecil complained the parents would not come but would send their children. This created some confusion because "they tattled and were troublesome." He had to assign adults to take care of them but those given that onerous duty were "not able to manage them." He was not resentful of the children's being there, however, because "here seems to be a large harvest." His way of teaching them was to speak in "terrible images" such as explaining salvation by "a house on fire."

Others tried their hand at giving advice. When it came time for J. Venn to contribute, he began by saying, "I once thought it absurd to teach

[1] John H. Pratt, Ed. *The Thought of Evangelical Leaders* (Edinburgh: The Banner of Truth Trust, 1978; first published by James Nisbet, 1856), 6.

children the Catechism, which they did not comprehend. So I determined to address their understandings." After trying this for a while, he compared their knowledge to that of one he described as a "stupid maidservant," who had been catechized in the old way. To his surprise, he found that her understanding and knowledge was best.

Venn then decided that the catechism method was appropriate as part of a scheme of education for children. One need not fear of "burdening their young memories." He had known children to learn 70 chapters by heart. One should be zealous thus to store the memory, because "children are machines." He recommended teaching several things by heart: the church catechism, the sermon broken into short questions, and Scripture. This time and energy should be directed solely at the children with no adult present, "because if others are there, the Minister will be aiming at them."

This is still good advice. Periodically the teaching of definite doctrine through catechetical instruction has fallen from favor. Sometimes the philosophical pressures of educational philosophy have relegated catechetical instruction to a category of irrelevance. Sometimes theological fads have so minimized the importance of definite truth or have disputed the possibility of systematic theology that churches have been brought to forsake their calling to protect "the form of sound words." Sometimes, as pointed out earlier, the knowledge of the answers of a catechism has been viewed as sufficient evidence of true Christian faith. This mistake leads those who know that the Father seeks worshippers who worship in spirit as well as truth to minimize the latter mistakenly thinking that they thereby enhance the former. In spite of this ebb and flow, it is a fact that when ministerial labor was warm and conscientious, and Christian truth transformed individuals and societies, catechetical instruction has abounded. One cannot help but think that catechism had an important part in creating that consensus of mind, heart, and culture.

On whose shoulders does responsibility fall for mastering the catechism? The Puritans made both pastor and parishioner share the load. In his *Christian Directory*, Richard Baxter gave directions for profitable hearing of the preached word. One of the practices essential for understanding what is heard is, "Learn first your catechism at home, and the great essential points of religion, contained in the creed, the Lord's prayer, and the ten commandments." Baxter called this investment of time in the catechism the "fruitfullest of all your studies."

John Flavel's admonition to ministers who would do their work well began with the "prudential expedient" of laying a "good foundation of knowledge in our people's souls, by catechizing and instructing them in the principles of christianity, without which we labour in vain."[2] Flavel believed that without a knowing people we should not have a gracious people. One may preach well, but "All your excellent sermons will be dashed to pieces, upon the rock of your people's ignorance." In light of the importance of a knowledge of divine truth, Flavel said, "You can never pitch upon a better project, to promote and secure the success of your labours, than catechizing."

Some mediating form of catechetical instruction that took advantage of the "most judicious and compendious system" ever to bless the church, that is, the Westminster Standards, would be very useful according to Flavel. The answers must not be as full as those in the primary documents but certainly must go beyond a mere "yes" or "no." This present catechism constitutes an attempt to meet this need. It introduces the theological ideas and much of the vocabulary of the *Shorter Catechism*, which is virtually the same as the catechism advocated by Baptist churches for its youth in the eighteenth and nineteenth centuries, while resisting the fulness of statement that will be reserved for a later adventure.

Theological Orientation

Several theological ideas are introduced which serve as large receptacles for future deposits of biblical truth. Fundamentally, emphases on the Trinity, Law/Gospel, Prayer, Covenant and Church determine the content and arrangement of the catechism. How each of these elements is related to the doctrine of salvation is a major concern of both the wording and the arrangement. A section on the Ten Commandments precedes the major soteriological section. The purpose of this is to emphasize the truth that by the law no flesh shall be justified, but rather through the law we become aware of sin. This should not be taken to imply that the law has no function subsequent to regeneration. For sure, that which revealed sin, corruption, and damnation to us is a sure guide to holiness. The indwelling of the Holy Spirit produces an increasing love for the perfect law of liberty, that same law whose initial glory was to bring condemnation (2 Corinthians 4).

The covenant of grace plays an integral part in and is one of the cohesive elements of this catechism. The approach emphasizes each person of the tri-une God and the function effected within the covenant respectively by the Father, the Son, and the Holy Spirit. Subjects such as election, justification, adoption, sanctification, atonement, regeneraton, sealing, and others are introduced in that context. The tri-fold office work of Christ

[2] John Flavel, "The Character of a True Evangelical Pastor," in *The Works of John Flavel*, 6 vols. (Edinburgh: Banner of Truth, 1968 [reprint]), 6:571.

as prophet, priest, and king discloses the all-sufficiency of the Lord Jesus Christ as Savior of fallen creatures.

Other sections add important material. Children are taught the centrality of the local church as an avenue of Christian discipleship. The ordinances, that is, baptism and the Lord's Supper, instututed by our Lord as representative of his death, burial and resurrection as an atoning work for sin and energizing power for life are explained. The reality of eternal destinies in heaven and hell cannot be omitted without an insult to the gospel itself. An exhortation for personal application of these eternal issues closes the catechism.

Suggestions for Use

The best use of this catechism would be as a supplement in Sunday School from the first to the fifth grades. A certain number of responses might be targeted each year as a goal for memorization. Perhaps five to ten minutes could be spent each week reviewing these. The children would be encouraged to involve their parents in the process at home. During the first year, a goal of mastering the first ten question and answer responses would be reasonable. Each year the number to be memorized would increase.

In grade five, a special catechism class led by the pastor could have several advantages. One, he could review all the material with the children and help them move toward a coherent understanding of the entire catechism. The logic of the movement of questions and the arrangement of sections should be part of this study. Two, the special class would help prepare the children for a more intense inductive Bible and doctrine study for the duration of their adolescent years. A beneficial activity at this stage is a "proofing" of the answers through Bible study and Bible memory. Passages within the proof section of each answer should be read and some verses might be selected for memorization. From time to time, the pastor, or other teacher, will help the young scholars determine if the passages of Scripture do indeed support the answer given in the catechism. Three, the pastor's involvement with the children in this kind of activity at this age will lay a foundation in a pastoral and teaching relationship that is sure, under God, to reap a gratifying spiritual harvest in the future.

Some have found that their children learn the responses easily and eagerly in the pre-school years. As part of a family worship practice, that method holds great promise. Families will find the catechism helpful, not only as a motivation, but as a guide in Bible-reading, discussion and prayer. Before beginning, however, parents must be convinced that it is the *right* thing to do. A purely pragmatic commitment will soon surrender to difficult circumstances: tiredness, busy schedule, apparent lack of success, periodic resistance and lack of responsiveness. Parents must, therefore, enter with conviction to persevere because of the rightness of teaching definite truth, because of affections set on things above, and because of the duty to rear children in the nurture and admonition of the Lord. It would not be a bad idea, also, to put a bit of creative time into thinking of interesting ways to present the material and making the memory work fun and rewarding as well as challenging. As a group exercise within the church, however, it probably is best to wait until first grade.

After the fifth grade, the young people may begin to learn and finally master the *Baptist Catechism* which was used for so many years within Baptist churches in both England and America. That catechism is included in this volume. Though some modernization of language may be necessary, its arrangement and content have achieved classical status and blessed three centuries of Christians in several denominations with its faithful, clear, reverent, biblical teachings.

Catechism for Girls and Boys

Part I
Questions about God, Man, and Sin

Q. 1.   **Who made you?**

A.   God made me (Genesis 1:26, 27; 2:7; Ecclesiastes 12:1; Acts 17:24–29).

Q. 2.   **What else did God make?**

A.   God made all things (Genesis 1, esp. verses 1, 31; Acts 14:15; Romans 11:36; Colossians 1:16).

Q. 3.   **Why did God make you and all things?**

A.   For His own glory (Psalm 19:1; Jeremiah 9:23, 24; Revelation 4:11; 4:15).

Q. 4.   **How can you glorify God?**

A.   By loving Him and doing what He commands (Ecclesiastes 12:13; Mark 12:29–31; John 15:8–10; 1 Corinthians 10:31).

Q. 5.   **Why ought you to glorify God?**

A.   Because He made me and takes care of me (Romans 11:36; Revelation 4:11; cp. Daniel 4:23).

Q. 6.   **Are there more gods than one?**

A.   There is only one God (Deuteronomy 6:4; Jeremiah 10:10; Mark 12:29; Acts 17:22–31).

Q. 7.   **In how many persons does this one God exist?**

A.   In three persons (Matthew 3:16, 17; John 5:23; 10:30; 14:9, 10; 15:26; 16:13–15; 1 John 5:20, 2 John 9; Revelation 1:4, 5).

Q. 8.   **Who are they?**

A.   The Father, the Son and the Holy Spirit (Matthew 28:19; 2 Corinthians 13:14; 1 Peter 1:2; Jude 20, 21).

Q. 9.   **Who is God?**

A.   God is a Spirit, and does not have a body like men (John 4:24; 2 Corinthians 3:17; 1 Timothy 1:17).

Q. 10.   **Where is God?**

A.   God is everywhere (Psalm 139:7–12; Jeremiah 23:23, 24; Acts 17:27, 28).

Q. 11.   **Can you see God?**

A.   No. I cannot see God, but He always sees me (Exodus 33:20; John 1:18; 1 Timothy 6:16; Psalm 139 esp. verses 1–5; Proverbs 5:21; Hebrews 4:12, 13).

Q. 12.   **Does God know all things?**

A.   Yes. Nothing can be hidden from God (1 Chronicles 28:9; 2 Chronicles 16:9; Luke 12:6, 7; Romans 2:16).

Q. 13.   **Can God do all things?**

A.   Yes. God can do all His holy will (Psalm 147:5; Jeremiah 32:17; Daniel 4:34, 35; Ephesians 1:11).

Q. 14.   **Where do you learn how to love and obey God?**

A.   In the Bible alone (Job 11:7; Psalm 119:104; Isaiah 8:20; Matthew 22:29; 2 Timothy 3:15–17).

Q. 15.   **Who wrote the Bible?**

A.   Holy men who were taught by the Holy Spirit (1 Peter 1:20, 21; Acts 1:16; 2 Timothy 3:16; 1 Peter 1:10, 11).

Q. 16.   **Who were our first parents?**

A.   Adam and Eve (Genesis 2:18–25; 3:20; 5:1, 2; Acts 17:26, 1 Timothy 2:13).

Q. 17.   **Of what were our first parents made?**

A.   God made the body of Adam out of the ground, and formed Eve from the body of Adam (Genesis 2:7; 21–23; 3:19; Psalm 103:14).

Q. 18.   **What did God give Adam and Eve besides bodies?**

A.   He gave them souls that could never die (1 Corinthians 15:45; Ecclesiastes 12:7; Zechariah 12:1).

Q. 19.   **Have you a soul as well as a body?**

A.   Yes. I have a soul that can never die (Matthew 10:28; Mark 8:34–38; 12:30).

Q. 20.   **How do you know that you have a soul?**

A.   Because the Bible tells me so (Matthew 10:28; Mark 8:34–38; 12:30).

Q. 21.   **What is your soul?**

A.   My soul includes all of me that should know and love God (Mark 8:34–38; Ephesians 3:16–19).

Q. 22.   **In what condition did God make Adam and Eve?**

A.   He made them holy and happy (Genesis 1:26–28; Psalm 8:4–8).

Q. 23.   **Did Adam and Eve stay holy and happy?**

A.   No. They sinned against God (Genesis 3:1–7; Ecclesiastes 7:29; Hosea 6:7 where "men" = Adam).

Q. 24.   **What was the sin of our first parents?**

A.   Eating the forbidden fruit (Genesis 2:16, 17; 3:6).

Q. 25.   **Why did they eat the forbidden fruit?**

A.   Because they did not believe what God had said (Genesis 3:1–6; cp. Hebrews 11:6).

Q. 26.   **Who tempted them to this sin?**

A.   The devil tempted Eve, and she gave the fruit to Adam (Genesis 3:1–13; 2 Corinthians 11:3; 1 Timothy 2:13, 14; cp. Revelation 12:9).

Q. 27. What happened to our first parents when they had sinned?

A. Instead of being holy and happy, they became sinful and miserable (Genesis 3:14–24; 4:1–24; James 1: 14, 15).

Q. 28. What effect did the sin of Adam have on all mankind?

A. All mankind is born in a state of sin and misery (Psalm 51:5; Romans 5:12, 18, 19; 1 Corinthians 15:21, 22; 1 John 5:19).

Q. 29. What do we inherit from Adam as a result of this original sin?

A. A sinful nature (1 Kings 8:46; Psalm 14:2, 3; 58:3; Ecclesiastes 9:3; Matthew 15:18–20; John 2:24, 25; Romans 8:7).

Q. 30. What is sin?

A. Sin is any transgression of the law of God (1 John 3:4; Romans 3:20; James 2:9–11).

Q. 31. What is meant by transgression?

A. Doing what God forbids (1 Samuel 13:8–14; 15:22, 23; Hosea 6:7; Romans 1:21–32).

Q. 32. What does every sin deserve?

A. The anger and judgment of God (Deuteronomy 27:26; Romans 1:18; 2:2; Galatians 3:10; Ephesians 5:6).

Q. 33. Do we know what God requires of us?

A. Yes, He has given us His law both in our hearts and in writing (Romans 2:14–15).

Part II
Questions about the Ten Commandments

Q. 34. How many commandments did God give on Mount Sinai?

A. Ten commandments (Exodus 20:1–17; Deuteronomy 5:1–22).

Q. 35.   **What are the ten commandments sometimes called?**

A.   God's moral law (Luke 20:25–28; Romans 2:14, 15; 10:5).

Q. 36.   **What do the first four commandments teach?**

A.   Our duty to God (Deuteronomy 6:5, 6; 10:12, 13).

Q. 37.   **What do the last six commandments teach?**

A.   Our duty to our fellow men (Deuteronomy 10:19; Micah 6:8; c.p. Galatians 6:10).

Q. 38.   **What is the sum of the ten commandments?**

A.   To love God with all my heart, and my neighbor as myself (Deuteronomy 6:1–15; 11:1; Matthew 22:35–40; James 2:8).

Q. 39.   **Who is your neighbor?**

A.   All my fellow men are my neighbors (Luke 10:25–37; 6:35).

Q. 40.   **Is God pleased with those who love and obey Him?**

A.   Yes. He says, "I love them that love me" (Proverbs 8:17; Exodus 20:6; 1 John 4:7–16).

Q. 41.   **Is God pleased with those who do not love and obey Him?**

A.   No. "God is angry with the wicked every day" (Psalm 7:11; Malachi 2:17; Proverbs 6:16–19; 1 Corinthians 16:22).

Q. 42.   **What is the first commandment?**

A.   The first commandment is, Thou shalt have no other gods before Me (Exodus 20:3; Deuteronomy 5:7).

Q. 43.   **What does the first commandment teach us?**

A.   To worship God only (Isaiah 45:5, 6; Matthew 4:10; Revelation 22:8, 9).

Q. 44.   **What is the second commandment?**

A.   The second commandment is, Thou shalt not make unto thee any graven image, or any likeness of any thing that is in heaven above, or that is in the earth beneath, or that is in the water under the earth: thou shalt not bow down thyself to them: for I, the Lord thy God, am a jealous God, visiting the iniquity of the fathers upon the children unto the third and fourth generation of them that hate Me; and showing mercy unto thousands of them that love Me, and keep My commandments (Exodus 20:4–6; Deuteronomy 5:8–10).

Q. 45.   **What does the second commandment teach us?**

A.   To worship God in the right way, and to avoid idolatry (Isaiah 44:9–20; 46:5–9; John 4:23, 24; Acts 17:29).

Q. 46.   **What is the third commandment?**

A.   The third commandment is, Thou shalt not take the name of the Lord thy God in vain; for the Lord will not hold him guiltless that taketh His name in vain (Exodus 20:7; Deuteronomy 5:11).

Q. 47.   **What does the third commandment teach us?**

A.   To reverence God's name, word, and works (Isaiah 8:13; Psalm 29:2; 138:2; Revelation 15:3, 4).

Q. 48.   **What is the fourth commandment?**

A.   The fourth commandment is, Remember the Sabbath day to keep it holy. Six days shalt thou labour, and do all thy work: but the seventh day is the Sabbath of the Lord thy God: in it thou shalt not do any work, thou nor thy son, nor thy daughter, nor thy manservant, nor thy maidservant, nor thy cattle, nor thy stranger that is within thy gates: for in six days the Lord made heaven and earth, the sea, and all that in them is, and rested the seventh day: wherefore the Lord blessed the Sabbath day, and hallowed it (Exodus 20:8–11; 23:12; Deuteronomy 5:12–15).

Q. 49.   **What does the fourth commandment teach us?**

A.   To keep the Sabbath holy (Leviticus 19:20; 23:3; Isaiah 58:13, 14).

Q. 50.   **What day of the week is the Christian Sabbath?**

A.   The first day of the week, called the Lord's Day (Acts 29:7; Revelation 1:10).

Q. 51.   **Why is it called the Lord's Day?**

A.   Because on that day Christ rose from the dead (Matthew 28:1; Mark 16:9; Luke 24:1–6; John 20:1).

Q. 52.   **How should the Sabbath be kept?**

A.   In prayer and praise, in hearing and reading God's Word, and in doing good to our fellow men (Isaiah 58:13, 14; Acts 20:7; 1 Corinthians 16:2; Luke 4:16; Matthew 12:10–13).

Q. 53.   **What is the fifth commandment?**

A.   The fifth commandment is, Honor thy father and thy mother that thy days may be long upon the land which the Lord thy God giveth thee (Exodus 20:12; Deuteronomy 5:16).

Q. 54.   **What does the fifth commandment teach us?**

A.   To love and obey our parents (Matthew 15:3–6; Ephesians 6:1–3; Colossians 3:20).

Q. 55.   **What is the sixth commandment?**

A.   The sixth commandment is, Thou shalt not kill (Exodus 20:13; Deuteronomy 5:17).

Q. 56.   **What does the sixth commandment teach us?**

A.   To avoid hatred (Matthew 5:21–24; 1 John 3:15).

Q. 57.   **What is the seventh commandment?**

A.   The seventh commandment is, Thou shalt not commit adultery (Exodus 20:14; Deuteronomy 5:18).

Q. 58.   **What does the seventh commandment teach us?**

A.   To be pure in heart, language and conduct (Matthew 5:27, 28; Ephesians 5:3–5; Philippians 4:8, 9).

Q. 59.   **What is the eighth commandment?**

A.   The eighth commandment is, Thou shalt not steal (Exodus 20:15; Deuteronomy 5:19).

Q. 60.   **What does the eighth commandment teach us?**

A.   To be honest and not to take the things of others (Exodus 23:4; Proverbs 21:6, 7; Ephesians 4:28).

Q. 61.   **What is the ninth commandment?**

A.   The ninth commandment is, Thou shalt not bear false witness against thy neighbor (Exodus 20:16; Deuteronomy 5:20).

Q. 62.   **What does the ninth commandment teach us?**

A.   To tell the truth and not to speak evil of others (Psalm 15:1–3; Zechariah 8:16; 1 Corinthians 13:6; James 4:11).

Q. 63.   **What is the tenth commandment?**

A.   The tenth commandment is, Thou shalt not covet thy neighbor's house, thou shalt not covet thy neighbor's wife, nor his manservant, nor his maidservant, nor his ox, nor his ass, nor any thing that is thy neighbor's (Exodus 20:17; Deuteronomy 5:21; Romans 7:7).

Q. 64.   **What does the tenth commandment teach us?**

A.   To be content with what we have (Philippians 4:11; 1 Timothy 6:6–8; Hebrews 13:5).

Q. 65.   **Can any man keep these ten commandments?**

A.   No mere man, since the fall of Adam, ever did or can keep the ten commandments perfectly (Proverbs 20:9; Ecclesiastes 7:20; Romans 3:19, 20; James 2:10; 1 John 1:8, 10).

Q. 66.   **Of what use are the ten commandments to us?**

A   They teach us our duty, make clear our condemnation, and show us our need of a Savior (1 Timothy 1:8–11; Romans 3:20; Galatians 3:24).

Q. 67.   **Does God condemn all men?**

A.   No. Though He could justly have done so He has graciously
          entered into a covenant to save many (Romans 3:19, 20, 23–
          25; John 17:11, 12; Isaiah 53:11).

Part III
Questions about Salvation

Q. 68.   **What is a covenant?**

A.   A covenant is an agreement between two or more persons
          (e.g., 1 Samuel 18:3; Matthew 26:14, 15).

Q. 69.   **What is the covenant of grace?**

A.   It is an eternal agreement within the Trinity to save certain
          persons called the elect, and to provide all the means for their
          salvation (Genesis 17:1–8; Romans 11:27; Hebrews 10:16, 17;
          13:20, 21; Jeremiah 31:31–34; Ezekiel 36:25–28).

Q. 70.   **What did Christ undertake in the covenant of grace?**

A.   Christ undertook to keep the whole law for His people, and to
          suffer the punishment due to their sins (Romans 8:3, 4; Gala-
          tians 4:4, 5; Hebrews 6:17–20; 7:22; 9:14, 15; 13:20, 21).

Q. 71.   **Did our Lord Jesus Christ ever sin?**

A.   No. He was holy, blameless and undefiled (Hebrews 7:26;
          Luke 23:47; Hebrews 4:15; 1 Peter 2:22; 1 John 3:5).

Q. 72.   **How could the Son of God suffer?**

A.   Christ, the Son of God, took flesh and blood, that He might
          obey and suffer as a man (John 1:14; Romans 8:3; Galatians
          4:4; Philippians 2:7, 8; Hebrews 2:14, 17; 4:15).

Q. 73.   **What is meant by the atonement?**

A.   The atonement consists of Christ's satisfying divine justice, by
          His sufferings and death, in the place of sinners (Mark 10:45;
          Acts 13:38, 39; Romans 3:24–26; 5:8, 9; 2 Corinthians 5:19–
          21; Galatians 3:13; 1 Peter 3:18).

Q. 74.   **For whom did Christ obey and suffer?**

A.   Christ obeyed and suffered for those whom the Father had given Him (Isaiah 53:8; Matthew 1:21; John 10:11, 15, 16, 26–29; 17:9; Hebrews 2:13).

Q. 75.   **What kind of life did Christ live on earth?**

A.   Christ lived a life of perfect obedience to the law of God (Matthew 5:17; Romans 10:4; 1 Peter 2:21, 22).

Q. 76.   **What kind of death did Christ die?**

A.   Christ experienced the painful and shameful death of the cross (Psalm 22; Isaiah 53; Gospel records).

Q. 77.   **Who will be saved?**

A.   Only those who repent of sin and believe in Christ will be saved (Mark 1:15; Luke 13:3, 5; Acts 2:37–41; 16:30, 31; 20:21; 26:20).

Q. 78.   **What is it to repent?**

A.   Repentance involves sorrow for sin, leading one to hate and forsake it because it is displeasing to God (Luke 19:8–10; Romans 6:1, 2; 2 Corinthians 7:9–11; 1 Thessalonians 1:9, 10).

Q. 79.   **What is it to believe in Christ?**

A.   A person believes who knows that his only hope is Christ and trusts in Christ alone for salvation (John 14:6; Acts 4:12; 1 Timothy 2:5; 1 John 5:11, 12).

Q. 80.   **How were godly persons saved before the coming of Christ?**

A.   They believed in the Savior to come (John 8:56; Galatians 3:8, 9; 1 Corinthians 10:1–4; Hebrews 9:15; 11:13).

Q. 81.   **How did they show their faith?**

A.   They offered sacrifices according to God's commands (Exodus 24:3–8; 1 Chronicles 29:20–25; Hebrews 9:19–23; 10:1; 11:28).

Q. 82.   What did these sacrifices represent?

A.   They were symbolic of Christ, the Lamb of God, who was to
            die for sinners (Exodus 12:46 cf. John 19:36; Hebrews 9 & 10;
            John 1:29; 1 Corinthians 5:7; 1 Peter 1:19).

Q. 83.   What does Christ do for His people?

A.   He does the work of a prophet, a priest and a king (Hebrews
            1:1–3; Revelation 1:5; Matthew 13:57; Hebrews 5:5–10; John
            18:37).

Q. 84.   How is Christ a prophet?

A.   He teaches us the will of God, reveals God to us, and really
            was God in human flesh. (Deuteronomy 18:15, 18; John 1:18;
            4:25; 14:23, 24; 1 John 5:20).

Q. 85.   Why do you need Christ as a prophet?

A.   Because I am ignorant (Job 11:7; Matthew 11:25–27; John
            6:67–69; 17:25, 26; 1 Corinthians 2:14–16; 2 Corinthians
            4:3–6).

Q. 86.   How is Christ a priest?

A.   He died for our sins and prays to God for us (Psalm 110:4;
            1 Timothy 2:5, 6; Hebrews 4:14–16; 7:24, 25; 1 John 2:1, 2).

Q. 87.   Why do you need Christ as a priest?

A.   Because I am guilty (Proverbs 20:9; Ecclesiastes 7:20; Romans
            3:19–23; Hebrews 10:14, 27, 28; 1 John 1:8, 9).

Q. 88.   How is Christ a king?

A.   He rules over us and defends us (Psalm 2:6–9; Matthew
            28:18–20; Ephesians 1:19–23; Colossians 1:13, 18; Revelation
            15:3, 4).

Q. 89.   Why do you need Christ as a king?

A.   Because I am weak and helpless (John 15:4, 5; 2 Corinthians
            12:9; Philippians 4:13; Colossians 1:11; Jude 24, 25).

Q. 90.   **What did God the Father undertake in the covenant of grace?**

A.   By His goodness and mercy, God the Father elected, and determined to justify, adopt and sanctify those for whom Christ should die (Exodus 33:18, 19; Ephesians 1:3–5; Romans 8:29–33; Galatians 4:4–7; Hebrews 10:9, 10; 1 Corinthians 1:8, 9; Philippians 1:6; 1 Thessalonians 4:3, 7).

Q. 91.   **What is election?**

A.   It is God's goodness as revealed in His grace by choosing certain sinners for salvation (Ephesians 1:3, 4; 1 Thessalonians 1:4; 1 Peter 1:1, 2).

Q. 92.   **What is justification?**

A.   It is God's regarding sinners as if they had never sinned and granting them righteousness (Zechariah 3:1–5; Romans 3:24–26; 4:5; 8:33; 2 Corinthians 5:21; Hebrews 8:12; Philippians 3:9).

Q. 93.   **What is righteousness?**

A.   It is God's goodness as revealed in His law, and as honored in Christ's perfect obedience to that law. (Exodus 33:19; 34:6; Psalm 33:5; Hosea 3:5; Romans 11:22).

Q. 94.   **Can anyone be saved by his own righteousness?**

A.   No. No one is good enough for God (Proverbs 20:9; Ecclesiastes 7:20; Romans 3:10–23; Philippians 3:8, 9).

Q. 95.   **What is adoption?**

A.   It is God's goodness in receiving sinful rebels as His beloved children (John 1:12; Ephesians 1:5; Ephesians 5:1; Galatians 4:7, 31; 1 John 3:1–3).

Q. 96.   **What is sanctification?**

A.   In sanctification God makes sinners holy in heart and conduct so that they will demonstrate His goodness in their lives (John 17:17; Ephesians 2:10; 4:22–24; Philippians 2:12–13; 1 Thessalonians 5:23).

Q. 97.   Is this process of sanctification ever complete in this life?

A.   No. It is certain and continual, but is complete only in heaven (Philippians 3:12–15; 2 Peter 1:4–8; 1 John 3:1–3).

Q. 98.   What hinders the completion of sanctification in this life?

A.   The Scripture says "The flesh lusts against the Spirit so that you cannot do the things you would" (Galatians 5:17).

Q. 99.   Since we are by nature sinful, how can one ever desire to be holy and to gain heaven where God lives?

A.   Our hearts must be changed before we can be fit for heaven (Ephesians 4:17–24; Colossians 3:5–12).

Q. 100.   Who can change a sinner's heart?

A.   Only the Holy Spirit can change a sinner's heart (John 3:3; Romans 8:6–11; 1 Corinthians 2:9–14; 2 Thessalonians 2:13, 14; Titus 3:5–6).

Q. 101.   What did the Holy Spirit undertake in the covenant of Grace?

A.   He regenerates, baptizes, and seals those for whom Christ has died (Ephesians 2:1–8; 1 Corinthians 12:13; Ephesians 1:13, 14; Ephesians 4:30; 2 Corinthians 1:22).

Q. 102.   What is regeneration?

A.   It is a change of heart that leads to true repentance and faith (Galatians 5:22; Ephesians 2:5–8; 2 Thessalonians 2:13).

Q. 103.   Can you repent and believe in Christ by your own power?

A.   No. I can do nothing good without God's Holy Spirit (John 3:5, 6; 6:44; Romans 8:2, 5, 8–11; 1 Corinthians 2:9–14; Galatians 5:17, 18; Ephesians 2:4–6).

Q. 104.   How does the Holy Spirit baptize believers?

A.   He puts them into the body of Christ by making them a living part of all those who truly believe in Him (1 Corinthians 12).

Q. 105.   How does the Holy Spirit seal believers?

A.   He comes to live within them to guarantee that they will re-
            ceive the wonders God has promised those who love Him
            (Ephesians 1:13, 14; Ephesians 4:30; 2 Timothy 1:9; 2 Corin-
            thians 1:22).

Q. 106.   How can you receive the Holy Spirit?

A.   God has told us that we must pray to Him for the Holy
            Spirit (Luke 11:9–13; John 4:10; 16:24); but the evidence of
            His presence is seen most clearly in our trusting and loving
            the Lord Jesus Christ (Luke 12:8–10; John 3:3–5, 16, 20, 21;
            14:17–21; 1 Corinthians 12:3; 1 Peter 1:2; 1 John 5:6–12).

Part IV
Questions about Prayer

Q. 107.   What is prayer?

A.   Prayer is talking with God (Genesis 17:22; 18:33; Nehemiah
            1:4–11; 2:4; Matthew 6:6; Romans 8:26, 27).

Q. 108.   In whose name should we pray?

A.   We should pray in the name of the Lord Jesus (John 14:13, 14;
            16:23, 24; Hebrews 4:14–16).

Q. 109.   What has Christ given to teach us how to pray?

A.   The Lord's Prayer (Matthew 6:5–15; Luke 11:1–13).

Q. 110.   Can you repeat the Lord's Prayer?

A.   Our Father which art in heaven, hallowed be Thy name. Thy
            kingdom come. Thy will be done in earth, as it is in heaven.
            Give us this day our daily bread. And forgive us our trespasses,
            as we forgive them that trespass against us. And lead us not
            into temptation, but deliver us from evil: For Thine is the king-
            dom, the power, and the glory, for ever and ever. Amen.

Q. 111.   How many petitions are there in the Lord's Prayer?

A.   Six.

Q. 112.   What is the first petition?

A.   'Hallowed be Thy name' (Matthew 6:9; Luke 11:2).

Q. 113.   What do we pray for in the first petition?

A.   That God's name may be honored by us and all men (Psalm
            8:1; 72:17–19; 113:1–3; 145:21; Isaiah 8:13).

Q. 114.   What is the second petition?

A.   'Thy kingdom come' (Matthew 6:10; Luke 11:2).

Q. 115.   What do we pray for in the second petition?

A.   That the gospel may be preached in all the world, and believed
            and obeyed by us and all men (Matthew 28:19, 20; John 17:20,
            21; Acts 8:12; 28:30, 31; 2 Thessalonians 3:1).

Q. 116.   What is the third petition?

A.   'Thy will be done in earth, as it is in heaven' (Matthew 6:20;
            Luke 11:2).

Q. 117.   What do we pray for in the third petition?

A.   That men on earth may serve God as the angels do in Heaven
            (Psalm 67; 103:19–22; John 9:31; Revelation 4:11).

Q. 118.   What is the fourth petition?

A.   'Give us this day our daily bread' (Matthew 6:11; Luke 11:3).

Q. 119.   What do we pray for in the fourth petition?

A.   That God will give us all things needful for our bodies (Psalm
            145:15, 16; Proverbs 30:8, 9; 1 Timothy 4:4, 5).

Q. 120.   What is the fifth petition?

A.   'And forgive us our trespasses, as we forgive them that trespass
            against us' (Matthew 6:12; Luke 11:4).

Q. 121.   What do we pray for in the fifth petition?

A.   That God will pardon our sins, and help us to forgive those who have sinned against us (Psalm 51; Matthew 5:23, 24; 18:21–35; 1 John 4:20, 21).

Q. 122.   What is the sixth petition?

A.   'And lead us not into temptation, but deliver us from evil' (Matthew 6:13; Luke 11:4).

Q. 123.   What do we pray for in the sixth petition?

A   That God will keep us from sin (1 Chronicles 4:10; Psalm 119:11; Matthew 26:41).

Part V
Questions about the Word, the Church, and the Ordinances

Q. 124.   How does the Holy Spirit bring us to salvation?

A.   He uses the Bible, which is the Word of God (1 Thessalonians 1:5, 6; 2:13; 2 Timothy 3:15, 16; James 1:18; 1 Peter 1:22, 23).

Q. 125.   How can we know the Word of God?

A.   We are commanded to hear, read, and search the Scriptures (1 Peter 2:2; Revelation 3:22; Matthew 21:42; 22:29; 2 Timothy 3:14–17).

Q. 126.   What is a church?

A.   A church is an assembly of baptized believers joined by a covenant of discipline and witness who meet together regularly under the preaching of the Word of God (Matthew 18:20; Acts 2:42).

Q. 127.   What two ordinances did Christ give to His Church?

A.   Baptism and the Lord's Supper (Matthew 28:19; 1 Corinthians 11:24–26).

Q. 128   **Why Did Christ give these ordinances?**

A.   To show that His disciples belong to Him, and to remind them of what He has done for them (Matthew 28:19; 1 Corinthians 11:24–26).

Q. 129.   **What is Baptism?**

A.   The dipping of believers into water, as a sign of their union with Christ in His death, burial, and resurrection (John 3:23; Acts 2:41; 8:12, 35–38; Colossians 2:12).

Q. 130.   **What is the purpose of baptism?**

A.   Baptism testifies to believers that God has cleansed them from their sins through Jesus Christ (Acts 22:16; Colossians 2:11–14).

Q. 131.   **Who are to be baptized?**

A.   Only those who repent of their sins, and believe in Christ for salvation should be baptized (Acts 2:37–41; 8:12; 18:8; 19:4, 5).

Q. 132.   **Should babies be baptized?**

A.   No; because they can show neither repentance nor faith and the Bible neither commands it, nor gives any example of it.

Q. 133.   **What is the Lord's Supper?**

A.   At the Lord's Supper, the church eats bread and drinks wine to remember the sufferings and death of Christ (Mark 14:22–24; 1 Corinthians 11:23–29).

Q. 134.   **What does the bread represent?**

A.   The bread represents the body of Christ, broken for our sins (Matthew 26:26; 1 Corinthians 11:24).

Q. 135.   **What does the wine represent?**

A.   The wine represents the blood of Christ, shed for our salvation (Matthew 26:27, 28; 1 Corinthians 11:25).

Q. 136.   Who should partake of the Lord's Supper?

A.   The Lord's Supper is for those only who repent of their sins, believe in Christ for salvation, receive baptism, and love their fellow men (Matthew 5:21–24; 1 Corinthians 10:16, 17; 11:18, 20, 27–33; 1 John 3:24–27; 4:9–11).

PART VI
Questions about Last Things

Q. 137.   Did Christ remain in the tomb after His crucifixion?

A.   No. He rose from the tomb on the third day after His death (Luke 24:45–47; 1 Corinthians 15:3, 4).

Q. 138.   Where is Christ now?

A.   Christ is in heaven, seated at the right hand of God the Father (Romans 8:34; Colossians 3:1; Hebrews 1:3; 10:12; 12:2).

Q. 139.   Will Christ come again?

A.   Yes. At the last day He will come to judge the world (Matthew 25:31–43; 2 Thessalonians 1:7–10; 2 Timothy 4:1).

Q. 140.   What happens to men when they die?

A   The body returns to dust, and the soul goes to be with God or to a place of suffering and waiting for judgement (Genesis 3:19; Ecclesiastes 12:7; 2 Corinthians 5:1–6; Hebrews 12:22, 23; Philippians 1:23; 2 Peter 2:9; Romans 2:5).

Q. 141.   Will the bodies of the dead be raised to life again?

A.   Yes. 'There shall be a resurrection of the dead, both of the just and unjust' (Acts 24:14, 15; John 5:28, 29; Daniel 12:2).

Q. 142.   What will happen to the wicked in the day of judgment?

A.   They shall be cast into hell (Psalm 9:16, 17; Luke 12:5; Revelation 20:12–15).

Q. 143.   What is hell?

A.   Hell is a place of dreadful and endless punishment (Matthew
            25:46; Mark 9:43–48; Luke 16:19–31).

Q. 144.   What will happen to the righteous in the day of judgement?

A.   They shall live with Christ for ever, in a new heaven and a new
            earth (Isaiah 66:22; 1 Thessalonians 4:16, 17; 2 Peter 3:10–13;
            Revelation 21:1–4).

Q. 145.   In light of these truths, what should you do?

A.   I should strive with all my energy to repent of sin and believe
            savingly in the Lord Jesus Christ (Luke 13:23, 24; John 6:27;
            Acts 16:31).

4

The First Principles
Of the Oracles of God

An Introduction

During the years immediately preceding the founding of the Particular Baptist Missionary Society in 1792, no pastor exerted more profound influence on the Northamptonshire Association than John Sutcliff of Olney. Sutcliff was born in 1752 in Yorkshire to pious parents who gave strict attention the proper instruction and training of their children. He was converted when about 16 years of age under the ministry of Mr. John Fawcett.[1] In 1769 Fawcett baptized Sutcliff who was received into the membership of Wainsgate Baptist Church. Fawcett received his first impression of conviction of sin under the preaching of George Whitefield. That kind of earnest evangelical Calvinism characterized Fawcett's ministry and helped form Sutcliff's views in the many conversations the two had. Sutcliff's spiritual zeal and sincerity prompted the Wainsgate congregation and John Fawcett to recommend that Sutcliff attend Bristol Baptist Academy in order to train for the Baptist ministry. In January, 1772, Sutcliff left

---

[1] Fawcett is the writer of the hymn "Blest be the Tie that Binds." Fawcett's evangelical theology and Whitefieldian understanding of evangelism did not stop John Gill from asking him to supply for him several times during Gill's sickness in 1772. Fawcett, upon the death of Gill received a call from the church. On preparing and packing to go, he became so concerned about the souls of his flock at Wainsgate that he unpacked his cart and decided to stay. On this occasion he wrote the great hymn sung so often as a benediction.

Yorkshire and walked 200 miles to Bristol, to enroll in the academy. After leaving the academy, Sutcliff settled into the pastorate of Olney in 1775.

Because he published little and the contributions and writings of Fuller and Carey are so overwhelming, Sutcliff's importance might be overlooked. The esteem his peers held for him, however, can be discerned in part by the number of circular letters he completed for the Association: "On Providence" (1779), "On the Authority and Sanctification of the Lord's Day" (1786), "On the Divinity of the Christian Religion" (1797), "On the Qualifications for Church Fellowship" (1800), "On the Lord's Supper" (1803), "On the Manner of Attending to Divine Ordinances" (1805), "On Obedience to Positive Institutions" (1808), and "On Reading the Word of God" (1813).

Twice Sutcliff led the Association into organized prayer for the success of the gospel. In 1784, the Association set apart one hour on the first Monday of every month for that purpose. His 1789 reprint of Jonathan Edwards's "Humble Attempt to Promote Explicit Agreement and Visible Union of God's People in Extraordinary Prayer for the Revival of Religion" renewed his call for prayer and had a considerable effect on those who eventually formed the Missionary Society.

His chief strengths seemed to be consistency, reliability, propriety, and devotional insight. Andrew Fuller described Sutcliff as not having "much brilliancy of imagination, but considerable strength of mind, with a judgment greatly improved by application." Robert Hall, Sr., once told Fuller, "Brother Sutcliff is a safe man: you never need fear that he will say or do an improper thing." His caution saved him from false steps and kept him will within the measures of orthodoxy. He was well known for seeking advice before taking any public stance. F. A. Cox said Sutcliff carried "caution and prudence to the utmost." [2]

Andrew Fuller first met John Sutcliff in 1776. In 1781 he consulted Sutcliff, along with others, about the pastoral move from Soham to Kettering that Fuller was contemplating. In 1784 William Carey joined the congregation at Olney, where Sutcliff was pastor, and soon the church at

---

[2] Michael A. G. Haykin, *One Heart and One Soul: John Sutcliff of Olney, his Friends and his Times* (Durham, England: Evangelical Press, 1994), 141. Haykin includes in this book the most carefully researched account of the famous "rebuke" administered to William Carey by the elder John Ryland. The account is contained on pages 193–197. Haykin's work is the most delightful and detailed account of Sutcliff available and includes pertinent discussion of Andrew Fuller, John Ryland, Jr., and a host of other contemporary Baptist leaders. It also is quite interesting and helpful in its discussion of late eighteenth and early nineteenth century evangelicalsim in England and has vaulable insights on some intricate theological issues.

Olney sent Carey into the ministry. Sutcliff also aided Carey in his study of Latin and gave him an advanced Latin grammar.

In 1791, it was Sutcliff's sermon on "Jealousy for God," from 1 Kings 19:10 that crystallized the conviction of Carey that something must be done immediately for evangelizing the heathen. Sutcliff pled for "hearts which embrace a globe and every habitable shore." After the sermon, Carey perceived the impression that had been made by the sermon, asked that some course of action immediately be taken, and as a result, Carey was asked to prepare and publish his ideas on missions. The famous *Enquiry* of Carey came from the press in 1792.

It is highly likely that Sutcliff discerned the critical theological flaw in hyper-Calvinism even before Fuller, John Ryland, Jr., and Carey. Fuller remarks that when he met Sutcliff in May, 1776, at the meeting of the Northamptonshire Association, Sutcliff had already been reading Jonathan Edwards, Joseph Bellamy, and David Brainerd. Fawcett had been familiar with Edwards and possibly opened Sutcliff's interests in that direction. For certain, Caleb Evans, one of the instructors at Bristol Academy, enforced the importance of Edwards on the students. In a list of "useful books," the works of Edwards received the highest recommendation, even above that of the prominent and revered Baptist theologian, John Gill. The effect this course of personal study had on Sutcliff had world-shaking implications.

> He drank deeply into them: particularly, into the harmony between the law and the gospel; between the obligations of men to love God with all their hearts, and their actual enmity against him; and between the duty of ministers to call on sinners to repent and believe in Christ for salvation, and the necessity of omnipotent grace to render the call effectual. The consequence was, that while he increased in his attachment to the Calvinistic doctrines of human depravity, and of salvation by sovereign and efficacious grace, he rejected as unscriptural, the high, or rather, hyper Calvinistic notions of the gospel, which went to set aside the obligations of sinners to every thing spiritually good, and the invitations of the gospel as being addressed to them. [3]

Sutcliff's settlement in Olney in 1775 had given him contact with the great hymn writer and Anglican minister, John Newton. This contact served to reinforce the benefits of this theological pilgrimage. Newton also engaged in correspondence with John Ryland, Jr. Newton loaned to Ryland a pamphlet by John Smalley entitled *The Consistency of the Sinner's Inability to Comply with the Gospel; with his Inexcusable Guilt in not Comply-*

---

[3] Andrew Fuller, *The Complete Works of Andrew Fuller*, 3 vols., ed Joseph Belcher (Philadelphia: The American Baptist Publication Society, 1845), 1:350.

ing with it. Newton also at this time, 1775, corresponded with the young Thomas Scott, a sceptic soon to be a convert and remarkable Bible scholar/ theologian. In this correspondence, Newton could say that in the fall man's "moral image … was totally lost by sin." Nevertheless, "His natural powers, though doubtless impaired, were not destroyed." Because of this, he still retains "understanding, reason, memory, imagination, etc. and by application is able to attain a considerable knowledge in natural things;" but "ten thousand instructors and instructions cannot instill good into them, so as to teach them to love their Creator, unless a divine power co-operates."[4]

In 1783, even before Fuller had published his justly applauded book, *The Gospel Worthy of All Acceptation*, Sutcliff had published this catechism. The theological questions relevant to the relationship between duty and grace were addressed clearly and forcefully, particularly the distinction between "Natural" inability and "Moral" inability. Fuller had spoken of the distinction as pivotal in his understanding of the obligation of all sinners to love God, though they are unable to do so if God does not grant them efficacious grace. Fuller argued that it was useless to speak of a moral inability without asserting the existence of a natural ability at the same time.

> A moral inability supposes a natural ability. He who never, in any state, was possessed of the power of seeing, cannot be said to *shut his eyes* against the light. If the Jews had not been possessed of natural powers equal to the knowledge of Christ's doctrine, there had been no justice in that cutting question and answer, "Why do ye not understand my speech? Because ye *cannot* hear my word." A total physical inability must, of necessity, supersede a moral one. To suppose, therefore, that the phrase, "No man *can* come to me," is meant to describe the former; and, "Ye *will not* come to me that ye may have life," the latter; is to suppose that our Saviour taught what is self-contradictory.[5]

Fuller knew that some confusion about the term "natural" might render discussion of the issue irrelevant. He was careful, therefore, to define *natural depravity*, not as "an essential part of human nature, or of the constitution of man as man." It involves the intrusion of sin in such an insidious way that from birth it is "so interwoven through all his powers, so ingrained, as it were, in his very soul, as to grow up with him, and become natural to him."[6]

---

[4] John Newton, *The Works of John Newton*, 6 vols. (Edinburgh: The Banner of Truth Trust, 1985 [reprint of 1820 edition]), 1:576, 577.

Andrew Fuller, "The Gospel Worthy of All Acceptation," in *Complete Works*, 2:378.

[6] Ibid.

The performance of spiritual duties, and the blame for not performing them, assume the presence of natural abilities: "we must possess the powers of men in order to perform the duties of good men." The presence of natural power does not increase self-sufficiency one whit or diminish the necessity of divine grace. "If any person imagine it possible, of his own accord," Fuller challenges, "to choose that from which he is utterly averse, let him make the trial."[7]

This distinction, absorbed from the writings of Jonathan Edwards, undergirded every practical and theological enterprise of Sutcliff and his circle of friends. While some may view such careful distinctions in vocabulary as unnecessarily obtuse, for Sutcliff it became the golden key that opened the true treasure and powers of God's grace.

Especially strong in the theological arrangement of Sutcliff's catechism is the emphasis on the law. After a short introduction to the doctrines of God's attributes, divine revelation, and the Trinity, responses 14–70 center on the law and its implications. These implications include human depravity and the mediatorial work of Christ. Subsequent responses emphasize the sovereignty of God in salvation manifest in unconditional election and effectual calling. Questions concerning the necessity of a spiritual life which exhibits itself in repentance, faith, and love lead to a discussion on the nature of the new birth. The doctrines of pardon, justification, adoption, and sanctification are followed by question/answer responses on the church, its ordinances, and last things, including the doctrine of hell ("a state of sin and misery, where devils and wicked men shall be eternally punished.") The final question encourages the serious application of the issues in the catechism to human experience.

Q. To conclude; what do you learn from the catechism you have now been repeating?

A. I learn that the affairs of my soul are of the greatest importance, and ought to employ my chief concern.

Though focused on a rather unusual theological issue, Sutcliff's catechism still resounds with the strong evangelistic concern characteristic of Baptist catechisms. Andrew Fuller, in his funeral sermon for Sutcliff, summarized the theological concerns of Sutcliff succinctly, accurately, and powerfully. This description distills the concerns of this catechism.

> He dwelt much in his preaching on the glory of the Divine character and government, as displayed in the law and the gospel, and scrupled not to

[7] Ibid., 378, 379.

declare his firm persuasion that all religious affections which disregarded this were spurious, and would prove of no account at the great day. He was persuaded that as sin must be hated as sin, or it is not hated at all; so God must be loved as God, or he is not loved at all. But to love God as God is to love him for what he is, as well as for what he has done for us. He had, indeed, no such notion of loving God for his own excellency as should render us indifferent to our own salvation. On the contrary, he considered it as essential to the love of God to desire his favour as our chief good. But we can no more desire this, irrespective of what he is, than we can desire any other object without considering it as in itself desirable. Unless we love God in respect of his character, his favour would be no enjoyment to us.[8]

[8] Andrew Fuller, *Complete Works*, 1:344, 345. Fuller clearly distances Sutcliff, and himself as well, from the false inference some theologians drew from the doctrine of disinterested benevolence of a willingness "to be damned for the glory of God." Jonathan Edwards himself strongly opposed such an inference as in no way harmonious with a true love for God and desire for his fellowship. Sutcliff and his circle followed Edwards instead of Hopkins on this point.

THE

FIRST PRINCIPLES

OF THE

ORACLES of GOD,

REPRESENTED IN

A PLAIN AND FAMILIAR

CATECHISM,

For the Use of Children.

By JOHN SUTCLIFF, A. M.

" BRING UP YOUR CHILDREN IN THE NURTURE AND ADMONITION OF THE LORD." Eph. vi. 4.

Third Edition.

PRINTED AND SOLD AT EWOOD HALL, NEAR HALIFAX.

Sold alfo by the Author, at OLNEY, and by W. BUTTON, No. 24, Paternofter-Row, LONDON.

(Price 1d, or 7s 6d. per Hundred.)

The
First Principles
of the

Oracles of God

represented in
a plain and familiar
Catechism
for the Use of Children

By John Sutcliff, A.M.
(3rd Edition, Printed and sold at Ewood Hall, Near Halifax)

"Bring up your children in the nurture and admonition of the Lord."
(Eph. 6:4)

For the ease of a young child in first going over the ensuing catechism, some parts, which are enclosed in Parentheses, may be conveniently omitted, and taken in when going over it the second time.

Q. 1. **My dear child, why should you wish to learn your catechism?**

A.   I should wish to learn it, that through a divine blessing, I may gain some acquaintance with those things which are of the greatest importance.

Q. 2. **What are those things which are of the greatest importance?**

A.   The knowledge of God and myself, with what concerns my relation to, and enjoyment of Him.

Q. 3. **How do you know there is a God?**

A.   I learnt it from the works of creation and providence.

Q. 4. **What does God appear to be from these His works?**

A.   He appears to be an eternal, almighty, wise, good and ever-present Being, far above all our thoughts of Him.

Q. 5.   And what are you?

A.   I am a creature, consisting of a body formed by God, out of the dust of the ground, into which He has breathed a rational and immortal soul.

Q. 6.   What is your soul?

A.   My soul is that in me which thinks and reasons, loves and hates, rejoices and is sorrowful.

Q. 7.   And where do you go for farther instruction?

A.   A. I go to the Holy Scriptures, commonly called the Bible, which are the Word of God.

[Q. 8.   Why do you call the Bible the Word of God?

A.   The Bible was wrote by men inspired of God for that end, and contains a revelation of His will.

Q. 9.   What does it teach you concerning God?

A.   It teaches me, that He is infinitely holy, just and true, yet gracious and merciful.

Q. 10.   Are there more Gods than one?

A.   The Scriptures assure me, there is but one living and true God.

Q. 11.   But do not the sacred Scriptures sometimes speak as if there were more persons than one in the Deity?

A.   Yes, for the one living and true God does subsist in three distinct persons, bearing the names of Father, Son and Holy Spirit.]

Q. 12.   And how do you stand related to God?

A.   I stand related to God, as my great creator, kind benefactor, and righteous governor.

Q. 13.   And what follows?

A.   It follows, that by all the ties of love, gratitude and interest, I am bound to serve Him.

Q. 14.   How ought you to serve Him?

A.   I ought to serve Him by a perfect and perpetual conformity to His moral law.

Q. 15.   What do you mean by His moral law?

A.   I mean His revealed will, particularly as contained in the Ten Commandments given to Israel at Mount Sinai.

Q. 16.   Into how many parts is this law divided?

A.   It is divided into two; the first contains my duty to God; the second my duty to my neighbour and myself.

Q. 17.   What is the sum of the first part respecting God?

A.   The sum of the first part is, that I should love God with all my heart, soul, mind, and strength.

[Q. 18.   Is this demand reasonable?

A.   Yes, for the character of God is infinitely lovely.

Q. 19.   And is it unalterable?

A.   Yes, for the character of God is unchangeable.

Q. 20.   And is it a kind and good law?

A.   Yes, for to love God perfectly, is to be completely happy.

Q. 21.   And yet is it not very extensive?

A.   Yes, for the sum of it shows it to be exceeding broad.

Q. 22. Does it mean that you should take pleasure in thinking of God?

A. Yes, for if I love any object, I shall naturally take pleasure in thinking about it.

Q. 23. And in praying to Him?

A. Yes, for if I love a person, I shall wish to associate and converse with him.

Q. 24. And in obeying Him?

A. Yes, for if I love my master, I shall cheerfully obey him.

Q. 25. And in searching His Word?

A. Yes, for if I love an absent friend, I shall rejoice to hear from him.

Q. 26. And in associating with His people?

A. Yes, for if I love God, I shall love to unite with His people.

Q. 27. And in attempting to promote His interest?

A. Yes, for if I love my king, I shall seek the good of his kingdom.

Q. 28. Does it mean that you should be very tender and fearful of offending Him?

A. Yes, for if I love my parents, I shall study to do all I can to please them.

Q. 29. And that you should abhor and shun whatever God abhors?

A. Yes, for to take pleasure in what God abhors, is to hate God, and not to love Him.

Q. 30. And that you should prefer God above every other object?

A. Yes, for if I love any object more than God, I shall be guilty of idolatry.

Q. 31.   But suppose you should sin against God, does this mean that you should repent, and be heartily grieved for it?

A.   Yes, for it is not possible that I should love Him, if I can offend Him, and not be grieved for it.

Q. 32.   And that you should believe whatever He declares?

A.   Yes, for if I believe not what God says, I make Him a liar, and that is not loving Him.

Q. 33.   And that you should heartily approve and love it too?

A.   Yes, for if I love God, I shall love whatsoever comes from Him.]

Q. 34.   Having given me an account of the first part of God's holy law, let me hear the sum of the second, relating to your neighbour and yourself?

A.   The sum of the second is, that I should love my neighbour as myself.

Q. 35.   How ought you to love yourself?

A.   I ought so to love myself, as warmly to pursue my most important interests.

Q. 36.   And who is your neighbour?

A.   Every person as a fellow creature, so far as I have any connection with him, is to be considered as my neighbour.

Q. 37.   How ought you to love him?

A.   I ought so to love him, as sincerely and fervently to wish and seek his welfare, even as I do my own.

Q. 38.   What general rule of conduct flows from this part of the divine law?

A.   This, that I ought to act towards others in every station in life, just as I might reasonably wish they would act towards me, were I in their situation, and they in mine.

Q. 39.	Is the same general line of duty binding with respect to persons in every situation?

A.	No, for peculiar relations have peculiar duties belonging to them.

Q. 40.	Suppose a person should hate you, or fail in his duty towards you, does the obligation on your part cease?

A.	No, for as he is still my fellow-creature, the relation still remains, and so does the obligation.

Q. 41.	Do you perfectly keep His holy law?

A.	No, to my shame I must own, I daily break it in thought, word and deed, and so am a sinner before God.

Q. 42.	Is this the general case among the sons of men?

A.	Yes, it is the case of all without exception, for there is none righteous, no not one.

[Q. 43.	But why do men thus break and transgress the law of God?

A.	The reason is, the reigning aversion of their wicked hearts to it so that they are unable to keep it.

Q. 44.	And does not this their inability release from obligation?

A.	No, for it is of such a nature as tends not in the least to break or weaken our obligations.

Q. 45.	Of what kind is it then?

A.	It is not of a natural, but of a moral kind.

Q. 46.	What is natural inability?

A.	Natural inability consists in a defect of rational faculties, bodily powers, or external advantages.

Q. 47.   **What is moral inability?**

A.   Moral inability consists in a want of proper disposition of
              heart to use our natural ability aright.

Q. 48.   **Can you illustrate the distinction by producing an instance.**

A.   Yes, the case of Joseph's brethren, who hated him so, that they
              could not speak peaceably to him.*

---

*Thus we say of a man destitute of an honest principle, that he cannot
refrain from cheating you, if he has an opportunity; that some are such
profane wretches they cannot open their mouths without an oath, and
others are such liars, that they cannot speak the truth; that some are so
revengeful they cannot forgive an injury; and others so easily provoked,
they cannot keep their temper if you contradict them. So a carnal mind
cannot be subject to God's law; for a man that hates God cannot serve
Him, cannot rejoice in seeing Him glorified, cannot love His image, cannot see any comeliness in Christ, nor fall in with the gospel plan of salvation. See Scripture examples of a vicious moral inability, in Jeremiah 6:10,
15; Matthew 7:24; John 5:44, 7:8, 43. And of a virtuous moral inability
in Gen. 39:9; Esther 8:6; Acts 4:20; 2 Corinthians 13:8; Titus 1:2.

The difference between this kind of inability, and that which is termed
natural, is plain and self evident. It is said of the mariners, that they
rowed hard to bring the ship unto the land, but could not, Jonah 1:13.
Also of Joseph's brethren, that they could not speak peaceably to him,
Genesis 37:4. In the former case there was a natural, but in the latter a
moral inability. Thus the inability of Zacharias to speak, Luke 1:22. was
widely different from that mentioned in 1 Samuel 25:17.

The importance of a proper attention to this distinction appears, when
we observe, that the former releases from obligation, but the latter not. It
was no crime in Isaac, being old, that he could not see, Genesis 27:1, but
the case seems very different with such as have eyes and see not, Jeremiah
5:21. or such as have eyes full of adultery, though it is expressly said of
them they cannot cease from sin, 2 Peter 2:14.

Moral inability is so far from affording an excuse for the sinner, that it is
crime itself seeing it consists in vitiosity or depravity of disposition; and
the stronger it grows, the more criminal it becomes, unless any can prove,
that a wicked heart delivers from a charge of guilt; or, that the strength of
our hatred destroys our obligation to love; or that some are so very bad,
they are not at all to blame.

Q. 49. But was man first formed by God in such a state?

A. No, for he was at first formed by God in a state of perfect holiness and happiness.

Q. 50. What is holiness?

A. Holiness is conformity to the divine law, in heart, lip, and life.

Q. 51. Wherein consisteth his happiness?

A. It consisteth in conformity to, and communion with, God.

Q. 52. How did he lose this his happy situation?

A. By sinning against God, He fell from it.

Q. 53. And did his fall affect us?

A. Yes, for by it he communicated sin and wretchedness to all his posterity.

Q. 54. How came this to pass?

A. Adam being the covenant head and representative of all his posterity, we sinned and fell in him.

Q. 55. How do men manifest their depravity of disposition?

A. By turning aside from God, rebelling against Him, and delighting in what He has forbidden.]

Q. 56. Are not the consequences of such conduct very awful?

A. Yes, for we lie under a most heavy charge of guilt, and are involved in misery beyond conception.

Q. 57. What is guilt?

A. Guilt is a charge of criminality proved against us, on account of which we deserve punishment.

Q. 58.   Wherein consists our misery?

A.   Our misery consists in having lost the enjoyment of God, and being liable to pains, sorrows, death and eternal ruin.

Q. 59.   And is this your condition?

A.   Yes, and is the condition of all mankind.

Q. 60.   Cannot we claim any degree of favour at the hand of God?

A.   No, for we are all righteously condemned, and lie entirely at His discretion.

Q. 61.   This is awful indeed, but is there no hope?

A.   There is yet hope, for the word of God reveals a way of salvation through rich and sovereign grace.

Q. 62.   What is grace?

A.   Grace is free and undeserved favour, manifested in saving those who justly deserve to perish.

Q. 63.   What is salvation?

A.   Salvation is a deliverance from sin, and all its awful consequences.

Q. 64.   And how is salvation enjoyed?

A.   Salvation is enjoyed through the mediation of the Lord Jesus Christ applied to the soul by the Holy Spirit.

Q. 65.   Who is the Lord Jesus Christ?

A.   The Lord Jesus Christ is the eternal Son of God in our nature.

Q. 66.   What has He done as mediator?

A.   As mediator, having obeyed the precepts of the moral law in His life, and borne its penalty in His death, He rose from the dead, to live and reign for evermore.

[Q. 67.   In what light does the mediation of Christ represent the character of God?

A.   The mediation of Christ represents the character of God as holy, just, and good.

Q. 68.   In what light does the mediation of Christ represent the moral law?

A.   The mediation of Christ represents the moral law as holy, just, and good.

Q. 69.   In what light does the mediation of Christ represent sin?

A.   The mediation of Christ represents sin as an infinite evil.

Q. 70.   In what light does the mediation of Christ represent the penalty threatened against the breaker of the moral law?

A.   The mediation of Christ represents the penalty threatened against the breaker of the moral law, as perfectly just and righteous.]

Q. 71.   And is this salvation sufficient for any who apply?

A.   Yes, for the chief of sinners.

Q. 72.   Have any who hear it liberty to apply?

A.   Yes, for an invitation is given to guilty sinners, in generous and unlimited terms.

Q. 73.   And it may be done with certain assurance of success?

A.   Yes, for its divine author has said, him that cometh He will in no wise cast out.

Q. 74.   And are men universally disposed to apply?

A.   No, for there are many who choose rather to hazard the eternal welfare of their souls, than part with their sins.

Q. 75.   And what does this evidence?

A.   It evidences the awful depravity of the carnal mind, which is
          enmity against God.

Q. 76.   How then do any come to apply?

A.   They apply then because the great God, as an act of rich grace
          inclines them to do so, by the work of His Holy Spirit on their
          souls.

[Q. 77.   Who are they that the Holy Spirit thus works upon?

A.   The Holy Spirit thus worketh on whom the blessed God
          pleaseth, "for He hath mercy on whom He will have mercy,
          and compassion on whom He will have compassion."

Q. 78.   Is there any rule by which the Holy Spirit thus acts?

A.   Yes, for He thus worketh on the minds of all those who were
          foreordained to eternal life.

Q. 79.   Did the infinitely-wise God determine long beforehand
          whom to call thus by grace? .

A.   Yes, for He elected or chose them to eternal life, through the
          Lord Jesus Christ, before the foundation of the world.

Q. 80.   Is this conduct becoming the character of God?

A.   Yes, for seeing He is not bound to save any, He may certainly
          act as He pleaseth.

Q. 81.   Does the doctrine of election discourage you in returning to
          God through Christ?

A.   No, for God's gracious invitation, in His Holy Word, is a suf-
          ficient warrant for all who will, to return.]

Q. 82.   Well, and wherein consists the work of the Holy Spirit?

A.   It consists in renewing in us a right spirit or temper of mind.

Q. 83. Cannot you tell me more particularly wherein the work of the Holy Spirit consists?

A. It consists in the communication of spiritual light and life, which are manifested in the exercises of repentance, faith and love.

Q. 84. Wherein consists spiritual light?

A. Spiritual light consists in having such a view of things as is contained in the Word of God.

Q. 85. What is spiritual life?

A. Spiritual life is a holy principle or disposition in the heart.

Q. 86. How does it shew itself?

A. It shews itself in breathing after, and acting for God.

Q. 87. What is repentance?

A. Repentance is a change of mind, arising from a conviction that we have been in an error.

Q. 88. Wherein is repentance discovered?

A. Repentance is discovered in sorrow for, and forsaking of whatever we see was wrong.

Q. 89. What is faith?

A. Faith is a cordial belief of the testimony God has given us in His Word.

Q. 90. How does it appear to be genuine?

A. It appears to be genuine, by the influence of divine truth, working effectually in the heart and life.

Q. 91. What is love?

A. Love is an esteem of, and delight in the moral character of God, as infinitely excellent and amiable; and in whatever bears His holy likeness.

Q. 92.   How is it seen?

A.   It is seen in reverencing His authority, and obeying His commands.

Q. 93.   And is such a change an important one?

A.   Yes, for we must be born again, and become new creatures, before we can either serve or enjoy God, here or hereafter.

[Q. 94.   Why is such a change necessary?

A.   It is necessary on account of the reigning enmity of the heart against God.

Q. 95.   But cannot such a change be effected without an almighty work of the Spirit of God?

A.   No, for the enmity of the heart is so strong and deeply rooted, that none but an almighty power can overcome it.

Q. 96.   But cannot we understand the Scriptures aright without His divine teachings?

A.   No, for the depravity of our hearts has corrupted our judgments, and blinded our minds.

Q. 97.   And what does a person spiritually enlightened think of the great God?

A.   He views the great God, as an infinitely holy, glorious, and amiable being.

Q. 98.   And what does he think of the moral law?

A.   He views the moral law as exceeding broad, yet holy, just and good.

Q. 99.   What does he think of the gospel?

A.   He views the gospel as a rich display of sovereign love, revealing a gracious, yet holy method of salvation for lost sinners.

Q. 100.   What does he think of sin?

A.   He views sin as infinitely hateful, and abhors himself as defiled with it.

Q. 101.   What does he think of holiness?

A.   He views holiness as the brightest ornament of a rational being.

Q. 102.   What does he think of the Lord Jesus Christ?

A.   He views the Lord Jesus Christ as infinitely lovely in His person, office and work.]

Q. 103.   Are not such in a very happy state and condition?

A.   Yes, for they now share the rich blessings of special grace, and are heirs of eternal glory.

[Q. 104.   What are the blessings of special grace which they now share?

A.   They now share the blessings of pardon, justification, adoption, and sanctification.

Q. 105.   What is pardon?

A.   Pardon is God's gracious forgiveness of all our sins for the sake of the death of Christ.

Q. 106.   What is justification?

A.   Justification is God's acquitting us from every criminal charge, and accepting us as righteous through the righteousness of Christ.

Q. 107.   What is adoption?

A.   Adoption is an act of free favour, in which we are taken into the relation of children of God.

Q. 108.   What is sanctification?

A.   Sanctification is the work of the Holy Spirit, in which we are
          fitted to serve and enjoy God, by being gradually conformed
          to His image.

Q. 109.   But may not these blessings be lost or forfeited?

A.   No, for they are made secure to the people of God, in an ever-
          lasting and well ordered covenant.

Q. 110.   Have these persons, as children of God, any peculiar privi-
          leges of an outward nature in this world?

A.   Yes, they have a right to all the privileges of the Lord's house,
          particularly the holy ordinances of baptism and the Lord's
          Supper.

Q. 111.   What is baptism?

A.   Baptism is a solemn immersion or burial in water, of the party
          to whom it is administered, in the name of the Father, Son and
          Holy Spirit.

Q. 112.   What is the Lord's Supper?

A.   The Lord's Supper is a solemn eating of bread, drinking of
          wine, in commemoration of the death of Christ.

Q. 113.   By what authority are these ordinances thus administered?

A.   Our authority arises from the command and example of
          Christ, obeyed and imitated by His apostles.

Q. 114.   Have none else a right to either of these holy ordinances?

A.   No, for none else do properly understand their true design, or
          will observe them in a proper manner.

Q. 115.   And what is the grand end the great God has in view, in these
          displays of divine grace?

A.   His grand end is to form a people for Himself, that shall shew
          forth His praise.]

Q. 116.   **What will be the consequence of finally remaining destitute of a knowledge of these things?**

A.   The consequence will be eternal ruin and destruction.

Q. 117.   **What must you do to escape this dreadful end?**

A.   I must believe what God in His Word tells me of my vile and lost condition, and seek unto Him for salvation through the Lord Jesus Christ.

Q. 118.   **Have you then a very serious and important concern in these matters?**

A.   Yes, for the everlasting happiness of my soul in another world, is herein concerned.

Q. 119.   **Then you do not expect always to remain in this world?**

A.   No, for I must in a little while die, and be no more here.

Q. 120.   **What is death?**

A.   Death is a separation of soul and body.

Q. 121.   **What becomes of the body at death?**

A.   At death, the body returns to the earth whence it was taken.

Q. 122.   **And what becomes of the immortal soul?**

A.   The soul enters upon a new and unalterable state of existence.

Q. 123.   **How do good men die?**

A.   Good men die in the favour of God, and their souls enter heaven.

Q. 124.   **How do wicked men die?**

A.   Wicked men die under the wrath of God, and their souls enter into hell.

Q. 125.   Will the bodies of men always remain in their graves?

A.   No, for they will be raised, and again united to their souls at
           the day of judgment.

Q. 126.   What is the day of judgment?

A.   The day of judgment is a time fixed by God, when all mankind
           shall be placed at His bar, their real characters laid open, and a
           final sentence pronounced upon them.

Q. 127.   What is heaven?

A.   Heaven is a glorious state of holiness and happiness, where
           God, angels, and good men will dwell in society for ever and
           ever.

Q. 128.   What is hell?

A.   Hell is a state of sin and misery, where devils and wicked men
           shall be eternally punished.

Q. 129.   Must you in a little while enter into one of these places?

A.   Yes, I must in a little while enter into, and take up my eternal
           abode in one of them.

Q. 130.   To conclude; what do you learn from the catechism you have
           now been repeating?

A.   I learn that the affairs of my soul are of the greatest impor-
           tance, and ought to employ my chief concern.

5

Notes and Questions for the Oral Instruction of Colored People

An Introduction

In the summer of 1995, the Southern Baptist Convention meeting in Atlanta, Georgia, passed a resolution which included the words, "We lament and repudiate historic acts of evil such as slavery from which we continue to reap a bitter harvest, and we recognize that the racism which yet plagues our culture today is inextricably tied to the past."[1] Following the SBC action, many interviews provided a platform from which the sore of racism was lanced repeatedly. Words of repentance and recognition of wrong abounded, such as: "facing our history of support for slavery and racism head-on;" "I can't change my great-great-great grandfather's standing before God, but I can apologize for the consequences of the man's ownership of slaves;" "It's important that we come out in print and in fact stating our failings, because it cast a cloud over our Christian belief."

The long history of racial conflict and culture clash, particularly in the South, caused some degree of reserve among observers. Some held the opinion that most overtures of Baptists toward the black constituency have been "very paternalistic," and others seemed convinced that even subsequent to the 1995 Convention action "there would be considerable resistance" to meaningful involvement with blacks either in church life or

---

[1] This portion of the resolution is quoted from *The New York Times NATIONAL*, Wednesday, June 21, 1995. A13, column 1. The story began on page A1.

social life. Others expressed greater optimism about the future in light of the resolution. A black pastor in New York, Calvin O. Butts, III, called it "a marvelous statement" and said that it was a fitting response to Martin Luther King's "Letter from the Birmingham Jail." Emmanuel McCall, a black Southern Baptist pastor in Georgia said it would help the "Image of Southern Baptists … as we do outreach."

That issue, outreach, gave the picture of slavery in the South its greatest impression of ambivalence, and even contradiction. Abolitionists and emancipationists of other degrees all felt keenly that consistent Christian witness and slavery were mutually exclusive. English Baptists in a letter to Baptists in America spoke of the "unchristian character" of the institution and urged the obligation of Christian ministers "to protest against it." In so doing they would vindicate "the character of your most holy faith."[2] Henry C. Fish, pastor of First Baptist Church in Newark, New Jersey, expressed outrage at the physical attack on Sumner in the senate chamber and saw great danger in the extension of slave territories under the Missouri Compromise and the Kansas-Nebraska Act. Such an extension would be fatal to the preaching of the gospel.

> I maintain that the question of *Slave Extension* towers immeasurably above them all. This is something more than a so-called "political" question. It is interlinked with the most sacred interests of our holy religion. Is it nothing to the cause of Christianity whether the wide and glorious territory now the matter of dispute, be doomed to Slavery or not? Whether a full and free gospel, for the entire population, shall, or shall not, be preached in that territory? Whether the type of Christianity and of Christian churches there to be planted, be that of the free or of the Slave states? Is *Religion* no way concerned in all this?[3]

Francis Wayland, more reserved than many of his fellow northerners, felt keenly, nevertheless, that slavery and Christianity were not entirely consistent with each other and the preponderant tendency of the preaching of the gospel was toward emancipation of all the sons of Adam. In his *Elements of Moral Science*, Wayland argued that slavery violated liberties that were necessary for the full expression of God's image in man. Physical, intellectual, and religious liberty all suffered under the thralldom of slavery.

---

[2] Document included in Robert A. Baker, *A Baptist Source Book*, (Nashville: Broadman Press, 1966), 87, 88. The letter was written by the Board of Baptist Ministers in and near London, December 31, 1833.

[3] Henry C. Fish, *The Voice of Our Brother's Blood: Its Source and Its Summons* (Newark, N.J.: Douglas & Starbuck, 1856), 20.

Southern slavery supposed that the master had the right to determine how much knowledge a slave would have of his duty to God.

Baptists in the South, however, did not see Christian witness and slavery as clearly dichotomous as their brethren in England and the northern states. Some viewed the discipline of slavery necessary for the stability of society and to allow ample opportunity for the civilizing powers of the gospel to permeate an uncivilized sector of society. John L. Dagg, in his own version of *The Elements of Moral Science* said the "mistake" of the abolitionists was in seeking "the benefits of enlightened virtue, without its presence and use." The way of the gospel in abolishing "imprisonment, capital punishment, war, and involuntary servitude" was in making such restraints unnecessary by "making all men righteous." Abolitionism, like an unwise friend who removes nauseous medicines from a sick friend, may command its patient to rise and walk, and, by its unwise treatment of the case, "aggravate the disease."[4]

Such leavening immediately depends on whether such leaven actually is in the mix. Dagg thought it was and that the providence of God in bringing Africans to America was one of the greatest missionary opportunities in history.

> The benevolent design of Providence in bringing the sons of Africa into bondage in the United States, is too manifest to be misinterpreted. It may be regarded as a stupendous missionary movement, accomplishing more in the evangelizing of the heathen than all the missionary operations of Christian churches throughout the world.[5]

Other Christians in the South shared Dagg's missionary view. John A Broadus, after the Civil War, thought the southern Christians looked on their former slaves with "strange tenderness of feeling, like that of foreign missionaries for their lowly converts." Broadus also pointed out that numerous ministers, chiefly Baptist and Methodist, in the years before that great conflict "were faithfully laboring to convert and instruct the vast multitude of colored people among whom they found themselves called to the work of the ministry."[6]

When J. P. Boyce served as pastor at Columbia, South Carolina, he instructed the slaves of the community faithfully in Christian truth and "fundamental duties of a Christian life." Broadus described Boyce's interest

---

[4] John L Dagg, *The Elements of Moral Science* (Charleston: Southern Baptist Publication Society, 1859), 371, 372.

[5] Ibid., 345.

[6] John A. Broadus, *Memoir of James Petigru Boyce* (New York: A. C. Armstrong and Son, 1893), 91, 92.

in this evangelistic ministry by highlighting its appearance of incongruity: "A wealthy and highly educated young minister was fitly employed in such labor for the benefit of the slaves."[7]

Boyce, however, lamented the impending loss of slavery. In a letter to H. A Tupper in 1857, he foresaw the dissolution of the union but the fragmentation of the South as well. "Alas, my country," he cried, and along with his admission to be an "old fogy" (at 33!), who loved the past and all its relations, he sensed in all this "the end of slavery." Boyce continued, "I believe we are cutting its throat, curtailing its domain." Although Boyce considered himself "an ultra pro-slavery man," he knew that God's providence as a judgment would sweep it away for "our sins as to this institution have cursed us." The South had been careless in the "marital and religious relations" of the "negroes" and would never know "how great we might be, were we to act as we ought in this matter."[8]

Sometimes language from both sides was exaggerated and "brimful of wrath and fight,"[9] and some was mournful, filled with remorse and lamentation. Baptist leaders on both sides knew that a terrible ordeal lay ahead, which, according to Boyce, would probably be a "long and bloody war." Henry C. Fish agreed that such would probably be the case. In addition, he agreed that, unless God prepared "some strange deliverance that shall glorify His providence," He would bring a judgmental end to slavery. Fish, however, did not share Boyce's nostalgia concerning the peculiar institution. He welcomed its destruction though he feared the means: "One cannot but fear that God Almighty, in His just indignation for the wrongs and sins of this people, so long committed, is about to allow us to be precipitated into one general ruin."[10]

When Broadus looked back on the sectional hostilities definitively intrinsic to the horrific conflict of the Civil War, he attempted to sort out the complex relations that Christians in the South had toward their former slaves. With all of its errors (and even with the continuing paternalism and implicit condescension of Broadus's statement), the relationship nevertheless did produce some positive results for eternal good. Dagg's vision of the evangelistic advantages of the providence of slavery is not wholly

---

[7] Ibid., 91.

[8] J. P. Boyce in Ibid., 185.

[9] This phrase is used in a letter of Basil Manly, Jr., to Charles Manly on December 15, 1857, when a respected teacher at Richmond College had been accused of abolitionism. The editor who reported the accusation witheld the identity of his source leading Manly to give the source the apellation, "any anonymous whipper snapper."

Fish, *The Voice of Our Brother's Blood*, 13.

indefensible. Broadus beckons future generations to be sensitive, gentle, and balanced in evaluating the events of the time.

> And now that the long conflict is long past, and we are facing the most remarkable problem that any civilized nation was ever called to attempt, —the problem of slowly and patiently lifting these people up to all they can reach, — it were well if mutual misjudgments could be laid aside, if the faithful work of many Christians in those trying years could be on all sides appreciated, and the whole undertaking before us could be estimated in part by its best results, and not simply by its worst difficulties.[11]

The polemics that Broadus implies came to pass. The most ambitious attempt to categorize the literature into different types is that by Randall M. Miller and David Smith, who contend that the literature is so vast and complex that no scholar can pretend to master it within a life time.[12] They identify four periods of historiographical development of slavery: (1) the period of post-war polemics, (2) the period of the Nationalist historians, (3) the period of Scientific historians, and (4) the period of economic historians. Divisions over the nature of slavery, the condition of the slaves, the character in general of masters, the economics of slavery, and the nature of plantation life still persist in each of these periods. One of the most recent attempts to resurrect the old south argument that slavery is good, the black is inferior, and slaves were better off in bondage than they would have been free is by Ulrich Bonnell Phillips, *American Negro Slavery*. Phillips contended that slave treatment more characteristically was kind than severe.[13] His arguments quickly provoked the challenge of Kenneth Stampp's *The Peculiar Institution*. Although he condemns slavery as cruel and dehumanizing and driven by the profit motive of masters, Stampp sets forth the covertly prejudicial assertion that "the slaves were merely ordinary human beings, that innately Negroes are, after all, only white men with black skins, nothing more, nothing less."[14] That is only slightly different than the sense of superiority which infected Broadus when he wrote in 1893

> They were not black angels, as some romantic readers of romance half imagined, nor yet black demons, as some who hated them then and now would have us believe; they were and are simply black men, from among

[11] Broadus, *Memoir*, 92.

[12] Randall M. Miller & David Smith, eds. *A Dictionary of Afro-American Slavery*, (New York: Greenwood Press, 1967), x.

[13] Ulrich Bonnell Phillips, *American Negro Slavery*,(Baton Rouge: Louisiana State University Press, 1966), 306.

Kenneth M. Stampp, *The Peculiar Institution*, (New York: Alfred A Knopf, 1963), vii.

the lowest races of mankind, yet by no means beyond the reach of saving Christian truth and loving Christian culture.[15]

Broadus probably had no conception as to the severity of the "worst difficulties" that he recognized. Subsequent to his plea for understanding, more than a century of repression, reaction, and heightened tension at least and violent hate crimes at most has followed. The sub-Christian conduct of many churches and the hesitance of many white Southern Christians to support a number of rational and defensible parts of the civil rights agenda contributed to the negative part of this legacy. Systemic oppression and prejudice blinded the minds and sensibilities of Christians in the South (and in other areas) for decades. The 1995 Southern Baptist Convention meeting shows the dawning of that realization.

Broadus also used the term "best results" as one part of the legacy. A recent historian, Jon Butler, thinks that there can be no "best results" in the situation. In his book, *Awash in a Sea of Faith*, Butler includes a chapter entitled "Slavery and the African Spiritual Holocaust." In their enslavement, Africans lost their "rich religious systems" which "were breathtaking in their expanse of world view, causality, and supernatural vitality." Slavery's "cultural destructiveness" constituted "not only wholesale cultural robbery, but cultural robbery of a quite vicious sort."[16] Butler is right that African religion hardly survived one generation in slavery and is right that this severely altered the patterns of community life and the "traditional collective means of comprehending life and loss." Individuals indeed were awash and had to find something to fill the void. They were channeled, therefore, "to the most complete religious system available to them — Christianity."[17]

Though it did represent temporary loss, and in a sense may be justly called "robbery," one who knows the eternal benefits of Christ and his atoning work can never call this loss a tragedy. Those "best results" that Broadus hoped would be recognized can not be measured in terms of the integrity of those involved in evangelization. It must be seen in terms of the infinite worthiness of Christ himself and the eternal gifts and spiritual blessings that he gives his people. One can never over-estimate the revolutionary impact of the Gospel among the slave population. The irrepressible musical witness of "spirituals" to the hope that transcended the temporal condition of the slave is matched only by the presence of thousands of churches and millions of Christians among African-Americans in the United States. Most of these are Baptist and Methodist and have

[15] Broadus, *Memoir*, 92.

[16] Jon Butler, *Awash in a Sea of Faith*, (Cambridge, Massachcusetts: Haravard University Press, 1990), 159, 162.

[17] Ibid., 162, 163.

their origin in the separate black congregations of the South. Preachers such as John Jasper, orators such as Frederick Douglass, leaders such as Richard Allen, and inspiring examples such as Josiah Henson combine to give compelling evidence of both the sinful foolishness of brutalizing such people and the transforming, invigorating power of the gospel they heard in the context of their despair.

A recognition of the infinite excellence of the gifts received in the midst of deprivation does not justify American slavery, but it does pull back the curtains on the glorious wisdom of God's providence who spared not His own Son but delivered Him up because He had chosen the base things of the world and the despised and the things that are not, that He might nullify the things that are.

The varied labors performed among the slaves in the nineteenth-century included catechetical instruction. One example of this is Robert Ryland's "A Scripture Catechism for the Instruction of Children and Servants" written in 1848. Ryland, while president of Richmond College, also served as pastor of the First African Baptist Church of Richmond. Those who were taught it received exposure to a thoroughgoing biblical theology in systematic form. The content consists of evangelical Calvinism and emphasis on holy and grateful living. The answer to each question is a direct quote of Scripture. Examples from lesson 35 on "Divine Purposes" illustrate.

Q. **Is the salvation of God's people in accordance with his previous purpose?**

A. Yes: Who hath saved us, and called us with a holy calling, not according to our works but according to his own purpose and grace which was given us in Christ Jesus before the world began. 2 Tim i.9.

Q. **Did this purpose look immediately to the holiness of his people?**

A. `Yes: According as he hath chosen us in him before the foundation of the world, that we should be holy and without blame before him in love. Eph. i. 4.

Q. **Was Jesus Christ the model after whom they were to be fashioned?**

A. Yes: For whom he did foreknow, he also did predestinate to be conformed to the image of his Son, that he might be the firstborn among many brethren. Rom. viii. 29.

Q. And did this purpose look ultlimately to their salvation?

A. Yes: God hath from the beginning chosen you to salvation, through sanctification of the Spirit, and belief of the truth. 2 Thes. ii. 13.

Lessons on divine revelation, the attributes of God, the person and work of Christ, the parts of salvation, the church, angelic beings, eternal destinies, and the spread of the gospel are all included.

When, in 1857, The Southern Baptist Publication Society sensed a "great earnestness" and a "pious interest in the condition" of servants among its southern constituency, it called on E. T. Winkler to produce a work suitable for religious instruction. Winkler was pastor of the First Baptist Church in Charleston, SC. He already was noted, at 31 years of age, as a major theological and literary figure among Southern Baptists, having served as assistant editor of the *Christian Index* in 1845 when he was 22 years of age. Winkler had studied at Brown University and Newton Theological Seminary before that and was called as pastor to Albany, Georgia in 1846. He originally moved to Charleston to fill the position of corresponding secretary of the Southern Baptist Publication Society, but became such a popular speaker in Charleston that the church asked him to be pastor. He served from 1854 until June 4, 1868. At the founding of Southern Baptist Theological Seminary, Winkler received an invitation to be on the first faculty, which, at the sincere urging of his congregation, he refused.

Because of the large percentage of the population involved in plantation life in Charleston including many members of First Baptist Church, one of the great concerns of the church was the religious instruction of its slave population. The minutes of monthly business meetings record the baptism of large numbers of slaves.[18] The church felt strong conviction that greater efforts should be expended in evangelizing this group of the population. A separate meeting place, not to the exclusion of the slaves' meeting in the regular worship services, was established so that a preacher "suiting his discourse to their understanding" might preach regularly to them. This was the beginning of the Morris Street Church which received hundreds of the freed slaves after the Civil War. Another effort at fulfilling this evangelistic and educational goal consisted of the production of this present catechism.

The preface alleviated several disparaging misconceptions concerning the "piety of our negroes" and justified the catechism by asserting "that

---

[18] Robert A. Baker and Paul J. Craven, *Adventure in Faith: The First 300 Years of the First Baptist Church, Charleston, South Carolina*, (Nashville: Broadman Press, 1982), 295.

when instructed by competent religious teachers, as clear examples of intelligent faith and consistent practice are found among them, as among any other class of professing Christians." The writer of the preface found the arrangement of Winkler's document to be most advantageous. Scripture ["for it is these, and not the words of men, that are to bless and save them"], theological exposition ["truth … conveyed to the understanding"], question and answer ["these truths … still further impressed upon the mind"], and hymn selection ["Their fondness for music is well known"] provided material for worship and instruction for each week of the year.

The preface insisted that consistent and earnest efforts for the thorough religious education of the slaves, particularly through the establishing of Sabbath schools, must be a priority. While masters have an obligation in this task, the responsibility of the pastor "is deep and solemn" and without the use of these suggested means "we do not see how the full measure of that responsibility is to be met."

The first 28 of the 52 lessons are doctrinal: God, His Word, His perfections (7 lessons), the Trinity, Creation, Fall and Misery of Man, the Grace of the Father, the Grace of the Son (with 4 lessons on the incarnation and offices of Christ), the Grace of the Spirit, followed by lessons on Repentance, Faith, Justification, Adoption, and Sanctification. Two lessons on "The Law" and "Love" define the duty of man and introduce ten lessons on the Ten Commmandments. Expositions of the Beatitudes (7 lessons) constitute a section entitled "Christian Character and Needs." The Church, Baptism, and the Lord's Supper (Christian Institutions) precede the last section on "Last Things:" death, resurrection, judgment, heaven and hell.

The exposition of the fifth commandment, seen as a part of the first table, is entitled "Honor to Superiors." It is given over mostly to the relationship between parents and children but mentions, without extraordinary emphasis, the relation between servants and masters. The following sentences in the expository section define that relationship: "Servants should honor their masters;" "masters should care for their servants." In the catechetical section of 21 questions and answers, these exchanges are included: "Q. Whom should servants honor? A. Their masters and mistresses." "Q. Whom should masters care for? A. Their servants." The exposition of the Beatitude, "Blessed are the meek," could certainly be used with a prejudicial pragmatic emphasis to imply the goodness of the subservient state of the slave, but no direct application is made in that way. That section is included in this volume.

Ministers who worked consistently for many years in this task noticed a profound generational difference in the slave population. The enlightening and elevating effects of the gospel marked its recipients with distinct traits of intellectual and emotional maturity. Close observers agreed that the impact was remarkable.

> The religious intelligence of those who have been taught in childhood, has been always found far beyond that of those who have received instruction later in life. The perceptions of the young are less obtuse than those of their elders; Their memories are more retentive; their minds less occupied with superstitious notions; their habits less perverted, and their dispositions more teachable. It is an interesting fact, that inquirers are almost universally found among the young in these schools, and when they are converted and come before the church to relate their religious experiences, instead of recounting the wild fancies and absurd dreams, so common among the more adult applicants for membership, their statements of the work of grace upon their hearts are generally clear and evangelical, and in many cases most edifying and impressive.

Any group of people forced to grow up in ignorance living in repressive and destructive circumstances which have had the effect of brutalizing and stultifying the spirit and intellect would manifest the same distressing symptoms as those spoken of as adults by this witness. By the same token the regular opening of the gospel from the Word of God, beginning in childhood, has a constuctive and liberating effect on the intellect. Catechisms and gospel preaching, both in rationale and result, generated a foundation too broad and deep for the shabbiness of slave quarters, but fit perfectly for a house of manumission. The effort exemplified in the following excerpt from Winkler's catechism must be ranked as one of what Broadus called "best results."

NOTES AND QUESTIONS

FOR THE

ORAL INSTRUCTION

OF

COLORED PEOPLE.

WITH

APPROPRIATE TEXTS AND HYMNS.

BY

REV. E. T. WINKLER,

PASTOR OF FIRST BAPTIST CHURCH, CHARLESTON, S. C.

WITH AN

INTRODUCTION BY JAMES TUPPER, ESQ.

CHARLESTON:

SOUTHERN BAPTIST PUBLICATION SOCIETY

SMITH & WHILDEN, DEP. AGT'S.

229 King Street.

1857.

NOTES AND QUESTIONS
FOR THE
ORAL INSTRUCTION
OF
COLORED PEOPLE
BY
E.T. WINKLER

[PUBLISHED IN CHARLESTON
BY THE SOUTHERN BAPTIST PUBLICATION SOCIETY 1857]

NOTES AND QUESTIONS
LESSON I
GOD

TEXT: HEBREWS 2:6. He that cometh unto God must believe that He is, and that He is the rewarder of them that diligently seek Him.

I. God is the first of beings. He is the being who has made all things, and who rules and blesses all creatures. He is the great King of Heaven, and He is high above the earth. It is our duty to worship Him only; we were made to love Him with all our hearts, and to serve Him with all our powers; and we shall be indeed a happy people if our God is the Lord.

II. We shall do well to believe firmly in God, and to think often of Him. This is what the angels in heaven do. They rest not day and night, but are forever praising Him. As for us, it is shameful and sinful not to know our Maker. Those who forget God are without excuse.

III. We need not be ignorant of God. Our own souls tell us about Him. We see His works all around us in the world. Our lives are full of His judgments and His mercies. And, finally, God has given us His blessed Word, as a light that shineth in a dark place. This will teach us what His will is. And we may ask for His Spirit, so that we may understand what we hear, and become wise unto salvation.

Q. 1.   Who is the first of beings?

A.   God.

Q. 2.   What has He done?

A.   He has made all things.

Q. 3.   What does He do?

A.   He rules and blesses all creatures.

Q. 4.   What is our duty to God?

A.   To worship Him and to love and serve Him.

Q. 5.   Should we believe firmly in God?

A.   Yes, and we should often think of Him.

Q. 6.   What do the angels in heaven do?

A.   They praise Him forever.

Q. 7.   If we do not know God, how should we feel?

A.   We should be ashamed and afraid.

Q. 8.   Has God made Himself known in us?

A.   Yes, our own souls tell us about Him.

Q. 9.   Do we see any signs of God in the world?

A.   Yes, His works are all around us.

Q. 10.   How does God deal with us in our lives?

A.   By judgments and mercies.

Q. 11.   What teaches us most about God?

A.   His blessed Word.

Q. 12.   **Will God help us to understand His Word?**

A.   Yes. He will give His Holy Spirit to them that ask Him.

CALL TO PRAISE

Come, sound His praise abroad,
And hymns of glory sing;
Jehovah is the sovereign God,
The universal King.

Come, worship at His throne;
Come, bow before the Lord;
We are His work, and not our own;
He formed us by His Word.

Today attend His voice,
Nor dare provoke His rod;
Come, like the people of His choice,
And own your gracious God.

LESSON X
THE TRINITY

TEXT: MATTHEW 28:19. Go ye therefore, teach all nations, baptizing them in the name of the Father, and of the Son, and of the Holy Ghost.

I.   There are three persons in the Godhead. These are the Father, the Son and the Holy Ghost. The first person in the Godhead is the Father: He is to be honored as the Father of Christ and of all the people of Christ. The second person is the Lord Jesus Christ, the Son of God. In Him the fullness of the Godhead dwells; by Him the Father has showed Himself to us; and He with the Father is God over all. The third person is the Holy Ghost, who comes from the Father and the Son, but who is equal to them in power and glory. These three persons are one God.

II.   These three, Father, Son and Holy Ghost, must be honored and worshipped in the Christian Church. For the plan of mercy was contrived by the Father—was finished by the Son—and is brought home to our souls by the Holy Ghost. We must submit to the Father as dutiful children. We must have faith in the Son as our Lord and Savior. And the love of the Holy Ghost must be shed abroad in our hearts. Then we shall be near to God: He will be our God and we shall be His people.

Q. 1.   How many persons are there in the Godhead?

A.   Three.

Q. 2.   Who are they?

A.   The Father, the Son, and the Holy Ghost.

Q. 3.   Who is the First person?

A.   The Father.

Q. 4.   How is He to be honored?

A.   As the Father of Christ and of Christians.

Q. 5.   Who is the second person?

A.   The Lord Jesus Christ, the Son of God.

Q. 6.   What is He?

A.   God over all.

Q. 7.   Whom does He show to us?

A.   The Father.

Q. 8.   Who is the third person?

A.   The Holy Ghost.

Q. 9.   From whom does He come?

A.   From the Father and the Son.

Q. 10.   Is He equal to them in power and glory?
A.   Yes.

Q. 11.   What are these three persons?
A.   One God.

Q. 12.   By whom should these persons be especially honored?
A.   By the church.

Q. 13.   Why?
A.   Because we are saved by them.

Q. 14.   How do we honor the Father?
A.   By obeying Him as His children.

Q. 15.   How do we honor the Son?
A.   By faith in Him.

Q. 16.   How do we honor the Holy Ghost?
A.   By love to Him.

Q. 17.   If we do honor God will He be our God?
A.   Yes; He will be our God and we will be His people.

PRAISE TO THE TRINITY

To God the Father yield
Immortal praise and love,
For all our comforts here,
And all our hopes above;
He sent His own eternal Son,
To die for sins which man had done.

To God th' Eternal Son
Let praise immortal flow,

Who bought us with His blood,
Who saves from endless woe;
And now on high He lives and reigns,
And seeks the fruits of all His pains.

To God the Holy Ghost
Immortal honors give,
Whose new creating power
Can make the dead to live:
His work completes the great design,
And fills the soul with joy divine.

Immortal praise to Thee,
O Father, Spirit, Son,
The undivided Three,
The great mysterious One;
Where reason fails with all her powers,
There faith prevails, and love adores.

LESSON XII
THE FALL OF MAN

TEXT: PROVERBS 7:29. God made man upright, but they have sought out many inventions.

I.   God made our first parents holy and happy. He put them in the Garden of Eden to tend it. He gave them to eat its choice fruits, but commanded them not to eat of the tree of the knowledge of good and evil. This command they broke. They listened to the tempter and disobeyed God. And God drove them from Paradise and punished their sin with labor, and sorrow, and death.

II.   We have all shared in the fall. We have received the fallen nature of Adam. We have followed his wicked example. We are now far off from God. Our minds are darkened. Our holiness is lost. It is easy for us to do wrong, and hard to do right. We are by nature the servants of sin. We are under the curse of God. We are in danger of eternal damnation. Our iniquities have separated between us and our God. Unless we repent and believe in Christ, we shall surely perish forever.

Q. 1.   What was the state of our first parents?

A.   Holy and happy.

Q. 2.   Where did God put them?

A.   In the Garden of Eden.

Q. 3.   What should they do there?

A.   They should tend it and feed on its fruits.

Q. 4.   Of what tree should they not eat?

A.   The tree of the knowledge of good and evil.

Q. 5.   Should we obey God's smallest commands?

A.   Yes.

Q. 6.   Did they obey?

A.   No; they listened to the tempter.

Q. 7.   Say what then happened.

A.   God drove them from Paradise.

Q. 8.   How did He punish their sin.

A.   With labor, and sorrow, and death.

Q. 9.   Have we shared in the fall?

A.   Yes.

Q. 10.   Whose nature have we received?

A.   Adam's fallen nature.

Q. 11.   Whose example have we followed?

A.   His wicked example.

Q. 12. Are we near to God now?

A. No; we are far off from God.

Q. 13. Is it easy for us to obey Him?

A. No; it is hard to do right, but easy to do wrong.

Q. 14. What do we serve?

A. Sin.

Q. 15. Is God pleased with us?

A. No; we are under His curse.

Q. 16. What are we in danger of?

A. Eternal damnation.

Q. 17. What has separated between us and our God?

A. Our iniquities.

Q. 18. How then shall we be saved?

A. By repenting and believing in Christ.

THE WANDERER INVITED TO RETURN

Return, O wanderer, now return,
And seek an injured Father's face;
Those warm desires that in [thee] burn,
Were kindled by the Spirit's grace.

Return, O wanderer, now return,
And seek a Father's melting heart;
His pitying eyes thy grief discern,
His love shall peace and joy impart.

Return, O wanderer, now return,
Thy dying Savior bids thee live;
Go to His bleeding cross, and learn
How freely Jesus can forgive.

Return, O wanderer, now return,
And wipe away the falling tear;
'Tis God who says, "No longer mourn,"
'Tis mercy's voice invites thee near.

LESSON XIII
THE MISERY OF MAN

TEXT. ISAIAH 57:21: There is no peace, saith my God, to the wicked.

I.   Fallen men receive punishment from the God of holiness. He suffers many outward evils to befall them. Their bodies are wasted by sickness and old age. They must eat their bread in the sweat of their face. They look for much and it comes to little. Sometimes their families disappoint them. Sometimes their blessings are taken away. Sometimes their neighbors injure and reproach them. They seem born to trouble as the sparks fly upward. And at last they have the wages of their sin, which is death.

II.   And they have many evils within them. The bitterness of sin reaches even to the heart. They go astray believing lies, and following vile passions which cannot make them happy. They came to think of the great God whom they have offended, without shame and fear, and great distress of mind. And they will be more miserable after they are dead. They will lose all their blessings. They will go down quick into hell, to be punished with everlasting pains. There is no peace saith my God to the wicked.

Q. 1.   **What does the holy God do to the wicked?**

A.   He punishes them.

Q. 2.   **What does He send upon their bodies?**

A.   Sickness and old age.

Q. 3.   How must they eat their bread?

A.   In the sweat of their face.

Q. 4.   What must they expect here?

A.   Disappointments, and losses, and troubles.

Q. 5.   What will they have at last?

A.   The wages of sin, which is death.

Q. 6.   Must they have evils within them?

A.   Yes.

Q. 7.   How far does sin reach?

A.   Even to the heart.

Q. 8.   How do they go astray?

A.   They believe lies and follow vile passions.

Q. 9.   Can these passions make them happy?

A.   No.

Q. 10.   How do they think of God?

A.   With shame and fear and great distress of mind.

Q. 11.   When will they be more miserable?

A.   After they are dead.

Q. 12.   What will happen to them then?

A.   They will lose everything, and go down to hell.

Q. 13.   What will become of them there?

A.   They will be punished with everlasting pains.

Q. 14.   Can the wicked have peace?

A.   No; my God says there is no peace to the wicked.

BELIEF IN GOD ONLY

How helpless guilty nature lies,
Unconscious of its load!
The heart unchanged, can never rise
To happiness and God.

Can aught beneath a power divine
The stubborn will subdue
'Tis Thine, eternal Spirit, Thine
To form the heart anew.

'Tis Thine the passions to recall,
And upward-bid them rise;
And make the scales of error fall
From reason's darkened eyes.

To chase the shades of death away,
And bid the sinner live,
A beam of heaven, a vital ray,
'Tis Thine alone to give.

O, change these wretched hearts of ours,
And give them live [life] divine;
Then shall our passions and our powers,
Almighty Lord, be Thine.

LESSON XIV
THE GRACE OF GOD, THE FATHER

TEXT.   1 THESSALONIANS 6:9. God hath not appointed us to
wrath, but to obtain salvation.

I.   Although we deserve to suffer and die, because we are sinners, God in His good pleasure and mercy, has provided salvation for us. Long before the world was made, He knew that men would fall into sin and misery. He resolved to help them. He resolved to send His Son to make satisfaction for sins, so that all those who are chosen in Christ, all who repent of their sins and turn to God, should be saved.

II.   This plan of mercy has been carried out. Christ has redeemed us. His gospel is sent to every kindred and tongue, and people, and nation. There is hope for the chief of sinners. The Lord Jesus will not cast out any who is willing to come to Him; but will keep him in this world and will at last give him eternal life. Wherefore strive to enter in at the strait gate.

Q. 1.   What are we?

A.   Sinners.

Q. 2.   What do we deserve?

A.   To suffer and to die.

Q. 3.   What has God provided for us?

A.   Salvation.

Q. 4.   Why did he provide salvation for us?

A.   Because of His good pleasure and His mercy.

Q. 5.   When did He know that men would fall?

A.   He knew it before the world was made.

Q. 6.   What did he resolve to do?

A.   To help them.

Q. 7.   Whom would He send to help them?

A.   His Son.

Q. 8. How would Christ help them?

A. By making satisfaction for sin.

Q. 9. Who will be saved?

A. The chosen in Christ.

Q. 10. How may we know the chosen in Christ?

A. They are those who repent of their sins and turn to God.

Q. 11. Has this plan of mercy been carried out?

A. Yes; Christ has redeemed us.

Q. 12. To whom is His gospel sent?

A. To all men.

Q. 13. May all men have it if they will?

A. Yes; even the chief of sinners.

Q. 14. If any comes to Christ, will he be cast out?

A. No.

Q. 15. What blessings shall he have?

A. He will be kept in this world, and he will have eternal life.

Q. 16. What should we do then?

A. We should strive to enter the strait gate.

GRACE ACKNOWLEDGED AND PRAISED

Grace! 'tis a charming sound;
Harmonious to the ear;
Heaven with the echo shall resound,
And all the earth shall hear.

Grace first contrived the way
To save rebellious man;
And all the steps that grace display,
Which drew the wondrous plan.

Grace led my roving feet
To tread the heavenly road;
And new supplies each hour I meet,
While pressing to God.

Grace all the work shall crown,
Through everlasting days;
It lays in heaven the topmost stone,
And well deserves the praise.

LESSON XV
THE GRACE OF GOD, THE SON

TEXT. ACTS 4:12. Neither is there salvation in any other, for there is none other name given under heaven whereby we must be saved.

I. The Lord Jesus Christ is our Savior. When we were in bondage to sin and hell He gave Himself for us. Although He was the glorious Son of God, He came to earth for our sakes. Although He was higher than the angels, He consented to dwell with men. He took upon Himself the form of a servant. He even consented to die, that we poor, perishing sinners might live. He went up to heaven to plead for us with His Father. He sends His Spirit down to make us holy and fit to dwell with Him. There is no Savior but Jesus Christ.

II. All this had to be done to save us from ruin. Our sins could not be pardoned, if Christ had not obeyed, and suffered, and prayed for us. What a dreadful evil is sin, that such a price must be paid for it! Let us not neglect this great salvation. And how wonderful was the love of Christ, that He should be willing to do so much for his enemies! O this love should win us to our Savior. We should feel that we are not our own. We are bought with a price. Wherefore let us glorify Him with our bodies and our spirits which are His.

Q. 1.   Who is our Savior?

A.   The Lord Jesus Christ, the glorious Son of God.

Q. 2.   From what does He save us?

A.   From sin and hell.

Q. 3.   Where did He come for us?

A.   To earth.

Q. 4.   Whom did He dwell with?

A.   With men.

Q. 5.   What form did He take upon Himself?

A.   The form of a servant.

Q. 6.   What did He consent to do for us?

A.   He consented to die.

Q. 7.   What does He now do in heaven?

A.   He pleads for us and sends His Spirit down upon us.

Q. 8.   Why does He send His Spirit?

A.   To make us holy and fit for heaven.

Q. 9.   Is there any Savior besides Him?

A.   No; there is none.

Q. 10.   What if Christ had not done all this?

A.   Then our sins could not have been pardoned.

Q. 11.   When such a price was paid for sin, what should we think of it?

A.   That sin is a dreadful evil.

Q. 12.   Should we neglect this great salvation?

A.   No.

Q. 13.   What makes Christ's love so wonderful?

A.   Because He did all this for His enemies.

Q. 14.   To whom should this love win us?

A.   To our Savior.

Q. 15.   How should it make us feel?

A.   That we are not our own.

Q. 16.   What should it lead us to do?

A.   To glorify God with our bodies and spirits, which are His.

GLORY AND GRACE OF JESUS

Come, ye that love the Savior's name
And joy to make it known;
The Sovereign of your hearts proclaim,
And bow before His throne.

Behold your King, your Savior, crowned
With glories all divine;
And tell the wondering nations round
How bright those glories shine.

Infinite power, and boundless grace,
In Him unite their rays;
You that have e'er beheld His face,
Can you forbear His praise?

When in His earthly courts we view
The glories of our King,
We long to love as angels do,
And wish like them to sing.

And shall we long and wish in vain?
Lord, teach our songs to rise!
Thy love can animate the strain,
And bid it reach the skies.

O, happy period! Glorious day!
When heaven and earth shall raise,
With all their powers, the raptured lay,
To celebrate thy praise.

LESSON XX
THE GRACE OF GOD THE SPIRIT

TEXT. JOHN 16:13. When He, the Spirit of Truth is come, He will guide you into all truth.

I.   When Christ went up to heaven He sent His Spirit down to earth. This Spirit was the Holy Ghost, the Spirit of truth. He came to teach the apostles the things of Christ and to give saving knowledge to the world. First He convinces men of sin. He teaches them how foolish, how filthy and how dangerous it is. He shows them that the greatest of all sins is the sin of unbelief. This is the only sin that cannot be forgiven. Then he convinces them of righteousness. He teaches that Christ has gone to the Father, and that all who become members of Christ shall also have a place in heaven. And then, He convinces them of judgment, that the world is judged, that all its joys and gains are less than the blessings of religion.

II.   In this way the Spirit persuades us to embrace the Gospel. He gives new light to our minds such as we never had before. He turns our hearts to Christ and to heaven. He strengthens us to resist the world, the flesh and the Devil. He shows us the great love which God has for us, and fills our souls with penitence and prayer, and praise. Let us not strive against the Holy Ghost, for sin against the Holy Ghost will certainly destroy us.

Q. 1.   **Whom did Christ send from heaven?**

A.   His Spirit.

Q. 2.   How does the Spirit act on earth?

A.   As the Spirit of Truth.

Q. 3.   What did He teach the Apostles?

A.   The things of Christ.

Q. 4.   What does He give to the world?

A.   Saving knowledge.

Q. 5.   What does He first convince them of?

A.   Of Sin.

Q. 6.   What does He teach them about sin?

A.   That it is foolish, filthy and dangerous.

Q. 7.   What is the greatest of all sins?

A.   The sin of unbelief.

Q. 8.   Can this sin be forgiven?

A.   No, it cannot.

Q. 9.   What then does he convince them of?

A.   Of righteousness.

Q. 10.   How do you know that Christ was righteous?

A.   Because He went to the Father.

Q. 11.   What shall the members of Christ have?

A.   A place in heaven.

Q. 12.   What does the Spirit then convince men of?

A.   Of judgment.

Q. 13.   What does He judge?

A.   The world.

Q. 14.   What does He show the gains and joys of the world to be?

A.   To be less than the blessings of religion.

Q. 15.   What does the Spirit give to our minds?

A.   A new light.

Q. 16.   Where does He turn our hearts?

A.   To Christ and heaven.

Q. 17.   What does [He] strengthen us to resist?

A.   The world, the flesh and the Devil.

Q. 18.   What does He show to us?

A.   The great love of God.

Q. 19   What does He fill our souls with?

A.   Penitence, prayer and praise.

Q. 20.   Why should we not strive against the Holy Ghost?

A.   Because this will destroy us.

THE SPIRIT INVOKED

Come, Holy Spirit, heavenly Dove,
With all thy quickening powers,
Kindle a flame of sacred love
In these cold hearts of ours.

Look, how we grovel here below,
Fond of these trifling toys!
Our souls can neither fly nor go
To reach eternal joys.

In vain we tune our formal songs,
In vain we strive to rise;
Hosannas languish on our tongues,
And our devotion dies.

Dear Lord, and shall we ever live
At this poor dying rate?
Our love so faint, so cold to thee,
And thine to us so great?

Come, Holy Spirit, heavenly Dove,
With all thy quickening powers;
Come, shed abroad a Savior's love,
And that shall kindle ours.

LESSON XXIII
JUSTIFICATION

TEXT.   ROMANS 5:1. Being justified by faith, we have peace with God through our Lord Jesus Christ.

I.   Those who believe in Christ are justified. Their sins are pardoned. However great they may have been God forgives and forgets them. Though they were as deep as scarlet, they shall become as white as snow: though they were large as mountains, God shall cast them into the depths of the sea. If we trust in the dear Savior, we shall never be condemned. God will receive us, just as if we had never done any wrong. He will spare us as a man spares his own son. He will look kindly on all our services. He will save our souls.

II.   Jesus poured out his blood to purchase for us this blessing. And God showed that the price pleased Him, by raising Jesus from the dead and setting Him on the throne of Heaven. And now the faithful and true God forgives the sins of the people of Jesus. If we are the disciples of Jesus, we have peace with God. And we shall know that we are pardoned by the good works that he helps us to do.

Q. 1.   Who are justified?

A.   Those who believe in Christ.

Q. 2.   What becomes of their sins?

A.   Their sins are pardoned.

Q. 3.   Are their greatest sins pardoned?

A.   Yes; God forgives and forgets them.

Q. 4.   If we trust in the Savior, shall we be condemned?

A.   No; never.

Q. 5.   How will God receive us?

A.   Just as if we had done no wrong.

Q. 6.   How will He spare us?

A.   As a man spares his own son.

Q. 7.   How will He look on our services?

A.   Kindly.

Q. 8.   What will He do to our souls?

A.   He will save them.

Q. 9.   What did Jesus do to purchase for us this blessing?

A.   He poured out His blood.

Q. 10.   Did God show that this price pleased Him?

A.   Yes; He raised Jesus from the dead and gave Him a throne in
          Heaven.

Q. 11.   Whose sins does the faithful and true God forgive?

A.   The sins of the people of Jesus.

Q. 12.   If we are disciples of Jesus, what have we?

A.   Peace with God.

Q. 13.   How shall we know that God has pardoned us?

A.   By the good works he helps us to do.

PARDON THROUGH CHRIST'S SACRIFICE

Not all the blood of beasts,
On Jewish altars slain,
Could give the guilty conscience peace,
Or wash away the stain.

But Christ, the heavenly Lamb,
Takes all our sins away;
A sacrifice of nobler name,
And richer blood than they.

My faith would lay her hand
On that dear head of Thine,
While, like a penitent, I stand,
And there confess my sin.

My soul looks back, to see
The burdens Thou didst bear,
When hanging on the cursed tree,
And hopes her guilt was there.

Believing, we rejoice
To see the curse remove,
We bless the Lamb with cheerful voice
And sing His bleeding love.

LESSON XL
MEEKNESS

TEXT.   MATTHEW 5:5. Blessed are the meek, for they shall inherit
the earth.

I.   The meek are those who submit to God's will. They patiently suffer affliction and wrong. If they suffer at the hands of God they do not murmur or complain against Him. They are sure that God corrects them in wisdom and mercy. They trust that their troubles will be for their eternal good. If they suffer at the hands of men, they are not carried away with passion. They do not take revenge into their own hands. In every time of distress they cast their cares on Him who careth for them.

II.   The meek shall receive a rich blessing. Their prayer is: Thy will be done. They desire that God will do with them as He pleases. They submit their wills to His. And He in return blesses them on earth. He causes things present and things to come to work for their good. They bear reproach like the meek and lowly Savior; and they shall have their portion in that new world where Christ reigns, the prince of glory and the captain of their salvation.

Q. 1.   Who are the meek?
A.   Those who submit to God's will.

Q. 2.   How do they bear affliction and wrong?
A.   Patiently.

Q. 3.   How do they act when they suffer at the hands of God?
A.   They do not murmur or complain.

Q. 4.   How does God correct them?
A.   In wisdom and mercy.

Q. 5.   What will all their troubles end in?
A.   Their eternal good.

Q. 6.   How do they act when they suffer at the hands of men?
A.   They are not carried away with passion.

Q. 7.   What do they in times of trouble?
A.   They cast their cares on God.

Q. 8.   Why do they cast their cares on God?

A.   Because He cares for them.

Q. 9.   What is the prayer of the meek?

A.   Thy will be done.

Q. 10.   How do they wish God to deal with them?

A.   As He pleases.

Q. 11.   How does God treat them?

A.   He blesses them.

Q. 12.   What blessing do they have on earth?

A.   All things work for their good.

Q. 13.   Who are they like on earth?

A.   Like the meek and lowly Saviour.

Q. 14.   Where shall they have their portion at last?

A.   In the world where Jesus reigns.

THE CHASTENED SON

And can my heart aspire so high
To say, "My Father, God?"
Lord, at Thy feet I fain would lie,
And learn to kiss the rod.

I would submit to all Thy will,
For Thou are good and wise;
Let every anxious thought be still,
Nor one faint murmur rise.

Thy love can cheer the darkest gloom,
And bid me wait serene,
Till hopes and joys immortal bloom,
And brighten all the scene.

"My Father," — O, permit my heart
To plead her humble claim,
And ask the bliss those words impart,
In my Redeemer's name.

LESSON LII
HELL

TEXT.   PSALMS 9:17. The wicked shall be turned into Hell and all the nations that forget God.

I.   Hell is the home of the wicked. Fallen angels and sinful men will dwell forever in that land of darkness and despair. They will be tormented in fires; they will cry in vain for a drop of water to cool their parching tongues. The worm of a guilty conscience will gnaw into their souls. They will be driven from the presence of God. They will have no good, and no hope forever. Their misery will be everlasting.

II.   O let men be wise in time! Let them not serve Satan, lest they share in his awful punishment. Let them not cling to the sins that will sink them into an eternal Hell. Now is the time of grace for sinners. They shall never be condemned if they now take Christ Jesus as their Savior. O let them not say to God: Depart from us, lest he shall say to them, Depart from me, ye cursed, into everlasting fire prepared for the devil and his angels.

Q. 1.   **Where shall the wicked have their home?**

A.   In hell.

Q. 2.   **What is hell?**

A.   A world of darkness and despair.

Q. 3.   Who live in hell?

A.   Fallen angels and sinful men.

Q. 4.   In what shall they be tormented?

A.   In fire.

Q. 5.   Will they also suffer from a guilty conscience?

A.   Yes; it will be like a gnawing worm in their souls.

Q. 6.   From what shall they be driven?

A.   From the presence of God.

Q. 7.   What will be taken from them?

A.   All good and all hope.

Q. 8.   What will they bear forever?

A.   Misery.

Q. 9.   What should this fact teach us?

A.   To be wise in time.

Q. 10.   If we serve Satan what will become of us?

A.   We will share in his punishment.

Q. 11.   If we cling to sins, what will they do to us?

A.   They will sink us into an eternal hell.

Q. 12.   What is the time of grace for sinners?

A.   Now is the time.

Q. 13.   How may sinners be saved from hell?

A.   By taking Christ as their Savior.

Q. 14.   If they bid God to depart from them, what will he say to them
          at the judgment?

A.   Depart from me, ye cursed, into everlasting fire prepared for
          the devil and his angels.

THE SINNER AT THE JUDGMENT

When thy mortal life is fled,
When the death-shades o'er thee spread,
When is finished thy career,
Sinner, where wilt thou appear?

When the world has passed away,
When draws near the judgment day,
When the awful trump shall sound,
Say, O where wilt thou be found?

When the Judge descends in light,
Clothed in majesty and might,
When the wicked quail with fear,
Where, O where, wilt thou appear?

What shall soothe thy bursting heart?
When the saints and thou must part?
When the good with joy are crowned,
Sinner, where wilt thou be found?

While the Holy Ghost is nigh,
Quickly to the Savior fly;
Then shall peace thy spirit cheer,
Then in heaven shalt thou appear.

6

A Brief Catechism
Of Bible Doctrine

An Introduction

Broadus, in his *Memoirs of J. P. Boyce*, gives 1874 as the date Boyce issued his *"Brief Catechism of Bible Doctrine."* He then states that a revised edition appeared in 1878. These dates are right as far as they go, but they fail to draw attention to the first appearance of the catechism in 1864. A report from the Sunday School Board in 1864 lists Boyce's catechism as one of its publications. The notice summarized the vital information.

> *A Brief Catechism of Bible Doctrine*, by J. P. Boyce contains twenty lessons, suited to children of ten or twelve years, and upwards. It brings out the "doctrines of grace" and the views of Baptists. Of this, 2,500 were issued in June, 1864, and 7,500 more in September, of which about 2,000 remain.

Ten thousand of these catechisms were in print within a four month period in 1864. This was during the most distressing period of the Civil War when church activity and finance suffered desperately. According to Broadus, the catechism went through at least two more editions.

Boyce and Doctrine

That Boyce should produce a catechism for children is consistent with his passion for truth. The dominant concern of his life was personal growth in understanding God's revelation in Scripture and for the integrity of the theology of Southern Baptists. Born in 1827 as son of one of the wealthiest men in South Carolina, Boyce received an excellent education. He studied under Francis Wayland at Brown (1845–1847) and under Charles Hodge at Princeton (1849–1851). In October of 1851, Boyce entered on the duties as pastor at First Baptist Church Columbia, SC (1851–1855). When he was ordained, in November, Dr. Thomas Curtis asked him if he intended to make preaching a life-long matter. Boyce replied, "Yes, provided I do not become a professor of theology."[1]

In 1856 his prognostication was realized when he became professor of theology at Furman University in Greenville, SC. Even then he was developing his theory of theological education for Southern Baptists. His inaugural address, entitled "Three Changes in Theological Institutions," called for a plain English education for those who had not the advantages of a preparatory education, an advanced education to train teachers and scholars for Baptist life, and a disciplinary confession of faith to guide the instruction, give accountability to the instructors, and to give confidence to contributors to the school.

After raising money for its support, Boyce chaired the faculty of The Southern Baptist Theological Seminary when it opened in Greenville, SC, in 1859. Not only did he take the lead in founding the seminary, his "Three Changes" established the principle that each professor would sign and adhere to a confession of faith in order to teach there. A document known as the "Abstract of Principles" was adopted by the faculty and trustees. Professors pledged to "teach in accordance with, and not contrary to," this guiding document. Around 1879, when divergence from the confession arose in a much beloved professor, C. H. Toy, Boyce encouraged Toy to a course of action designed to halt theological shift. In fact, as early as 1876 Boyce informed Broadus in a letter, "In a postscript to a letter to Toy I broke into a gentle remonstrance and earnest entreaty on inspiration."[2] When Toy found he could not continue in the path Boyce suggested, Boyce's remonstrance led to the eventual resignation of Toy. This separation gave personal pain to Boyce (He said he would give his right arm to have Toy reestablished in theological orthodoxy) but it was followed faithfully in the path of duty.

Boyce's correspondence with H. A. Tupper, corresponding secretary of the Foreign Mission Board, led to the rescinding of a call of two mission

---

[1] John A. Broadus, *Memoir of James Petigru Boyce* (New York: A. C. Armstrong & Son, 1893), 88.

[2] A. T. Robertson, *The Life and Letters of John Albert Broadus* (Philadelphia: American Baptist Publication Society, 1909), 301.

volunteers for China, T. P. Bell and John Stout. He provided information which led to the realization that they adhered to Toy's view of the inspiration of Scripture. Again, this was a painful action for Boyce, Tupper, and the mission in China, but viewed as necessary for the doctrinal integrity of the mission.

Boyce taught systematic theology at the seminary with an intense earnestness to see his students embrace orthodox theology including the "doctrines of grace" outlined so clearly in this catechism. Eventually, he produced his own textbook for systematic theology, *Abstract of Systematic Theology*. The textbook could be described as a "fleshing out" of the catechism and the "*Abstract of Principles*." The order in which Boyce treats doctrinal topics is virtually the same in all three. The textbook greatly expands the number of chapters but begins with the same foundational issues of the other texts. As essential to the entire theological enterprise and guaranteeing its legitimacy, even its possibility, Boyce's initial discussion unfolds divine revelation in all its manifestations and concludes that the present corpus of divine revelation is found in the error-free Bible. Having established the authority for the rest of the discussion, the order continues with the attributes of God, creation, providence, the fall, the mediatory work and person of Christ, the order of salvation, and eschatology. The catechism and the confession include sections on the church and ordinances not contained in the textbook since those items were taught in a separate course in the seminary. The section on "Election" follows "Providence" in the confession; in the textbook and the catechism the discussion of the topic of "Election" follows Boyce's discussion of the "Work of Christ." On the order of salvation all three move from regeneration to repentance and faith, then justification, sanctification, assurance and perseverance. Each discusses regeneration as the "change of heart" or the giving of a "new heart" necessary for the production of repentance and faith.

In addition, the wording within one document is remarkably reminiscent of that in the other two documents when defining parallel issues. For example, the article on "God" in the "Abstract of Principles" says that God has "in and of himself, all perfections" and is "infinite in them all; and to Him all creatures owe the highest love, reverence and obedience." Combining several catechism questions and answers we learn that God has "every perfection … to an equally boundless extent" and that "all his creatures" owe him their "supreme love and obedience." *The Abstract of Systematic Theology* speaks of his having "absolute perfection" (62) and being "infinite and eternal in his moral perfections" (66) or "infinite, eternal, and unchangeable in all the perfections that belong to his nature," (11) and because of these he "ought to be reverenced and worshipped" (9). Of course, in the textbook each attribute is discussed fully and affirmed to be infinitely perfect.

The questions and answers in this catechism are well-suited for children—simple, clear, and accurate, while at the same time challenging and fulsome. The doctrines of grace are taught in a forthright manner. The sections of election, the sacrifice of Christ, the offer of salvation, assurance, and perseverance contain specific question and answer exchanges designed to teach the Calvinistic doctrine of salvation. The death of Christ delivers "those for whom he died … from the guilt and punishment of all their sins." Although when left to their own powers, men universally reject the offer of salvation, God "effectually calls many to the knowledge and belief of His truth."

Those effectually called are known as the "elect or chosen ones of God," because "before the foundation of the world," not on the basis of any good, piety, or faith that God foresaw in the creature, but on the basis of "his own sovereign will," he chose them to salvation through Christ Jesus. Those thus chosen and called pursue lives of true repentance and good works done to the glory of God. By God's grace they persevere to the end and none in whom the work of grace is begun ever "finally fall."

For Boyce, this naturally gave coherence to the entire theological scheme; these doctrines of grace, therefore, have no appearance of disproportion or of having been forcefully infused into the stream of thought. They do not awkwardly bulge out of the banks of the catechism but flow smoothly within its parameters and give beauty of strength to the whole. Boyce's treatments of Scripture, the attributes of God, creation, providence, the fall of humanity, and the person and work of Christ are fully connected with biblical and logical coherence to support the doctrines of grace; sections on the offer of salvation, regeneration and sanctification, repentance and faith, justification, and good works complement the whole to produce a profoundly balanced catechism.

A

𝕭𝖗𝖎𝖊𝖋 𝕮𝖆𝖙𝖊𝖈𝖍𝖎𝖘𝖒

OF

BIBLE DOCTRINE.

BY

REV. JAMES P. BOYCE, D. D.,

PROFESSOR OF SYSTEMATIC AND POLEMIC THEOLOGY IN
THE SOUTHERN BAPTIST THEOLOGICAL SEMINARY.

REVISED EDITION.

LOUISVILLE:
CAPERTON & CATES, PUBLISHERS.
1878.

A

Brief Catechism

of
Bible Doctrine
By Rev. James P. Boyce, D.D.

The Bible

Q. 1.   **What book have we that teaches about God?**

A.   The Bible.

Q. 2.   **By what other name is it known?**

A.   The Scriptures.

Q. 3.   **Into what two parts is it divided?**

A.   Into the Old and New Testaments.

Q. 4.   **How came it to written?**

A.   God inspired holy men to write it.

Q. 5.   **Did they write it exactly as God wished?**

A.   Yes; as much as if He had written every word Himself.

Q. 6.   **Ought it, therefore, to be believed and obeyed?**

A.   Yes; as much so as though God had spoken directly to us.

Q. 7.   **Does it teach us every thing about God?**

A.   It does not; no language could teach us the full glory of God, nor could we ever comprehend it.

Q. 8.   **How much does it teach us?**

A.   It teaches us all that is necessary about God, our duty to Him, our condition as sinners, and the way of salvation.

God

Q. 1.   Who is God?

A.   He is the Maker and Supreme Rule of all things, and the greatest and best of beings.

Q. 2.   Is there but one God?

A.   There is but one God.

Q. 3.   For what purpose did He create all things?

A.   That He might show forth His glory.

Q. 4.   Does He not also delight in the happiness and goodness of His creatures?

A.   Yes; and these ends are secured by the display of His glory.

Q. 5.   How did He make the worlds?

A.   He made them out of nothing.

Q. 6.   Of what did He make man?

A.   He formed man of the dust of the ground, and breathed into his nostrils the breath of life.

Q. 7.   What may we learn from these acts of creation?

A.   That He is a being of boundless power, wisdom and goodness.

Q. 8.   Has He all other perfections?

A.   Yes; He has every perfection, and to an equally boundless extent.

Q. 9.   What is due to this glorious Being?

A.   The supreme love and obedience of all His creatures.

Providence

Q. 1.   Does God take notice of every thing that takes place?

A.   Yes; nothing comes to pass without His knowledge and permission.

Q. 2.   When did He determine what things He would do, and what He would permit?

A.   In Eternity; before He had created anything.

Q. 3.   Has He ever permitted His creatures to do wrong?

A.   Yes, when they have wilfully chosen to do so.

Q. 4.   Has He not, however, warned them of the consequences of sin?

A.   He has always warned them that He would surely punish them if they should sin.

Q. 5.   Can God be regarded as approving sin under any circumstances?

A.   On the contrary, the Scriptures teach us that He is of purer eyes than to behold evil, and cannot look on iniquity.

Q. 6.   Does He not influence men to do right?

A.   He does; and it is owing to His grace that we do anything that is good.

Q. 7.   Does He ever make men do right against their will?

A.   He never does; but He so leads them to see and love what is right, that they choose to do it.

Original and Present Condition of Man

Q. 1.   In what condition was man originally created?

A.   He was created in the image of God, and free from sin.

Q. 2.   How did he fall from that condition?

A.   Satan tempted him to disobey God, and he did so.

Q. 3.   Did Satan himself tempt Adam?

A.   No; he tempted Eve, and used her as his instrument in tempting Adam.

Q. 4.   In what form did he present himself to Eve?

A.   In the form of a serpent.

Q. 5.   What evil effect followed the sin of Adam?

A.   He, with all his posterity, became corrupt and sinful, and fell under the condemnation of the law of God.

Q. 6.   Have not all men been wilful transgressors of the law in their own persons also?

A.   Yes; as soon as they have become old enough to know what is right and wrong.

Q. 7.   What has been the only exception to this universal prevalence of sin?

A.   The Lord Jesus Christ.

Q. 8.   Was He a descendant of Adam in the same way as all others?

A.   He was not.

Jesus Christ—A Man

Q. 1.   We have learned that Jesus was descendant of Adam; was He then, a man?

A.   He was a man in every respect; but He was without sin.

Q. 2.   Mention some respects in which He was a man.

A.   He had a human body and soul and could not only suffer, but was also liable to temptation.

Q. 3.   **Was He ever tempted?**

A.   Yes; Satan tried in every way to make Him sin, but could not.

Q. 4.   **Was He made subject to the law of God?**

A.   He was, and rendered perfect obedience to it.

Q. 5.   **Had He the same bodily desires and appetites that we have?**

A.   Yes; He felt hunger and thirst, and was liable to all sinless in-
         firmities.

Q. 6.   **Was His soul also liable to suffer?**

A.   Yes; it was His soul that suffered most severely in fulfilling the
         work which He came to do.

Q. 7.   **For what did this human nature fit Him?**

A.   Not only to die for us, but also to sympathize with us in our
         trials and temptation.

Jesus Christ—God

Q. 1.   **Was Christ merely a man?**

A.   No; He was God also.

Q. 2.   **By what name is He called as such?**

A.   The only Begotten Son of God.

Q. 3.   **How is He described in Hebrews?**

A.   As the brightness of the Father's glory and the express image
         of His person.

Q. 4.   **What language does God use to the Son?**

A.   Unto the Son He says, "Thy throne, O God, is forever and
         ever."

Q. 5.   Is Jesus Christ called God in any other place in the Bible?

A.   Yes; in the first Epistle of John, speaking of Him, it says, "This is the true God."

Q. 6.   Did He ever allow Himself to be addressed as God?

A.   Yes; Thomas said to Him, "My Lord and My God."

Q. 7.   In what other ways does the Bible teach the divinity of Christ?

A.   It ascribes to Him the possession of every perfection ascribed to God.

Q. 8.   Mention some of these.

A.   Omniscience, omnipresence and eternity of existence.

Q. 9.   Is the work of creation ever ascribed to Him?

A.   Yes; the Bible says all things were made by Him.

The Trinity

Q. 1.   Does not the title "Son of God" indicate to us that Jesus is not the only person that is God?

A.   Yes; it suggests to us the Father.

Q. 2.   What other person is also called God?

A.   The Holy Spirit.

Q. 3.   Does this imply that there is more than one God?

A.   No, the Bible teaches that the Father is God, that the Son is God, and that the Spirit is God, and yet that there is but one God.

Q. 4.   Can we understand the nature of God as thus revealed to us?

A.   We cannot; but we can believe and know that it is such as God teaches us.

Q. 5.   **Why can we not understand the nature of God?**

A.   Because our minds are limited in power, and the glorious mystery of the nature of God is boundless.

Q. 6.   **Is it in His nature only that God is beyond our knowledge?**

A.   No, He is mysterious also in all His works and ways.

Q. 7.   **What should we learn from this?**

A.   To trust Him, both in what he does and what He teaches.

The Mediator

Q. 1.   **What is a Mediator?**

A.   One who leads persons who are at enmity to become friends, or to be reconciled to each other.

Q. 2.   **Why is Christ called the Mediator?**

A.   Because He comes between man and God, and reconciles them to each other.

Q. 3.   **What offices does Christ discharge as Mediator?**

A.   The offices of Prophet, Priest and King.

Q. 4.   **Why is Christ called a Prophet?**

A.   A Prophet is one who speaks for God, and Christ is the Great Teacher of Divine Truth.

Q. 5.   **Why is He called a Priest?**

A.   It was the duty of the Priest to offer sacrifice for sin, and to pray to God to pardon the sinner. Christ is in both these respects the High Priest of His people.

Q. 6.   **In what sense is He a King?**

A.   He has no earthly kingdom; but He reigns in the hearts of saints and angels.

Q. 7.   Is He not King of the universe?

A.   He is and hence is called the King of kings and Lord of lords.

Q. 8.   Will this reign ever be acknowledged by all?

A.   It will at the judgment day.

The Sacrifice of Christ

Q. 1.   What was the sacrifice which Christ offered?

A.   He offered up Himself for sin.

Q. 2.   In what way did He become the sacrifice?

A.   He took our sin upon Him and suffered the penalty in our place.

Q. 3.   When did He suffer that penalty?

A.   When He died on the cross.

Q. 4.   Did He suffer in both natures?

A.   No; in the human nature only. The divine nature cannot suffer.

Q. 5.   Was not the union of the divine and the human nature necessary in the work of salvation?

A.   It was necessary; otherwise the human nature could not have sustained the sufferings it endured.

Q. 6.   For what else was that union necessary?

A.   To give value and efficacy to sufferings which, but for that union, would have been those of a mere creature.

Q. 7.   Why would not the sufferings of a mere creature have sufficed?

A.   Because every creature is bound, as his own duty, to do and suffer all that God wills, and therefore can do nothing to secure merit or pardon for others.

Q. 8.   Of what value is this sacrifice to those for whom He died?

A.   It delivers them from the guilt and punishment of all their sins.

The Offer of Salvation

Q. 1.   To whom does God offer the salvation in Jesus?

A.   He has ordered it to be offered to every creature.

Q. 2.   Upon what conditions?

A.   Upon that of repentance and faith.

Q. 3.   Are not these terms easy?

A.   They are so easy that all who refuse are without excuse.

Q. 4.   Do all men accept them?

A.   They do not; they universally reject them where left without divine influence.

Q. 5.   Has God thus left all mankind?

A.   He has not; but effectually calls many to the knowledge and belief of His truth.

Q. 6.   What agent accomplished this work?

A.   The Holy Spirit.

Q. 7.   Do those who accept the gospel deserve any reward for so doing?

A.   No, for their acceptance is entirely due to the grace of God.

Q. 8.   How will God punish those who reject it?

A.   Far more severely than He will those who have never heard it.

Q. 9. Upon what grounds will He punish any who have not heard the gospel?

A. Because they, too, are sinners, and have disobeyed the law of God written in their hearts and in nature.

Election

Q. 1. What name is given to those whom God effectually calls to salvation?

A. They are called the elect or the chosen ones of God.

Q. 2. Why are they so called?

A. Because God, before the foundation of the world, chose them unto salvation through Christ Jesus.

Q. 3. Did God make this choice because He foresaw that these persons would be pious and good people?

A. He did not; for the goodness and piety of any are due to the influences of the Spirit.

Q. 4. Was it, then because He foresaw that they would believe?

A. On the contrary, it is through His choice that they are led to believe.

Q. 5. What, then, was the ground of that choice?

A. His own sovereign will.

Q. 6. How may we know if we be of the elect of God?

A. Only by perceiving that the Holy Spirit has led us to repentance and faith and loving obedience to God.

Q. 7. Ought we not diligently to watch for such assurance of our calling and election?

A. Yes; and besides this we ought to pray to God to give His Spirit thus to work in us.

Regeneration and Sanctification

Q. 1.   **What is the first work that the Spirit accomplished in those who are saved?**

A.   The work of regeneration.

Q. 2.   **What is meant by our Regeneration?**

A.   Our being born again.

Q. 3.   **What does the Spirit do in the act of Regeneration?**

A.   He gives us a new heart, inclined to love and practice holiness.

Q. 4.   **How does Regeneration affect the mind?**

A.   It enlightens the mind to understand savingly the Word of God.

Q. 5.   **Is Regeneration necessary to salvation?**

A.   Yes, "Except a man be born again, he cannot see the kingdom of God."

Q. 6.   **Are we made perfectly holy in Regeneration?**

A.   No, this is only attained in our perfect Sanctification.

Q. 7.   **What is meant by our Sanctification?**

A.   It means our being made holy or free from sin.

Q. 8.   **Is such perfection attained in this life?**

A.   It is not.

Q. 9.   **What, then, is the Sanctification which we have experienced?**

A.   It is a change produced by the influence of the Spirit, by which we gradually increase in the love and practice of holiness.

Repentance and Faith

Q. 1. **What is Repentance?**

A. It is sorrow for sin, accompanied by a determination, with the help of God, to sin no longer.

Q. 2. **Do we truly repent every time we are sorry for sin?**

A. No; our sorrow may be from wrong motives.

Q. 3. **Suppose our sorrow arises merely from the fear of detection or punishment?**

A. In that event, it is not true repentance.

Q. 4. **What kind of sorrow, then, is involved in true repentance?**

A. A sorrow which makes us hate sin because it is sin, and because it is wrong to commit it.

Q. 5. **What is Faith?**

A. It is believing what the Bible tells us about Jesus, and trusting our salvation in His hands.

Q. 6. **Is this belief an act of the mind only?**

A. No; it is with the whole heart, so that we are led to love and obey Christ.

Q. 7. **Are there many who believe the Bible who do not exercise faith?**

A. Yes; the greater part of those who have the Bible believe it with the mind, but do not trust with the heart also.

Justification

Q. 1. **What is Justification?**

A. It is an act of God, by which He fully acquits us of all sin.

Q. 2.   Is it based upon any works of our own?

A.   It is not; by our own works we could never secure it.

Q. 3.   Is it not, however, intimately connected with some act of ours?

A.   Yes, with the exercise of faith.

Q. 4.   Is it due to our faith in Christ?

A.   It is not; that faith becomes the instrument only, not the cause of our justification.

Q. 5.   To what, then, is it due?

A.   Simply to the merits and sufferings of Christ, which are accounted by God as ours.

Q. 6.   What do the Scriptures mean when they say that we are justified by faith?

A.   In part, they are teaching that our justification is not by works.

Q. 7.   What else do they mean?

A.   They also speak thus, because in the act of faith the believer takes hold of the meritorious work of Christ, which is the true ground of justification.

Q. 8.   Why does the Apostle James say that we are justified by works and not by faith only?

A.   He refers to the fact that every one that has true faith also performs good works.

Good Works

Q. 1.   Has not God offered life and happiness upon the performance of good works?

A.   He has.

Q. 2.   Have any of mankind ever been justified in that way?

A.   None have been thus justified.

Q. 3.   Why is this?

A.   Because, having a sinful nature, no man can perform good works in an acceptable manner.

Q. 4.   Since, then, we are saved by faith alone, does God still require good works?

A.   He does, and gives us grace to help us to do them.

Q. 5.   Are they to be performed with any hope of attaining salvation?

A.   They are not: for we can never perfectly perform them in this life.

Q. 6.   From what motive then?

A.   From a spirit of love and obedience.

Q. 7.   What, then, is the position of works in God's way of justification?

A.   They are the fruits and evidence of a change of heart and of love to God.

Q. 8.   With what motive should we let men see our good works?

A.   With the hope that thus they may be led to glorify God.

Assurance and Perseverance

Q. 1.   What is meant by assurance of Salvation?

A.   It is an undoubting conviction of our acceptance in Christ.

Q. 2.   Do all the people of God attain it?

A.   It is not attained by all.

Q. 3.   Is not assurance an essential of saving faith?

A.   It is not, doubts and fears assail believers sometimes to the end of life.

Q. 4.   Is it not desirable to attain this grace?

A.   It is not only very desirable, but we are expressly commanded to seek for it.

Q. 5.   Do any in whom the work of grace has begun ever finally fall?

A.   They do not.

Q. 6.   How do we know this?

A.   We learn it from the Scriptures; moreover, salvation is the work of God, who cannot fail in what He undertakes.

Q. 7.   Do not such persons sometime fall into grievous sin?

A.   They do; and years may elapse before they are finally rescued therefrom.

Q. 8.   Can a child of God be contented in this state?

A.   No; the renewed nature God has given him must be disturbed at the presence of sin.

Q. 9.   What is his plain duty when he finds himself in this condition?

A.   Still to trust in his Savior, praying to Him for pardon and for help to avoid sin.

The Future Life

Q. 1.   What do the Scriptures teach about the immortality of the soul?

A.   They teach that the soul will never die, but will live forever.

Q. 2. Do not our bodies die?

A. They do, and after death return to dust.

Q. 3. Will these bodies ever be raised to life again?

A. They will, at the judgment day.

Q. 4. What is the judgment day?

A. It is the day God has appointed in which to judge the world.

Q. 5. By whom will He do this?

A. By His Son, Jesus Christ.

Q. 6. What will be done with the wicked?

A. He will send them away into everlasting punishment.

Q. 7. Into what place will He send them?

A. Into Hell, the place of torment.

Q. 8. What will He do for the righteous?

A. He will give them life everlasting.

Q. 9. Where will they live?

A. In heaven with Jesus - the home of all the good.

Q. 10. Who alone of mankind will be the righteous?

A. Those who have attained to the righteousness of God in Christ Jesus.

Baptism

Q. 1. What duty has God intimately associated with Faith?

A. The profession of that faith in the ordinance of Baptism.

Q. 2.   **What is Baptism?**

A.   It is the immersion of the body in water, in the name of the Father, the Son and the Holy Ghost.

Q. 3.   **Why is it done in the name of the Father, the Son and the Holy Ghost?**

A.   To denote that the person baptized thus professes to believe these three to be God, and to devote himself to His service.

Q. 4.   **What does the use of water in Baptism represent?**

A.   The washing away of our sins by the cleansing influences of the Holy Spirit.

Q. 5.   **What does the act of immersion represent?**

A.   The union of the believer with Christ in His death.

Q. 6.   **Do the Scriptures assign this union as a reason why we are to profess Christ by immersion?**

A.   They do; they tell us that it is on this account that we are buried with Christ by baptism unto death.

Q. 7.   **Who alone are the fit subjects of Baptism?**

A.   Those who exercise faith; for they only can properly profess to have experienced the things which Baptism represents.

The Lord's Supper

Q. 1.   **What other ordinance has Christ established?**

A.   The Lord's Supper.

Q. 2.   **In what does this ordinance consist?**

A.   In eating bread and drinking wine in remembrance of Christ.

Q. 3.   Who alone are authorized to receive it?

A.   The members of His churches.

Q. 4.   In what way is it to be observed?

A.   As a church ordinance, and in token of church fellowship.

Q. 5.   Is there any established order in which these ordinances are to
         be observed?

A.   Yes; the believer must be baptized before he partakes of the
         Lord's Supper.

Q. 6.   What does the Lord's Supper represent?

A.   The death and sufferings of Christ.

Q. 7.   Does the mere partaking, either of Baptism or the Lord's
         Supper confer spiritual blessings?

A.   No; they are worthless, if not injurious, to those who do not
         exercise faith.

Q. 8.   But how is it when they are partaken of by those who do exer-
         cise faith?

A.   The Spirit of God makes them, to such persons precious means
         of grace.

Q. 9.   Whom has Christ appointed to administer Baptism and the
         Lord's Supper?

A.   The authorized ministers of His churches.

The Sabbath

Q. 1.   What is the Sabbath?

A.   It is one day of the week, which God requires to be kept as a
         day of rest, and holy to Him.

Q. 2.   What day of the week did the Jews observe?

A.   The seventh, which we commonly call Saturday.

Q. 3.   What day do Christians keep?

A.   The first day of the week or Sunday.

Q. 4.   Why do Christian keep Sunday as the Sabbath?

A.   Because it was on that day of the week that Christ rose from the dead.

Q. 5.   What name is given to it on this account?

A.   The Lord's Day.

Q. 6.   Did the Apostles and the Christians of their day observe the first day of the week?

A.   They did, and that is our authority for observing the first instead of the seventh day.

Q. 7.   What truth was the Sabbath appointed to commemorate?

A.   The completion of God's work of Creation.

Q. 8.   What additional truth does the Christian Sabbath teach?

A.   The triumphant completion of the still more glorious work of Redemption.

7

A Catechism of Bible Teaching

An Introduction

That John A. Broadus would be selected by both the American Baptist Publication Society and the Sunday School Board to write a Baptist catechism should come as no surprise. Called by A. H. Newman, "perhaps the greatest man the Baptists have produced," he was the most highly respected Baptist of his day, and in scholarship was without peer. Even as early as 1859, J. P. Boyce recognized the strength of Broadus's influence and implied that his presence was needed for the successful founding of The Southern Baptist Theological Seminary. "If you cannot consent to a lifetime of work," Boyce pleaded, "try it for a while in order to inaugurate the matter. Your simple name will be a tower of strength to us."

Broadus

Born in Culpepper County, Virginia, John A. Broadus was educated by Mr. Albert Tutt, his sister Martha, his father, and Albert G. Simms, Broadus's uncle and one of the best teachers in Virginia in those days. During his last year of school he assisted Simms in teaching, a profession he pursued from 1844 to 1848. He enrolled in the University of Virginia in 1846 and graduated in June 1850, two days after his father died. A graduation speech, undelivered but eventually published, was entitled *Human Society in its Relation to Natural Theology*. After graduation, Broadus served as pastor in Charlottesville Baptist Church in Virginia, tutored Greek at the University of Virginia, and helped found Albemarle Female Institute.

J. P. Boyce asked Broadus to leave the pastorate to teach in a new seminary to be located in Greenville, South Carolina. Broadus declined the first invitation, but at a second election, and after much soul-searching, he accepted the position of Professor of New Testament Interpretation and Homiletics at the newly founded Southern Baptist Theological Seminary in 1859. As well as being one of the best scholars and teachers of his generation, he was universally recognized as one of its most powerful and effective preachers.

J. H. Farmer said, "There was the warmth and fervor, without the luxuriant extravagance of the South, combined with the matter of fact directness and sturdy vigor of the North. He was always interesting, instructive, persuasive." His eloquence, which was always impressive and sometimes impassioned, "exalted not the speaker but the truth." Farmer reported, "I have seen stated that Spurgeon himself pronounced him the greatest of living preachers."

Except for a brief intermission during the Civil War, Broadus spent the remainder of his days at the Seminary. He succeeded Boyce as President in 1889 and served until his death March 16, 1895. Upon Broadus's death, the great Baptist historian A. H. Newman said, "I have long regarded Doctor Broadus as the finest and most perfect specimen of Christian manhood I have ever known, and I look in vain for his superior in the history of the church since the apostolic age." Perhaps his best known publications were *On the Preparation and Delivery of Sermons* and his commentary on "Matthew" in the American Commentary series.

Form

Broadus's catechism includes 15 lessons and a section of suggested biblical passages for memorization. Each lesson consists of two types of questions: the first set is for all students and the second is for advanced students. This method arose from much earnest contemplation on the part of Broadus. Originally, the publishing houses sponsoring the project desired separate catechisms for three different age levels. Settling, however, for two different levels within one catechism, this format appeared to pose special problems. As Broadus struggled with the problem confronting him, he set forth a tri-fold qualification serving as his guidelines. His marvelous implementation of this set of criteria should certainly aid anyone in evaluating the usefulness of catechisms. In December 1891, having finished lesson one in the catechism he wrote thoughtfully, "It is, of course, an extremely difficult task to make questions and answers about the existence and attributes of the Divine Being, that shall be intelligible to children, adequate as the foundation for future thinking, and correct as far as they go."[1]

---

[1] A. T. Robertson, *Life and Letters of John A. Broadus* (Philadelphia: American Baptist Publication Society, 1909), 398.

The catechism begins with God as "the only being that has always existed, … the Creator and Preserver of all things." Following this basic assumption, Broadus continued to move from the broad and general to the more particular and precise. God is known "partly from his works" (general), "mainly from his Word" (precise and particular). The next two lessons follow logically: "Providence of God:" and "The Word of God." The Lesson on Scripture, divided into two parts, is the longest in the catechism. The next seven lessons (IV –X) are basically soteriological in nature. Lesson IV discusses man, especially as a fallen creature completely unable to redeem himself. Lesson V, "The Saviour," treats the person of Christ and introduces his work. Lesson VI completes the Trinitarian picture of God, "The Holy Spirit and the Trinity." Lesson VII resumes discussion on the work of Christ in a dialogue entitled "The Atonement of Christ." Lessons VIII, IX, X complete the soteriological section with respective treatments of "Regeneration," "Repentance and Faith," and "Justification and Sanctification." The subjects of the church and the Christian life are treated in Lessons XI-XIV. Beginning with "Baptism and the Lord's Supper," Broadus moves through the queries and responses to the "Lord's Day" and "Some Duties of the Christian Life," and capsules this subject area with a lesson entitled "Imitation of Christ." His brief treatment of eschatology forms the final lesson (XV) entitled "The Future Life."

Theology

Broadus's theological stance might be described as thoroughly Baptistic and cautiously Calvinistic. A comparison of Broadus's catechism with that of his good friend J. P. Boyce reveals that Boyce has a full chapter on only one subject not treated equally fully by Broadus, That chapter is election. Broadus, however, affirms that "both divine predestination and human freedom must be true … and both are plainly taught in the Bible." His view of providence is "There is no such thing as chance or luck; everything is controlled by the providence of God: and God has always intended to do whatever he does." In spite of these strong statements discussed directly under the headings of providence, Broadus does not have a specific statement relating to the election of certain persons to salvation. In fact, Broadus quotes 1 Timothy 2:4 as evidence that, at least in some way, God desires the salvation of all men. Boyce taught election more explicitly affirming that "God before the foundation of the world, chose them [the elect] unto salvation through Christ Jesus." Similarly, the catechism leaves the reader to implication in discerning Broadus's view concerning the particularity of atonement. In the advanced section of the catechetical heading "Man," Broadus posed the following exchange:

Q. (d)   What does the New Testament reveal that corresponds to the effect of Adam's sin upon his descendants?

A.   The benefits of Christ's salvation for his people correspond to the effect of Adam's sin upon his descendants.

This implies a direct imputation of the work of Christ to "his people," a statement at least consistent with particular atonement if not consonant solely with that view. Broadus discussed the atonement as a substitutionary and propitiatory sacrifice willingly undertaken by Christ in accordance with God's will. He made the Calvinistic distinction between the "sufficiency" of Christ's death for all men and its actual salvific effect for those who repent and believe. In this way he aligned himself with historic Calvinism and but avoided some of the complexities of a fuller statement. Broadus clearly taught the particularity of salvation as he discussed the effectual work of the Spirit. According to Broadus, this is a particular and sovereign work. Regeneration is "God's causing a person to be born again." "The Holy Spirit regenerates." Faith does not precede the new birth but "it is the new heart that truly repents and believes." An answer to one of the "Advanced Questions" states, "God gives his renewing Spirit to those whom he always purposed to save. Eph 1:3, 4." The implications of Broadus's discussion of the work of the Spirit, combined with Broadus's understanding of the eternal unity of the purposes of the triune God and the chasteness of his language in questions on the atonement, elicit the just conclusion that Broadus believed in both particular election and particular atonement.

He was not hesitant to solicit the aid of theological ideas in his interpretation of Scripture and his organization of it into a harmonious system. Broadus spoke of the "covenant of redemption formed in eternity," and employed it as a possible interpretation of Jesus words in Matthew 11:27, "All things were delivered to me of my Father." Broadus taught a historic Calvinist position on perseverance of the Saints. In addition to this confidence that "God will preserve a true believer in Christ to the end," he also stated "the only sure proof of being a true believer is growing in holiness and in usefulness, even to the end." This treatment properly respects the power and intent of God to accomplish a full salvation in his elect and, at the same time, recognizes that his effectual calling produces a pursuit of holiness throughout life.

Such an apparently clandestine approach to some of the doctrines of grace may find explanation in the criteria Broadus established for himself in constructing the catechism—"intelligible to children, adequate as the foundation for future thinking, and correct as far as they go." One must know that he was not always quite so oblique in his approach to these strong and mighty doctrines. On a summer trip to Europe in 1891, Broadus took a steamer trip to Geneva on which he had a vivid view of Mont Blanc. That one of the councilors of Geneva was named "Turretin" reminded Broadus of the great text by the theologian Turretin used by his late friend J. P. Boyce in the class on Latin Theology. In a letter to the *Western Recorder* he reminisced on the influence of that text on students.

> Several great departments of systematic theology seem to me more thoroughly discussed and luminously stated by Turretin's noble work than by any other of the great theologians. The people who sneer at what is called Calvinism might as well sneer at Mont Blanc. We are not in the least bound to defend all of Calvin's opinions or actions, but I do not see how any one who really understands the Greek of the Apostle Paul or the Latin of Calvin and Turretin can fail to see that these latter did but interpret and formulate substantially what the former teaches.[2]

Appreciation for the spiritual and biblical power of the doctrines of grace was a consistent element in Broadus's evaluation of theological issues. Two friends of Broadus, James P. Boyce and Basil Manly, Jr., had studied at Princeton Theological Seminary under the great theologian Charles Hodge. Broadus described him as a "man of marked Christian earnestness and fervor, with whom the great doctrines were living facts." Boyce and Manly had great esteem for this teacher, "It was a great privilege to be directed and upborne by such a teacher in studying that exalted system of Pauline truth which is technically called Calvinism," Broadus remarked. Not only did such a teacher inspire but that particular system of truth, Calvinism, was one to compel "an earnest student to profound thinking." Then affirming the value of thinking both systematically and piously about the truths of Scripture, Broadus added that the system of Calvinism "when pursued with a combination of systematic thought and fervent experience, makes him at home among the most inspiring and ennobling views of God and of the universe he has made."[3]

Without such a commitment to systematic thought, Broadus would never have consented to produce a catechism. The lessons of "Baptism" and "The Lord's Supper" give expression to Broadus's thoroughly baptistic stance. Among the lessons taught are the following. 1: Only believers are to be baptized. 2: Only immersion is baptism. Other modes are not baptism. Strict obedience to the word of God requires this belief. 3: Baptist does

---

[2] Ibid., 396–397.
[3] John A. Broadus, *Memoir of J. P. Boyce* (New York: A. C. Armstrong & Son, 1893), 73.

not regenerate. 4: The Lord's Supper is a symbolic ordinance. 5: It is to be taken in a church context only. 6: Baptists should not partake with other denominations.

Broadus published several items dealing with baptism including a tract on immersion issued by the American Baptist Publication Society. His commentary on Matthew contains a lengthy note on baptism in the discussion of Mathew 3:6. Broadus discussed the term etymologically, lexically, and historically and also interacted with some of the polemics concerning the initiatory ordinance of the church. The number of considerations involved in the discussion should, according to Broadus, "promote charity" as they explain why so much controversy is engendered "about a very plain word." After having given deference to other views, however, Broadus returned with conviction to his original affirmation—"It thus appears that in none of the ways mentioned is warrant found for giving *baptizo* any such meaning as pour, sprinkle, or wash religiously, or any other than its own proper and well-known sense," i.e. immerse. It is therefore with a great deal of time and thought invested that he included in his advanced questions, "Can there be Christian baptism without immersion?" He then answered in light of his thorough study, "No, Christ was immersed, and commanded us to be immersed, and sprinkling or pouring water will not represent burial and rising again (Romans 6:4; Colossians 2:12)." He further adds that the principle driving this teaching "is that of strict obedience to the Word of God."

The following catechism is copied from the 1892 edition. Its style has been amended slightly in arrangement of the questions and answers.

A CATECHISM

OF

BIBLE TEACHING.

BY

JOHN A. BROADUS, D. D., LL.D.

———•———

PHILADELPHIA:

AMERICAN BAPTIST PUBLICATION SOCIETY,

1420 CHESTNUT STREET,

AND

NASHVILLE:

SUNDAY-SCHOOL BOARD OF SOUTHERN
BAPTIST CONVENTION.

A Catechism
of
Bible Teaching

by
John A. Broadus, D.D., LL.D.

LESSON I
GOD

Q. (1)   Who is God?

A.   God is the only Being that has always existed, and He is the
           Creator and Preserver of all things.

Q. (2)   How do we know that God Exists?

A.   We know that God exists from the worlds He has made, and
           from our own sense of right and wrong; and the Bible above
           all tells us of God.

Q. (3)   Have men any reason for denying God's existence?

A.   It is foolish and wicked to say there is no God (Psalm 14:1;
           Romans 1:20).

Q. (4)   How may we learn the character of God?

A.   We learn the character of God partly from His works, mainly
           from His Word.

Q. (5)   What does God know?

A.   God knows all things, even the secrets of our hearts; God is
           omniscient (Hebrews 4:13; Ecclesiastes 12:14).

Q. (6)   What power has God?

A.   God has all power; God is omnipotent.

Q. (7)   Where is God?

A.   God is everywhere, and all things are present to Him; God is omnipresent (Genesis 16:13; Psalm 139:7).

Q. (8)   What do we know as to the holiness of God?

A.   God is perfectly holy; the angels praise Him as holy (Isaiah 6:3; Revelation 4:8).

Q. (9)   Is God just?

A.   God is always perfectly righteous and just (Psalm 145:17).

Q. (10)   Is God loving and good?

A.   God is love, and He is good to all (1 John 4:8; Psalm 145:9).

Q. (11)   Is God all love?

A.   God's justice is as truly a part of His nature as His love (Revelation 15:3).

Q. (12)   How ought we to feel and act toward God?

A.   We ought to love God with all our heart and serve Him with all our powers (Deuteronomy 6:5; 1 John 5:3).

Q. (13)   Is it our duty to fear God?

A.   It is our duty to obey God in filial fear, and to fear His wrath if we sin (Ecclesiastes 12:13; Hebrews 10:31).

ADVANCED QUESTIONS

Q. (a)   May little children easily recognize that there is a God?

A   Young children often think and speak about God (Psalm 8:2; Matthew 21:16).

Q. (b)   How do many persons practically deny that there is a God?

A.   People practically deny that there is a God by living as if He did not exist.

Q. (c)   Why is it wrong to use images of God in worship?

A.   Men would soon worship the image instead of God, and so
          God has positively forbidden such use of images (Exodus
          20:4, 5; Romans 1:23, 25).

Q. (d)   Is it possible for God to do wrong?

A.   For God to do wrong would be contrary to His very nature;
          He cannot deny Himself (2 Timothy 2:13).

LESSON II
PROVIDENCE OF GOD

Q. (1)   What is meant by the providence of God?

A.   God cares for all His creatures and provides for their welfare.

Q. (2)   Does God's providence extend to the wicked?

A.   God gives to the wicked, sunshine and rain and all the com-
          mon blessings of life, thereby calling them to repentance
          (Matthew 5:45; Psalm 145:9; Romans 2:4).

Q. (3)   Does God exercise any special providence over the righteous?

A.   God makes all things work together for good to them that
          love Him (Romans 8:28; Psalm 23:1).

Q. (4)   Is God's providence confined to great things?

A.   God notices and provides for even the least things (Luke
          12:7).

Q. (5)   Is there really any such thing as chance or luck?

A.   There is no such thing as chance or luck; everything is con-
          trolled by the providence of God.

Q. (6)   Does God act according to purposes formed beforehand?

A.   God has always intended to do whatever He does (Ephesians
          1:11; 1 Peter 1:20).

Q. (7) Do God's purposes destroy our freedom of action?

A. We choose and act freely, and are accountable for all we do (Joshua 21:15; Romans 14:12).

Q. (8) Does God cause evil?

A. God permits evil, but does not cause it.

Q. (9) Does God ever check and overrule evil?

A. God often prevents evil, and often brings good out of evil (Genesis 45:5; Psalm 76:10).

Q. (10) What is the greatest example of God's bringing good out of evil?

A. The crucifixion of Christ is the greatest example of God's bringing good out of evil.

Q. (11) How ought we to think and feel about the providence of God?

A. We ought always to remember our dependence on God, and to trust His providential guidance (James 4:15; Jeremiah 10:23).

Q. (12) When God in His providence sends upon us something painful, how ought we to feel?

A. When God sends on us something painful we ought to be patient, obedient, and thankful (1 Samuel 3:18; 1 Thessalonians 5:18).

ADVANCED QUESTIONS

Q. (a) Would it be possible to control great events while disregarding all little things?

A. Great things and little things are inseparable and dependent on each other.

Q. (b) If all things take place according to fixed laws, how can it be that God controls them?

A. God created all the forces of nature, and made them without violating the laws.

Q. (c)   Can God then answer prayer by His providential control without violating the laws of nature?

A.   Yes, the Bible assures us that God does answer prayer.

Q. (d)   What instances can you give of special providence in the story of Joseph?

A.   Genesis 37:28; 39:2, 3, 21–23; and Chapter 45.

Q. (e)   What example of speedy answer to prayer in the story of Hezekiah?

A.   2 Kings 20:1–6.

Q. (f)   If we cannot explain the relations between divine predestination and human freedom, does that warrant us in rejecting either?

A.   Both divine predestination and human freedom must be true from the very nature of God and man, and both are plainly taught in the Bible.

LESSON III
THE WORD OF GOD

PART I. THE BOOKS OF THE BIBLE

Q. (1)   How many separate books are there in the Bible?

A.   There are thirty-nine books in the Old Testament and twenty-seven in the New Testament.

Q. (2)   What are the five books of Moses?

A.   The five books of Moses are Genesis, Exodus, Leviticus, Numbers, Deuteronomy.

Q. (3)   What are the other historical books in the Old Testament?

A.   The twelve other historical books in the Old Testament are Joshua, Judges, Ruth, 1 and 2 Samuel, 1 and 2 Kings, 1 and 2 Chronicles, Ezra, Nehemiah, Esther.

Q. (4)   What are the five poetical books?

A.   The five poetical books are Job, Psalms, Proverbs, Ecclesiastes, Song of Solomon.

Q. (5)   Which are the four greater prophets?

A.   The four greater prophets are Isaiah, Jeremiah (with Lamentations), Ezekiel, Daniel.

Q. (6)   Which are the twelve lesser prophets?

A.   The twelve lesser prophets are Hosea, Joel, Amos; Obadiah, Jonah, Micah; Nahum, Habakkuk, Zephaniah; Haggai, Zechariah, Malachi.

Q. (7)   What are the five historical books of the New Testament?

A.   The five historical books of the New Testament are Matthew, Mark, Luke, John, Acts.

Q. (8)   What are the fourteen epistles of Paul?

A.   The fourteen epistles of Paul are Romans, 1 and 2 Corinthians, Galatians; Ephesians, Philippians, Colossians; 1 and 2 Thessalonians; 1 and 2 Timothy, Titus; Philemon; Hebrews.

Q. (9)   What are the seven other epistles?

A.   The seven general epistles are James, 1 and 2 Peter, 1, 2, and 3 John, Jude.

Q. (10) What is the last book in the Bible?

A.   The last book in the Bible is Revelation.

PART II. INSPIRATION AND AUTHORITY OF THE BIBLE

Q. (11) Were the books of the Bible written by men?

A.   The books of the bible were written by men, but these men were moved and guided by the Holy Spirit (2 Peter 1:21; 1 Corinthians 14:37).

Q. (12) What special proof have we that the entire Old Testament is inspired?

A. Christ and His apostles speak of "Scripture" or "the Scriptures," as inspired by God, and we know that they meant exactly what we call the Old Testament (John 10:35; 2 Timothy 3:16).

Q. (13) Does the Bible contain any errors?

A. The Bible records some things said by uninspired men that were not true; but it is true and instructive that these men said them.

Q. (14) What authority has the Bible for us?

A. The Bible is our only and all-sufficient rule of faith and practice.

Q. (15) What things does the Bible teach us?

A. The Bible teaches all that we need to know about our relations to God, about sin and salvation.

Q. (16) How ought we to study Bible history?

A. We ought to study the Bible as a history of providence and a history of redemption.

Q. (17) Who is the central figure of the Bible history?

A. The central figure of the Bible history is Jesus Christ, the hope of Israel, the Savior of mankind.

Q. (18) What does the Bible do for those who believe in Jesus Christ?

A. The Bible makes those who believe in Jesus wise unto salvation (2 Timothy 3:15).

Q. (19) What does the Bible contain besides history?

A The Bible contains doctrines, devotional portions, precepts, and promises; it teaches us how to live and how to die.

Q. (20)   With what disposition ought we to study the Bible?

A.   We ought to study the Bible with a hearty willingness to believe what it says and to do what it requires (John 7:17).

Q. (21)   What great help must we all seek in studying the Bible?

A.   We must pray that the Holy Spirit who inspired the Bible will help us to understand it (Psalm 119:18; Luke 24:45).

ADVANCED QUESTIONS

Q. (a)   How do we know that Christ and His apostles meant by "the Scriptures" what we call the Old Testament?

A.   We know from Jewish writers and early Christian writers, that those who heard Christ and His apostles would understand them to mean the Old Testament; and therefore they must have meant it so.

Q. (b)   What promise did our Lord give His apostles as to the Holy Spirit?

A.   Our Lord promised His apostles that the Holy Spirit should bring all his teachings to their remembrance, and guide them into all the truth (John 14:26; 16:13).

Q. (c)   Did the inspired writers receive everything by direct revelation?

A.   The inspired writers learned many things by observation or inquiry, but they were preserved by the Holy Spirit from error, whether in learning or in writing these things.

Q. (d)   What if inspired writers sometimes appear to disagree in their statements?

A.   Most cases of apparent disagreement in the inspired writings have been explained, and we may be sure that all could be explained if we had fuller information.

Q. (e)   Is this also true when the Bible seems to be in conflict with history or science?

A.   Yes, some cases of apparent conflict with history or science have been explained quite recently that were long hard to understand.

Q. (f)   Has it been proved that the inspired writers stated anything as true that was not true?

A.   No; there is no proof that the inspired writers made any mistake of any kind.

LESSON IV
MAN

Q. (1)   How did men begin to exist?

A.   God created Adam and Eve, and from them are descended all human beings.

Q. (2)   What sort of character had Adam and Eve when created?

A.   Adam and Eve were made in the image of God, and were sinless.

Q. (3)   Who tempted Eve to sin against God by eating the forbidden fruit?

A.   Eve was tempted by the Devil, or Satan, who is chief of the fallen angels, or demons.

Q. (4)   What was the beginning of Eve's sin?

A.   The beginning of Eve's sin was that she believed Satan rather than God (Genesis 3:4, 5).

Q. (5)   What was the first sign that Adam and Eve gave of having fallen into sin?

A.   Adam and Eve showed that they had become sinful by trying to hide from God (Genesis 3:8).

Q. (6)   **What was the next sin?**

A.   Adam and Eve tried to throw the blame on others (Genesis 3:12, 13).

Q. (7)   **How did God punish their wilful disobedience?**

A.   God condemned Adam and Eve to death, physical, spiritual, and eternal (Genesis 2:17; Romans 6:23; Ephesians 2:1).

Q. (8)   **How does this affect Adam and Eve's descendants?**

A.   All human beings are sinful and guilty in God's sight (Romans 5:12).

Q. (9)   **How does this sinfulness show itself?**

A.   All human beings actually sin as soon as they are old enough to know right from wrong (Romans 3:23).

Q. (10)   **Will those who die without having known right from wrong be punished hereafter for the sin of Adam and Eve?**

A.   Those who die without having known right from wrong are saved in the way God has provided.

Q. (11)   **Can any human beings be saved through their own merits from the guilt and punishment of sin?**

A.   No; the second Adam, the son of God, is the only Savior of sinners (Acts 4:12; Genesis 3:15).

ADVANCED QUESTIONS

Q. (a)   **Was man to be idle in the garden of Eden?**

A.   No, man was to keep the garden and to have dominion over the animals (Genesis 2:15; 1:26).

Q. (b)   **Is work a curse?**

A.   Work is not a curse, but anxious and wearing toil is a curse and a fruit of sin (Genesis 3:17).

Q. (c)   **Does the Bible elsewhere speak of Satan as a serpent?**

A.   Satan is called a serpent in the book of Revelation (Revelation 12:9; 20:2).

Q. (d)   **What does the New Testament reveal that corresponds to the effect of Adam's sin upon his descendants?**

A.   The benefits of Christ's salvation for His people correspond to the effect of Adam's sin upon his descendants.

Q. (e)   **How does the apostle Paul state this parallel?**

A.   "Through one man sin entered into the world, and through sin, death," so likewise through one man came justification, and through justification, life. (Romans 5:12–19).

LESSON V
THE SAVIOR

Q. (1)   **Who is the Savior of men?**

A.   Jesus Christ, the Son of God, is the Savior of men.

Q. (2)   **Was Jesus Himself really a man?**

A.   Yes, Jesus Christ was really a man; He was the son of Mary.

Q. (3)   **Was Jesus the son of Joseph?**

A.   No, people called Jesus the son of Joseph, but he was really the Son of God (Luke 1:35).

Q. (4)   **Can you give any express statement that Jesus was God?**

A.   "The Word was God … And the Word became flesh, and dwelt among us, full of grace and truth" (John 1:1, 14).

Q. (5)   **What then is Jesus Christ?**

A.   Jesus Christ is both God and man, the God-man.

Q. (6) How does this fit Jesus to be the Savior of men?

A. Jesus the God-man can stand between men and God as Mediator.

Q. (7) Can you tell the meaning of the two names, Jesus Christ?

A. Jesus means Savior, and Christ means Anointed, like the Hebrew word Messiah (Matthew 1:21; John 4:25).

Q. (8) What did Christ do on earth for us?

A. Christ taught the highest truths, He lived as a perfect example, and He died and rose again to redeem us.

Q. (9) What is Christ doing for us now?

A. Christ dwells in His people, intercedes for them, and controls all things for their good (John 14:23; Hebrews 7:25; Matthew 28:18).

Q. (10) What will Christ do hereafter for us?

A. Christ will come a second time and receive us unto Himself, to be with Him forever (John 14:3; Hebrews 9:28).

Q. (11) What must we do to be saved through Jesus Christ?

A. We must believe in Christ, must turn from our sins to love and obey Him, and must try to be like Him.

ADVANCED QUESTIONS

Q. (a) How did Christ take our place?

A. He who knew no sin was made sin for us, that we might become righteous in God's sight through Him (2 Corinthians 5:21).

Q. (b) Was Christ's work necessary to make God willing to save men?

A. No, Christ simply made it right that God should save those who trust in Him (Romans 3:26).

Q. (c)   What was the origin of Christ's mission to save?

A.   The origin of Christ's mission to men was in God's pitying
          love for the world (John 3:16; 1 John 4:10).

Q. (d)   Does God offer to save all men through Christ?

A.   Yes, whosoever will may have salvation without cost (Revela-
          tion 22:17; Isaiah 55:1).

Q. (e)   Ought we to make this salvation known to all men?

A.   Yes, it is our solemn duty to carry the gospel to all nations
          (Luke 24:47).

Q. (f)   How can we carry the gospel to distant lands?

A.   We can go ourselves as missionaries, or help to send others.

LESSON VI
THE HOLY SPIRIT AND THE TRINITY

Q. (1)   Who is the Holy Spirit?

A.   The Holy Spirit is the Spirit of God, and is called the third
          person in the Trinity.

Q. (2)   What did the Holy Spirit do for the prophets and apostles?

A.   The Holy Spirit inspired the prophets and apostles to teach
          men their duty to God and to each other.

Q. (3)   What did the Holy Spirit do for all the writers of the Bible?

A.   The Holy Spirit inspired them to write just what God wished
          to be written.

Q. (4)   Did the Holy Spirit dwell also in Jesus Christ?

A.   Yes, the Holy Spirit was given to Jesus without measure (Luke
          4:1; John 3:34).

Q. (5)   When Jesus ascended to heaven, what did He send the Holy
          Spirit to do?

A.   Jesus sent the Holy Spirit to take His place and carry on His
          work among men (John 14:16, 17).

Q. (6)   What does the Holy Spirit do as to the world?

A,   The Holy Spirit convicts the world of its sin and its need of
          Christ's salvation (John 16:8).

Q. (7)   What work does the Holy Spirit perform in making men
          Christians?

A.   The Holy Spirit gives men a new heart, to turn from sin and
          trust in Christ (John 3:5; Ezekiel 36:26).

Q. (8)   How does the Holy Spirit continue this work?

A.   The Holy Spirit helps those who trust in Christ to become
          holy in heart and life (Galatians 5:22; 1 Corinthians 3:16).

Q. (9)   Is the Holy Spirit Himself divine?

A.   Yes, the Holy Spirit is God (Acts 5:3, 4).

Q. (10)   If the Father is God, and the Savior is God, and the Holy
          Spirit is God, are there three Gods?

A.   No, there are not three Gods; God is one (Deuteronomy 6:4;
          Mark 12:20).

Q. (11)   What then do we mean by the doctrine of the Trinity?

A.   The Bible teaches that the Father is God, and the Son is God,
          and the Holy Spirit is God, and yet God is one.

Q. (12)   Are we able to explain the Trinity?

A.   We cannot explain the Trinity; and need not expect to under-
          stand fully the nature of God; we cannot fully understand even
          our own nature.

Q. (13) How is the Trinity recognized in connection with baptism?

A.   We are told to baptize "in the name of the Father and of the Son and of the Holy Spirit" (Matthew 28:19).

Q. (14) How is the Trinity named in a benediction?

A.   "The grace of the Lord Jesus Christ, and the love of God, and the communion of the Holy Spirit, be with you all" (2 Corinthians 13:14).

ADVANCED QUESTIONS

Q. (a)   Did the Holy Spirit give men the power of working miracles?

A.   Yes, the Holy Spirit gave to the apostles and others the power of working miracles (Acts 2:4; 1 Corinthians 12:11).

Q. (b)   What did the Savior mean when he spoke of blaspheming against the Holy Spirit?

A.   Blaspheming against the Holy Spirit was saying that a work of the Holy Spirit was work of Satan (Mark 3:29).

Q. (c)   Is there any other unpardonable sin?

A.   The Savior says that every sin may be forgiven except the blasphemy against the Holy Spirit (Mark 3:23; Matthew 12:31, 32; 1 John 5:16).

Q. (d)   What is the meaning of the word Trinity?

A.   The word Trinity or Triunity means that God is in one sense three and in another sense one.

LESSON VII
THE ATONEMENT OF CHRIST

Q. (1)   What was Christ's chief work as Savior?

A.   Christ died and rose again for His people (2 Corinthians 5:15; Romans 4:25).

Q. (2) Did Christ voluntarily allow Himself to be slain?

A. Yes, Christ laid down His life of Himself (John 10:17, 18).

Q. (3) Was this Christ's design in coming into the world?

A. Our Lord says that He came "to give His life a ransom for many" (Mark 10:45).

Q. (4) For what purpose did the loving God give His only Son?

A. God gave His only Son "that whosoever believeth on Him should not perish, but have eternal life" (John 3:16).

Q. (5) How could Christ's dying give us life?

A. Christ took our place and died like a sinner, that we might take His place and be righteous in Him (2 Corinthians 5:21).

Q. (6) Was it right that the just should die for the unjust?

A. The Savior was not compelled, but chose to die for the benefit of others.

Q. (7) Is it right for God to pardon men because the Savior dies?

A. God declares it to be right for Him to pardon men if they seek salvation only through Christ (Romans 3:26).

Q. (8) May a man go on in sin and expect to be saved through Christ's atoning death?

A. No, we must live for Him who died for us (2 Corinthians 5:15).

Q. (9) Is salvation offered to all men through the atonement of Christ?

A. Yes, salvation is offered to all, and all are saved who really take Christ for their Savior (Ezekiel 18:23; 2 Peter 3:9).

Q. (10) What is Christ now doing for men's salvation?

A. Christ is interceding for all those who trust in His atonement (Hebrews 7:25; Romans 8:34).

ADVANCED QUESTIONS

Q. (a)   Is the atonement of Christ sufficient for all men?

A.   The atonement of Christ is sufficient for all, and would actu-
              ally save all if they would repent and believe (John 1:29; 3:17;
              1 John 2:2; 4:14).

Q. (b)   Does God desire the salvation of all men?

A.   God "wishes all men to be saved, and to come to the knowl-
              edge of the truth" (1 Timothy 2:4).

Q. (c)   If any who hear the gospel are not saved, can they justly com-
              plain?

A.   No, they cannot justly complain, for if they wished it, and
              would believe, they might be saved.

Q. (d)   Are the heathen, who never heard the gospel, condemned for
              not believing it?

A.   No, the heathen are judged by the light they have, and are
              condemned for violating the law that is written in the hearts
              (Romans 1:20; 2:14).

Q. (e)   Will God punish those who have not heard the gospel as se-
              verely as those who hear and reject it?

A.   No, those who have not heard the gospel will be punished for
              disregarding what they know, or might know, of the true God
              (Romans 2:13; 3:23).

Q. (f)   Has God commanded His people to proclaim salvation to all
              men?

A.   Yes, God commands His people to proclaim salvation to all
              men (Matthew 28:19; Romans 10:13–15).

LESSON VIII
REGENERATION

Q. (1)   What is meant by the word regeneration?

A.   Regeneration is God's causing a person to be born again.

Q. (2)   Are such persons literally born a second time?

A.   No, the regenerated are inwardly changed as if they were born over again.

Q. (3)   In what respect are men changed in the new birth?

A.   In the new birth men have a new heart, so as to hate sin and desire to be holy servants of God (Ezekiel 11:19, 20).

Q. (4)   Is this new birth necessary in order to salvation?

A.   Without the new birth no one can be saved (John 3:3).

Q. (5)   Who produces this great change?

A.   The Holy Spirit regenerates (John 3:5, 6).

Q. (6)   Are people regenerated through baptism?

A.   No, only those whose hearts are already changed ought to be baptized.

Q. (7)   Are people regenerated through bible teaching?

A.   Yes, people are usually regenerated through the Word of God (1 Peter 1:23; James 1:18).

Q. (8)   Can we understand how men are born again?

A.   No, we can only know regeneration by its effects (John 3:8).

Q. (9)   Does faith come before the new birth?

A.   No, it is the new heart that truly repents and believes.

Q. (10)   **What is the proof of having a new heart?**

A.   The proof of having a new heart is living a new life (1 John 2:29; 2 Corinthians 5:17).

ADVANCED QUESTIONS

Q. (a)   **Why is water mentioned in connection with the new birth?**

A.   Water is mentioned in connection with the new birth to show that this is a pure birth, leading to a new and pure life (John 3:5; Titus 3:5; Romans 6:4).

Q. (b)   **Does God give His renewing Spirit as He sees proper?**

A.   Yes, God gives His renewing Spirit to those whom He always purposed to save (Ephesians 1:3, 4).

LESSON IX
REPENTANCE AND FAITH

Q. (1)   **What is it to repent of sin?**

A.   Repenting of sin means that one changes his thoughts and feeling about sin, resolving to forsake sin and live for God.

Q. (2)   **Does not repenting mean being sorry?**

A.   Everyone who truly resolves to quit sinning will be sorry for his past sins, but people are often sorry without quitting.

Q. (3)   **What is the great reason for repenting of sin?**

A.   The great reason for repenting of sin is because sin is wrong, and offensive to God (Psalm 51:4).

Q. (4)   **Is repentance necessary to a sinner's salvation?**

A.   Those who will not turn from sin must perish (Luke 13:3; Ezekiel 33:11).

Q. (5)   What do the Scriptures mean by faith in Christ?

A.   By faith in Christ the Scriptures mean believing Christ to be
           the divine Savior, and personally trusting in Him for our salva-
           tion.

Q. (6)   Is faith in Christ necessary to salvation?

A.   No person capable of faith in Christ can be saved without it
           (John 3:6; Hebrews 11:6).

Q. (7)   Can those who die in infancy be saved without faith?

A.   Yes, we feel sure that those who die in infancy are saved for
           Christ's sake.

Q. (8)   Are they saved without regeneration?

A.   Infants are not saved without regeneration, for without holi-
           ness none shall see God (Hebrews 12:14; John 3:3).

Q. (9)   Can we see why persons capable of faith cannot be saved
           without it?

A,   Persons capable of faith must by faith accept God's offered
           mercy; and His truth cannot become the means of making
           them holy unless it is believed.

Q. (10)   Is refusing to believe in Christ a sin?

A.   It is fearfully wicked to reject the Savior and insult God who
           gave His Son in love (John 3:18; 1 John 5:10).

Q. (11)   Do faith in Christ and true repentance ever exist separately?

A.   No, either faith or repentance will always carry the other with
           it (Acts 20:21).

ADVANCED QUESTIONS

Q. (a)   How is it that some persons say they believe the Bible to be true, and yet are not Christians?

A.   Many persons who say they believe the Bible are not willing to forsake sin, and often they do not really believe what the Bible says about Christ (John 5:46).

Q. (b)   Is a man responsible for his belief as to the Bible?

A.   Yes, a man is responsible for his belief as to the Bible, because it depends partly on whether he is willing to know the truth, willing to forsake sin and serve God (John 7:17).

Q. (c)   Were not people in Old Testament times saved without faith in Christ?

A.   The truly pious in Old Testament times believed in God's promise of a future provision for salvation, and some of them looked clearly forward to Christ Himself (Genesis 3:15; John 8:45; Psalm 110:1; Psalm 53:6).

Q. (d)   How can we explain the statement that Judas repented and killed himself?

A.   When it is said that Judas repented, that is another Greek word, which means simply sorrow, and not at all the repentance that leads to salvation (2 Corinthians 7:10).

LESSON X
JUSTIFICATION AND SANCTIFICATION

Q. (1)   What is meant in the Bible by justification?

A.   God justifies a sinner in treating him as just, for Christ's sake.

Q. (2)   Can any person be justified by his own works?

A.   By works of the law shall no flesh be justified (Romans 3:20).

Q. (3)   How are we justified by faith?

A.   Believing in Christ our Savior, we ask and receive justification for His sake alone (Romans 3:24; 5:1).

Q. (4)   Has this faith that justifies any connection with our works?

A.   The faith that justifies will be sure to produce good works (Galatians 5:6; James 2:17).

Q. (5)   What is meant by sanctification?

A.   To sanctify is to make holy in heart and life.

Q. (6)   What connection is there between sanctification and regeneration?

A.   The new birth is the beginning of a new and holy life.

Q. (7)   Is justification complete at once?

A.   Yes, the moment a sinner really believes in Christ he is completely justified.

Q. (8)   Is sanctification complete at once?

A.   No, sanctification is gradual, and ought to go on increasing to the end of the earthly life (Philippians 3:13, 14).

Q. (9)   Is it certain that a true believer in Christ will be finally saved?

A.   Yes, God will preserve a true believer in Christ to the end (John 10:28; Philippians 1:6).

Q. (10)   What is the sure proof of being a true believer?

A.   The only sure proof of being a true believer is growing in holiness and in usefulness, even to the end (2 Peter 1:10).

Q. (11)   To what will justification and sanctification lead at last?

A.   Justification and sanctification will lead at last to glorification in heaven (Romans 5:2; 8:30; Matthew 25:21).

ADVANCED QUESTIONS

Q. (a)   How can it be right for God to treat a believing sinner as just, when he has only begun a holy life?

A.   God treats a believing sinner as just for Christ's sake, and God will be sure to make him completely holy in the end (Romans 3:26).

Q. (b)   Does faith in Christ procure justification by deserving it?

A.   No, faith does not deserve justification; it only brings us into union with Christ, for whose sake we are justified (Romans 8:1).

LESSON XI
BAPTISM AND THE LORD'S SUPPER

Q. (1)   Who ought to be baptized?

A.   Every believer in Christ ought to be baptized.

Q. (2)   Why ought every believer in Christ to be baptized?

A.   Because Christ has commanded us to declare our faith in Him by being baptized (Matthew 28:19; Acts 8:12; 10:48).

Q. (3)   What is the action performed in Christian baptism?

A.   The action performed in Christian baptism is immersion in water (Mark 1:9, 10; Acts 8:39).

Q. (4)   What does this signify?

A.   The water signifies purification from sin, and the immersion signified that we are dead to sin, and like Christ have been buried and risen again (Acts 22:16; Romans 6:4).

Q. (5)   Does baptism procure forgiveness or the new birth?

A.   No, baptism only represents regeneration and forgiveness like a picture (John 3:15; Acts 2:38).

Q. (6)   What is meant by our being baptized "in the name of the Father and of the Son and of the Holy Spirit"?

A.   It means that we take God the Father, the Son, and the Spirit as our Sovereign and Savior (Matthew 28:19).

Q. (7)   What is the solemn duty of all who have been baptized?

A.   It is the duty of all who have been baptized to live that new life of purity and obedience which their baptism signifies (Romans 6:4).

Q. (8)   What is the Lord's Supper?

A.   A church observes the Lord's Supper by eating bread and drinking wine to represent the body and blood of our Savior (1 Corinthians 11:20, 26).

Q. (9)   Why ought the bread and wine to be thus taken?

A.   Because Christ has commanded us to eat bread and drink wine in remembrance of Him (Luke 22:19).

Q. (10)   Who ought to partake of the Lord's Supper?

A.   Those ought to partake of the Lord's Supper who have believed in Christ, and have been baptized, and are trying to live in obedience of Christ's commands.

ADVANCED QUESTIONS

Q. (a)   Can there be Christian Baptism without immersion?

A.   No, Christ was immersed, and commanded us to be immersed, and sprinkling or pouring water will not represent burial and rising again (Romans 6:4; Colossians 2:12).

Q. (b)   If the person were very ill or the water could not be had, would not something else than immersion suffice?

A.   In cases of extreme illness or scarcity of water it is not a duty to be baptized.

Q. (c)   When we insist that nothing ought to be substituted for immersion, what is the principle involved?

A.   The principle we insist upon is that of strict obedience to the Word of God.

Q. (d)   Ought the bread and wine to be taken by one person alone?

A.   No, all the instances in the New Testament are of a church together taking the bread and wine.

Q. (e)   Does not the joint participation become a bond of fellowship?

A.   Yes, our partaking together promotes Christian fellowship, but the word "communion" means simply the partaking (1 Corinthians 10:16).

Q. (f)   Why ought Baptists not to take the Lord's Supper with believers of other denominations?

A.   Because we think they have not been baptized, or are not walking orderly as to church connection.

LESSON XII
THE LORD'S DAY

Q. (1)   What does the word Sabbath mean?

A.   The word Sabbath means rest.

Q. (2)   Why was the Sabbath at first appointed?

A.   The Sabbath was at first appointed to represent the rest of God after finishing the creation (Genesis 2:3).

Q. (3)   What says the fourth commandment given through Moses at Mount Sinai?

A.   Remember the Sabbath day to keep it holy (Exodus 20:8, 11).

Q. (4)   What does this show?

A.   The fourth commandment shows that the children of Israel knew about the Sabbath, but were apt to neglect it.

Q. (5) When the Saviour was charged with breaking the Sabbath, what did He teach about it?

A. The Savior taught that it was not breaking the Sabbath to heal the sick, to provide food for the hungry, or to do any work of necessity or mercy (Matthew 12:3; Mark 3:4; Luke 13:15, 16).

Q. (6) What change was gradually made under the direction of the apostles as to the day to be observed?

A. The day to be observed was changed from the seventh day to the first day of the week, the day on which the Lord Jesus rose from the dead (John 20:1, 19, 26).

Q. (7) What is this day called?

A. The first day of the week is called the Lord's day (Revelation 1:10).

Q. (8) What do we find the first Christians doing on the Lord's day?

A. They met for public worship, heard preaching, took the Lord's Supper, and gave money for religious objects (1 Corinthians 16:2; Acts 20:7).

Q. (9) Ought we to keep the Lord's day as the Sabbath?

A. Yes, we ought to keep the Lord's day as a day of rest and holy employments.

Q. (10) Ought we to keep the Lord's day as the first Christians did?

A. Yes, we ought to keep the Lord's day as a day for public worship, with Bible study and preaching, for religious gifts and ordinances, and for doing good in every way.

ADVANCED QUESTIONS

Q. (a) Does the New Testament say that the Sabbath was changed to the first day of the week?

A. No, the New Testament speaks of religious exercises on the first day of the week as something that everybody understood (1 Corinthians 16:1, 2; Acts 20:7; Revelation 1:10).

Q. (b)   What explanation have we of these statements?

A.   Several Christian writers just after the apostles speak of wor-
           ship on the first day of the week in such language as to show
           plainly what the New Testament references meant.

LESSON XIII
SOME DUTIES OF THE CHRISTIAN LIFE

Q. (1)   What is our duty as to speaking the truth?

A.   We must always speak truth and never lie (Ephesians 4:25;
           Exodus 20:16; Revelation 21:8).

Q. (2)   Is it possible to act a lie without speaking it?

A.   Yes, to act a lie may be one of the worst forms of falsehood
           (Acts 5:3).

Q. (3)   What is our duty as to speaking evil of others?

A.   We must never speak so as to wrong any person (John 4:11).

Q. (4)   What is meant by profane speech?

A.   Profane speech is cursing or swearing, or speaking in an irrev-
           erent way of God, or of the Bible, or of anything sacred.

Q. (5)   What does the Bible say about stealing?

A.   "Thou shalt not steal" (Exodus 20:15; Ephesians 4:28).

Q. (6)   Can you tell some things which this forbids?

A.   The commandment forbids all unfair buying and selling, and
           any failure to pay promised wages or perform promised work.

Q. (7)   Is it wrong even to wish to take away another person's prop-
           erty?

A.   Yes, the Bible says we must not covet what belongs to another
           (Exodus 20:17).

Q. (8)   May we properly strive to do better than others?

A.   Yes, we may strive to excel others, but we must not envy others nor try to pull them back (1 Peter 2:1).

Q. (9)   May we revenge ourselves on those who have wronged us?

A.   No, revenge is very wicked, and we must leave punishment of those who have wronged us with God (Romans 12:19).

Q. (10)   Ought we to love our enemies just as we love our friends?

A.   We ought to love our enemies as God loves His enemies, and so be ready always to do them a kindness (Matthew 5:44, 45).

Q. (11)   What is our duty as to purity?

A.   We must avoid all impure actions and words, thoughts and feelings.

Q. (12)   How many Christians hope to perform these and all duties of the Christian life?

A.   Christians may hope to perform their duties by watchful effort and constant prayer for the help of the Holy Spirit (Matthew 26:41; Luke 11:13).

ADVANCED QUESTIONS

Q. (a)   Does truthfulness require us to tell everything we know or think?

A.   No, we may keep to ourselves what others have no claim to know, when we are not professing to tell everything (1 Samuel 16:2).

Q. (b)   When may we say things that will damage others?

A.   We may say things that will damage others when the things said are true, and it is needful that they should be known to prevent wrong.

Q. (c)   What may we do for the punishment of one who has injured us?

A.   If a person has injured us we may help to secure his punishment according to law, not for private revenge, but for public good.

Q. (d)   Is it ever right to take an oath?

A.   It is right to take an oath only in court of justice or on some other important occasion, and always in a very solemn way (Matthew 16:63, 64; 2 Corinthians 1:23).

Q. (e)   Ought we to be careful about the example we set to others?

A.   Yes, it is the duty of Christians to be the salt of the earth, and the light of the world (Matthew 5:13, 14).

LESSON XIV
IMITATION OF CHRIST

Q. (1)   Did the Savior live a real human life?

A.   Yes, the Savior lived a real human life, but without sin of any kind.

Q. (2)   Was He tempted to sin?

A.   He was tempted in all points just as we are, but He always overcame the temptation (Hebrews 4:15).

Q. (3)   Is it the duty of the Christian to imitate Christ?

A.   Yes, Christ has left us a beautiful and perfect example, which we ought to imitate (1 Peter 2:21; 1 Corinthians 11:1).

Q. (4)   How may we hope to imitate Christ?

A.   We may hope to imitate Christ by the help of the Holy Spirit (Luke 4:1).

Q. (5)   What example did the Savior set as to obeying parents?

A.   The Savior did as His parents directed, and "was subject unto them" (Luke 2:51).

Q. (6)   What example did He set as to the Scriptures?

A.   The Savior attended a Bible Class, and had great knowledge of the Scriptures even when a child (Luke 2:46, 47).

Q. (7)   Did He use the Bible when tempted or suffering?

A.   Yes, the Savior quoted the Bible three times against the tempter, and twice while on the cross.

Q. (8)   What is His example as to public worship?

A.   Our Lord's custom was to go into the synagogue on the Sabbath day and worship (Luke 4:16).

Q. (9)   What example did Christ set as to private praying?

A.   Christ prayed often and much, sometimes through a whole night.

Q. (10)   What example in doing good to men?

A   Jesus all the time "went about doing good."

Q. (11)   What example as to the love of enemies?

A.   Jesus prayed for the men who were crucifying Him, "Father, forgive them, for they know not what they do" (Luke 23:34).

Q. (12)   What example as to loving Christians?

A.   Christ laid down His life for us, and we ought to lay down our lives for the brethren (1 John 3:16; John 13:34).

Q. (13)   What is our highest hope for the future life?

A.   "We shall be like Him" (1 John 3:2).

ADVANCED QUESTIONS

Q. (a)   Which books of the Old Testament did the Savior quote when tempted or suffering?

A.   In the great temptation Christ three times quoted Deuteronomy (8:3; 6:13, 16), and on the cross He twice quoted the Psalms (22:1; 31:5).

Q. (b)   Did He use the Old Testament Scriptures on other occasions?

A.   Yes, Christ often quoted Scripture to convince the Jews and to instruct the disciples.

Q. (c)   Can you mention some special occasions on which Jesus prayed?

A.   Luke 3:21; 6:12; 9:29; 11:1; John 17:1; Matthew 26:39, 42, 44.

LESSON XV
THE FUTURE LIFE

Q. (1)   Do men everywhere believe in a future life?

A.   In all nations and races men have generally believed in a future and endless life.

Q. (2)   Does the Bible confirm this belief?

A.   The Bible leaves no room to doubt that every human being will always continue to exist.

Q. (3)   What becomes of the soul at death?

A.   The soul is undying, and passes at once into blessedness or suffering (2 Corinthians 5:8; Luke 16:23, 28).

Q. (4)   What becomes of the body after death?

A.   The body returns to dust, but it will rise again (Genesis 3:19; Ecclesiastes 12:7; Acts 24:15).

Q. (5)   Will the same body live again?

A.   Yes, the very same body will live again, but greatly changed as
            to its condition and mode of life (1 Corinthians 15:42–44).

Q. (6)   What is meant by the day of judgement?

A.   The day of judgment means a great and awful day, on which
            the living and the dead will stand before Christ to be judged
            (Acts 17:31; Matthew 25:31, 32; 2 Corinthians 5:10).

Q. (7)   To what will Christ condemn the wicked?

A.   Christ will send the wicked away to everlasting punishment in
            hell (Matthew 25:41, 46).

Q. (8)   To what will Christ welcome the righteous?

A.   Christ will welcome the righteous to everlasting blessedness
            with Him in heaven (Matthew 25:34, 46).

Q. (9)   Will there be different degrees of punishment?

A.   The future punishment will be greater according to the de-
            grees of sin, and the knowledge men had of God's will and of
            the way of salvation through Christ (Luke 12:47, 48; Mark
            12:40).

Q. (10)   How is hell described in the Bible?

A.   Hell is a place of darkness and torment, of endless sin and
            endless suffering.

Q. (11)   How is heaven described?

A.   Heaven is a place of light and holiness, of freedom from all
            sorrow and temptation, of blessed society and thankful praise
            to God (Revelation 7:9, 10; 21:4).

ADVANCED QUESTIONS

Q. (a)   What do we know as to the period between death and resur-
           rection?

A.   We know that between death and the resurrection there will
           be conscious existence of the soul, either in torment or in
           blessedness with Christ (Luke 16:24; 23:43; Philippians 1:23).

Q. (b)   Is there any salvation provided in the future life for persons
           who died in their sins?

A.   The Bible does not reveal any provision for salvation in the
           future life for persons who died in their sins, nor does it au-
           thorize any such hope.

Q. (c)   Are we authorized to believe in heavenly recognition?

A.   The Bible warrants the hope that we shall know each other in
           heaven (1 Thessalonians 2:19; Matthew 17:3, 4).

Passages for Learning by Heart

It is an excellent thing for the young to commit to memory many portions of Scripture. The following passages are recommended as suitable, and it is hoped that many will learn some of them, and add other selections as thought best.

- The Ten Commandments, Exodus 20:1–17.

- Psalms 1, 16, 19, 23, 24, 27, 32, 34, 51, 84, 90, 92, 95, 100, 103, 115, 116, 130, 139, 145.

- Proverbs 3:1–20; 6:6–11; chapter 10; chapter 11, chapter 20;

- Ecclesiastes, chapter 12.

- Isaiah, chapter 40; chapter 53; chapter 55.

- Matthew 5:3–16; chapter 6; chapter 7; chapter 25; 28: 18–20.

- Mark 14:22–25; 32:2.

- Luke 15:11–32; 16: 19–31; 18:1–14; 24: 13–35.

- John 1:1–18; 14:1–15; 20: 1–23.

- Acts 17:22–31; 20:17–38.

- Romans 5:1–11; 8:28–39; chapter 12.

- 1 Corinthians, chapter 13; chapter 15.

- 2 Corinthians, chapter 5.

- Ephesians 3:14–21; 6:10–20.

- Colossians 3:1–4; 4:2–6.

- 1 Thessalonians 4:13–18.

- Titus 2:11–14.

- Hebrews 4:14–16, 11:1 to 12:3.

- 1 John 1:5 to 2:6; 3:13–24; chapter 4.

- Revelation 1:9–20; 7:9–17; 20:11–15; chapter 21; chapter 22.

Indices

Index of Catechisms

Index of Scripture References

Index of People

Index of Doctrines